# Party Finance and Political Corruption

*Also by Robert Williams*

EXPLAINING AMERICAN POLITICS: Issues and Interpretations (*editor*)
POLITICAL CORRUPTION IN AFRICA
POLITICAL SCANDALS IN THE USA

# Party Finance and Political Corruption

Edited by

Robert Williams
*Professor of Politics*
*University of Durham*

in association with

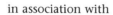

First published in Great Britain 2000 by
**MACMILLAN PRESS LTD**
Houndmills, Basingstoke, Hampshire RG21 6XS and London
Companies and representatives throughout the world

A catalogue record for this book is available from the British Library.

ISBN 0–333–73986–8

---

First published in the United States of America 2000 by
**ST. MARTIN'S PRESS, LLC,**
Scholarly and Reference Division,
175 Fifth Avenue, New York, N.Y. 10010

ISBN 0–312–23170–9

Library of Congress Cataloging-in-Publication Data
Party finance and political corruption / edited by Robert Williams.
p.   cm.
Includes bibliographical references and index.
ISBN 0–312–23170–9
1. Campaign funds. 2. Campaign funds—Case studies. 3. Political corruption. 4.
Political corruption—Case studies. I. Williams, Robert, 1946 Sept. 10–

JF2112.C28 P37   2000
324.7'8—dc21

00–035261

---

This book is printed on paper suitable for recycling and made from fully managed and sustained
forest sources.

10   9   8   7   6   5   4   3   2   1
09   08   07   06   05   04   03   02   01   00

Printed and bound in Great Britain by
Antony Rowe Ltd, Chippenham, Wiltshire

# Contents

# Preface and Acknowledgements

This book has its origins in a paper I presented on 'Corruption and Party Finance' to a European Association for Social Science Conference in Cyprus in 1997. I am grateful to the organizers and particularly to Professor Michael Johnston, who facilitated my contribution. I am also grateful to my former editor at Macmillan, Sunder Katwala, for encouraging me to develop my ideas for the book. In preparing this book, my editorial burden was greatly reduced by the professionalism and courtesy of the contributors. Most book editors have 'horror' stories to tell but in this case I am happy to record my sincere appreciation to the contributors for the quality of their work and their promptness in meeting deadlines.

My principal debt, as always, is to Jean Richardson, whose help and support made this book possible.

*Durham*                                                    ROBERT WILLIAMS

# Notes on the Contributors

**William A. Callahan** is Lecturer in Politics, University of Durham. He is the author of *Poll Watch: Civil Society and Elections in Southeast Asia* and of articles on vote buying in Thailand.

**Justin Fisher** is Senior Lecturer in Politics, London Guildhall University. He is the author of *British Political Parties* and a number of book chapters. He served as consultant to the Committee on Standards in Public Life inquiry into party finance in the UK.

**Dean McSweeney** is Principal Lecturer in Politics, University of the West of England. He is the co-author of *American Political Parties* and a number of book chapters on American politics.

**James Newell** is Lecturer in Politics, University of Salford. He is the co-author of *Italian Politics since 1945* and was co-editor of a special issue of *Corruption and Reform*.

**Thomas Saalfeld** is Lecturer in Politics, University of Kent. He is the author of a number of books and articles on political parties in Germany.

**Richard Sakwa** is Professor of Politics and International Relations, University of Kent. He is the author of *Russian Politics and Society* and *Gorbachev and His Reforms*.

**Robert Williams** is Professor and Head of the Department of Politics, University of Durham. He is the author of *Political Corruption in Africa* and *Political Scandals in the USA*. He has served as a consultant to the UK government on corruption.

# 1
# Aspects of Party Finance and Political Corruption

*Robert Williams*

The concept of party varies widely from north to south, from authoritarian to democratic regimes and from emerging to established democracies. But whatever form political organization takes, there is a common problem: how to find sufficient financial resources to fund the activities the political organizations wish to pursue. Competition between political parties divided on ideological, economic, social, factional or ethnic lines depends on finance, drives up the costs of campaigning and intensifies the search for additional or new income streams.

Money buys the access, favours, skills, goods and services that are essential to effective party activity. As Alexander notes, 'money is instrumental, and its importance lies in the ways it is used by people to try to gain influence, to convert into other resources, or to use in combination with other resources to achieve political power.'[1] Money compensates for a lack of volunteers and serves, in some societies, as a surrogate for individual commitment. In short, money is a transferable and convertible resource which helps mobilize support for, and secures influence with, political parties.

The role of money in politics, especially in funding political parties, has attracted much adverse attention in the past 20 years. Many countries have experienced major scandals involving political parties and the nature, sources and consequences of their financial support. The reform impulse is readily observed around the globe and a wide variety of reforms in political finance have been advocated. Attempts to regulate party finance are not new but the plethora of scandals has focused public and media attention and thereby encouraged political leaders to reform, or at least to be seen to reform, the ways in which political formations fund their activities. Inevitably, the scope of reform varies according to the type of political party, the nature of the political system, the perceived seriousness of the problem and the availability of alternative funding regimes.

While the contexts vary, the complaints and charges are remarkably similar: a lack of openness and transparency in party finance; ineffective or inadequate government regulation; an undesirable closeness between large financial contributors and the leadership of political parties leading to subversion of democratic processes; and, more simply, straightforward bribery. Such charges open up the debate about what sort of organizations political parties are and what constitutes legitimate and appropriate means of securing the financial resources necessary to their effective operation. At root, there is the underlying concern that, left unregulated, the problems of party finance will intensify and either corrupt the entire political process or, where such corruption is already entrenched, will preclude its control and eradication.

Before examining the particular issues in different systems, a preliminary general sketch of the sources of party finance will identify the key forms and their associated problems. Such a sketch will not do justice to the rich complexity of many contexts but it will serve to illustrate the range of common responses to the universal need to fund movements, formations or organizations which help structure political activity. The world of party finance can be divided up according to a variety of competing criteria. One recent study suggests that funding regimes 'can be classified under a number of bimodal headings'.[2] Thus, we can discuss party finance in terms of public versus private funding; legal versus illegal; domestic versus foreign; institutional versus individual; overt versus covert; or even large versus small. These are clearly not discrete closed categories and there is considerable overlap but the bimodality does draw attention to some key issues.

A European authority on the problem of party finance suggests there are three methods of party finance in Western democracies which should be seen not as alternatives but as running in parallel: they are internal finance, external finance and state finance.[3] But the problem with simple typologies or bimodalities is that what they conceal may be more important than what they reveal. In many jurisdictions it is, for example, unclear what constitutes a legal contribution and, when private finance can embrace everything from a trivial contribution from an individual to a large 'donation' from an organized crime syndicate, the typology's utility is questionable. It is, of course, possible to produce more elaborate typologies of party finance but the danger here is that we fail to see the wood for the trees. Party finance is a complex issue which is embedded in myriad and disparate political and legal contexts.

What is appropriate, practicable and desirable in a mature democracy and affluent society is not a recipe for all political contexts. Newly democratizing countries in Eastern Europe and East Asia are faced with very different political and economic realities, and their systems of political financing are unlikely to match closely those found in Western Europe or North America. Political parties are often looser, more transient, more personal political formations than their Western counterparts and even the term 'party' may give a spurious sense of their tangibility and durability. Some options, such as state financing, may be economically unrealistic while other options, such as external funding by foreign governments or international organizations, are attractive but raise political concerns. The attempts by advanced democracies, notably the United States, to help fund political parties in other advanced democracies, notably Italy, have not been widely admired or imitated.

If Beyme's suggestion that party financing has three main forms – internal, external and state – is unpacked, it is possible to see where the opportunities and incentives for what is commonly seen as corruption arise. Corruption is, of course, a contested concept but most approaches ultimately rest on a distinction between some formal obligation to pursue the public good, and conduct which is construed as private regarding and which serves to undermine the public good. In this context, it focuses attention on whether, or to what extent, political parties are seen as public rather than private organizations. This may have a legal dimension but it may also depend on popular and media perception. If parties are accorded a preferred legal status, the matter is clearer but where they are treated as if they were mere interest groups, the distinction is hard to make. One authority suggests that 'accusations of corruption do not distinguish between illegality and impropriety'[4] but, while this charge is obviously true, it is relevant neither to an appreciation of the political, as opposed to legal, consequences, nor to the impact of such accusations on levels of public trust and confidence in the political process.

Political activity in many countries is conspicuously and frequently interrupted by allegations of corruption, sleaze and scandal. Where corruption ends and where sleaze begins is an interesting question but not one that is central to how the legitimacy of funding political parties is perceived by the public and the media. The press and competing parties love a scandal and are not easily dissuaded by claims that the conduct was not illegal but only gave an appearance of impropriety. Scandals take on lives of their own and their consequences can be disproportionate to the gravity of the original offence. The important point here is that the 'dogs of scandal are always hungry and however many bones are tossed to them, their appetite for their quarry remains undiminished.'[5]

Beyme's first category of party finance, intra-party sources, is deceptively simple and innocuous. In its most rudimentary forms, it seems uncontroversial. Political parties recruit members who pay membership fees which finances the party's activities. But this leaves open the question of what constitutes membership and how much those members contribute. Some parties, notably the Labour Party in the UK, have different categories of membership and the status of affiliated bodies such as the co-operative movement, the trade unions and the Fabian Society is ambiguous. Political opponents tend to see trade unions as separate organizations which act as interest groups exercising their privileged status within the UK Labour Party. For most of its history, the UK Labour Party was heavily dependent on payments from affiliated trade unions and thus what it saw as internal financing was interpreted by its rivals in other parties as external financing. Moreover, the imbalance between members' contributions and the scale of trade union contributions suggested to critics that this financial dependency gave the trade unions disproportionate and improper political influence over the policies of the Labour Party.

If individuals choose to join a political party and thereby agree to pay the prevailing subscription, there seems little cause for concern. But if the level of subscriptions is determined by the individual, then wealthy individuals are always susceptible to the charge that their influence is proportionate to the scale of their contributions. The reality seems to be that a mass subscription base is both an unrealistic aspiration in developing and transitional countries and inadequate to meet the organizational and campaigning costs in developed countries.

When ordinary membership dues either do not exist or are insufficient to meet costs, political parties sometimes take steps to compel their supporters working in the executive and legislative branches of both national and local government to pay a special charge or even a percentage of their income. Thus, members of assemblies may, as in Germany, be required to contribute a fixed portion of their salaries to their parties. In the United States there was a long-established practice of imposing a levy on employees in local, state and federal government to compensate for the lack of income which parties with a stronger sense of membership are able to derive from subscriptions. In both examples, the justification seems to rest on the identity of the individual with the party. In the European cases, the argument seems to be that the election of a member of parliament has more to do with the appeal of their political party than with their individual qualities. Thus, if the individual benefits by being elected on a party ticket, it is only reasonable that the political party should share in that benefit. In the American case, the distribution of posts was long a matter of party patronage. Some posts, for example, in customs or the post office gave privileged access to opportunities to make additional, illicit income, and therefore appointments to such offices were effectively being sold. Patronage came at a price and, for some posts, there was a clamour to pay.

When party officials are required to pay a tithe to their employers, it might be thought unusual and even undesirable. But when public officials and elected representatives are forced to hand over part of their salaries to their parties, it could be argued that private organizations are effectively securing control of public resources by extortion. The extortion is not based on crude blackmail or the promise of violence but on the party's ability to determine re-selection and re-appointment. While the political levy has been outlawed in the United States, the practice is still well established in some European states.

Some political parties are effectively owned by individuals – Berlusconi and his *Forza Italia* is a leading example – and will also tend to own newspapers and other media outlets. In one sense, this is the purest form of internal financing but it raises questions about how the proprietor acquired his wealth, how he uses the political party to advance purely personal interests and what forms of accountability are available or appropriate. When the political party is essentially a vehicle for the personal ambitions of the owner, the ability of members and supporters to influence party conduct and party finance is correspondingly reduced.

Other sources of internal finance include income from investments, additional contributions from members and supporters through party rallies and similar events, and the sale of party newspapers and other publications. But the line between internal and external finance is difficult to sustain when parties have developed trading arms which inescapably bring them into contact with the business sector, and their financial success may be linked to a change in the party's public image and identity. However much this may be regretted by 'old guard' party members, all political parties are, in financial terms, hybrids in that they rely on more than one kind of funding.

External funding of political parties attracts the most adverse comment because, as the English saying puts it, 'he who pays the piper calls the tune.' When political parties and their leaders receive money from private organizations and individuals, who is beholden to whom and for what? The English saying and its typically terse American equivalent, 'money talks', express an important political truth. What Americans call influence peddling, what the French call pantouflage and what ordinary citizens everywhere call corruption tends to undermine public trust in parties and encourages cynicism about politicians, their motives and loyalties. But some sources invite greater concern than others. When trade unions give their financial support to progressive social democratic or labour parties, this is generally consistent with the declared aims of the parties they support. Where there is a mismatch between the ideological or policy stances of the political party and the known or assumed preferences of contributors, the possibility of the financial relationship having corrupt implications correspondingly increases.

The motives of those who make substantial contributions to political parties are often called into question and, when there are attempts to conceal or disguise donations, suspicions are aroused. While some may legitimately wish to protect their anonymity, others are concerned that the public disclosure of their contributions would excite public disapproval and even create a scandal. If the donor is a foreign national, their motives might more readily be impugned and the British Conservative Party was for many years keen not to disclose the large contributions it received from Hong Kong, Greece and elsewhere. In extreme cases, the contributions will simply be unlawful, both in the sense they violate regulations on party finance and in the sense that the donors themselves may be representatives of criminal organizations. In Italy and Russia, the interactions between party politics and organized crime are not to be underestimated.

In some contexts, external financing is derived from the close linkages which have developed between parties and large business enterprises. In Japan and Korea such arrangements are long established and raise issues about the preferential treatment such businesses enjoy in matters of trade, taxation and investment. In other countries, the costs of campaigning are so huge that parties and their leaders actively solicit funds from business enterprises. Such conspicuous fund-raising gives rise to concerns about what such business interests expect by way of a return on their political investment. The common fear is that the concerns of voters, or even party members and supporters, will be subordinated to the priorities of the party's financial backers. In the United States there have been demands for investigations of both President Clinton and Vice President Gore and some claim to detect links between the receipt of large donations and changes in the administration's policy. At the congressional level, similar concerns have been voiced and some argue that a primary reason for the failure to deal with the savings and loan scandal in a timely way was the dependence of so many legislators on campaign contributions from savings and loan owners.

State funding is sometimes presented as a way of freeing political parties from the obligations created by their dependence on income from trade unions or business groups. The danger here is that parties exchange one form of dependency for another. One study suggests that German parties have become addicted to public funds and their thirst for state funding is unquenchable. Allowing party politicians to determine levels of state funding for parties is likened to 'an alcoholic entering a self-service liquor store'.[6] As parties and their office holders become more dependent on the state, they are less beholden to their voters, supporters and members, and this may erode ties of loyalty and weaken accountability.

But those who placed faith in state funding as a means of rescuing political parties from the potentially corrupt influences of external finance both underestimated the escalating costs of modern political and campaign organizations and overestimated the effectiveness of laws regulating donations from external sources. Just as internal finance has generally proved inadequate, so too has state finance. Party funding is therefore dependent on multiple forms of funding and even where state funding of parties is relatively lavish, as in Germany, there is no automatic protection against corruption. All the major parties in Germany have experienced scandals and 'revelations of laundered money for party activities, with most cases involving illegal tax exemptions for political donations'.[7]

Corruption and party finance are inextricably linked. It is obvious that whatever the origins, structure, character and ideology of a political party and irrespective of the prevailing party system, political parties solicit funds over and above those received from their members or, where available, from state subsidies. The sources, scale, forms and distribution of party finance all have profound political implications. Political parties form linkages and conduits between executive, legislative and administrative institutions and between such institutions and the wider political, economic and social environment. In short, they provide a bridge between state and society. They offer the prospect of durable forms of political organization and a means of controlling and directing the power of the state. It is the prospect of the party capturing state power which attracts the attention of financial backers who require some benefit, favour or concession from government.

Where political parties have little prospect of power, the problems of funding are likely to be acute and they are not likely to be able to afford to be too discriminating. Many new democracies carry with them the baggage or legacy of authoritarian or autocratic rule, with their important influences on political attitudes and relationships, and political parties are challenged by and compete with other social forces. Patterns of party development depend on economic and cultural variations, the nature of the pre-democratic polity and the actual process of transition to democratic rule. All these factors will help shape the forms of party finance and political corruption. Not all parties endure and one key reason is a lack of finance. In the United States, it is said that those who run for office most often withdraw because they run out of money. In newer democracies, one study suggests unsurprisingly that 'there is a high mortality rate among political groupings; some are cannibalised by other parties, but the vast majority are cot deaths. They simply run out of breath.'[8]

The central concern is that financial aid rarely comes without strings attached. Money may create expectations of reciprocity and the result can be a form of dependency. In extreme cases, the party is effectively bought and owned by its financial backers and such dependency is seen as corrupt when it impacts upon the party's declared mission or purpose. The need for money can deflect a party from its stated aims or can constrain it from pursuing policies detrimental to the interests of its most influential financial supporters. Reliance on state funding does not create the same form of obligation but it may provide a means to deny entry to new parties. In some states there is effectively a political cartel, as to an extent there has been in Germany, which discourages 'extreme' or 'fringe' groups from organizing for electoral competition. Political parties can structure political competition and help promote political pluralism but state funding may also encourage the ossification of the party system and the development of the corporate state.

The above discussion underlines the importance of party finance and its associated problems, including corruption. In choosing the contributions to this volume, a number of criteria were used. The first was to present a reasonable cross-section of case studies.

While global coverage is impractical, there is a need to identify and illustrate the diverse forms of party finance and the ways in which corruption manifests itself. Although the party literature for the developed world is extensive, other regions are relatively neglected. This neglect is partly explicable in terms of the poor survival rates of political parties in particularly harsh and violent political environments. But political parties have emerged in difficult circumstances and there are acute problems of party finance and political corruption in developing and transitional countries.

In developed contexts, the key problem is often seen as corruption arising from the financial needs of competitive political parties. In other contexts, for example the countries of the former Soviet Union, the problems arise from the attempt to construct a new political order in the ruins of the old one. The corruption of the former Soviet Union was systemic and institutionalized in the sense that public trust was destroyed by the subversion of the formal processes and values of government. Sakwa's chapter illuminates the many problems of party finance and corruption which emerged during and following the collapse of communism, the intensifying economic crises and the rise of organized crime. His analysis penetrates the facade of formal structures and processes to reveal the realities of democratic transition in Russia and the consequences for corruption.

While it is obviously important to acknowledge that political parties vary in their form, cohesion and roles in different political contexts, it is also important to understand that the dynamic in generating corruption also varies. In many developed countries, the issue is defined in terms of economic elites buying political power and influence through their support of political parties but, as Callahan convincingly demonstrates, in much of Southeast Asia, the process is effectively reversed. Party leaders bribe the citizens for electoral support. He deals with political contexts far removed from the liberal democratic parties of Western Europe and North America and shows how the prevalence of vote buying, which disappeared from industrial democracies a century ago, is an integral part of party activity in some Asian countries. His analysis shows that simply eliminating such practices does not always result in more open and less corrupt forms of political competition. The electoral process can be corrupted by forces other than money and Callahan's chapter illustrates the different pathologies found in East Asia.

Developing and transitional countries exhibit very different patterns of party finance and corruption but it is equally the case that developed countries display a diversity of practice and varying degrees of corruption. Thus, a second criterion is to consider examples of developed states which reflect different party systems, different approaches to party finance and differing experiences of corruption. The selection of case studies, the United States, the United Kingdom, Germany and Italy, are major Western liberal democracies but their problems of party finance and political corruption are very different.

Party finance in Britain has recently been the subject of an extensive inquiry which has recommended radical reform. For many years, there seemed to be a degree of complacency about the integrity of British public life. Corruption was a problem for other countries which did not enjoy the benefits of the uniquely British way of regulating parties and elections. Such complacency has disappeared in the 1990s and the report on party finance of the Committee on Standards in Public Life[9] emphasized the urgent need for wholesale reform. Fisher's chapter examines how the British system evolved, the factors that encouraged the quest for reform and the shape of the new system to come.

The United States has long experienced problems with political finance. Its highly decentralized parties and the relative autonomy of party candidates has helped produce unusually expensive electoral campaigns and heightened concern about the corruption of the electoral process. Campaign finance reform is a perennial feature on most political agendas but effective reform remains elusive. Allegations of financial contributions playing an undue and improper influence have plagued presidential and congressional elections for over one hundred years. McSweeney explains how the unique features of the American system interact and how concerns about the current system are generated without serious prospect of reform.

The appeal of Germany as a case study arises both from its distinctiveness as a leading example of state funding for political parties and, as Saalfeld shows, as an example of judicial regulation of party finance. The resort to state finance can be seen as a possible defence against the corrupting influence of private funding but Saalfeld suggests that state funding has not prevented German political parties from being enmeshed in a number of scandals. He also demonstrates that the financial pressures on German political parties are more acute than elsewhere because the range of activities they engage in, especially through the party foundations, is much wider than in many other countries. Where state funding is lavish and party functions varied, the judiciary may offer the most likely source of protection against abuse.

Any modern study of party finance and political corruption which did not include a chapter on Italy would risk being characterized as eccentric or even perverse. The exposure of the corrupt nature of the Italian party system led to an implosion of the political system. Italy demonstrates the problems of party finance and corruption in their most acute and dramatic forms. Newell analyses the crisis of the Italian political system and traces it to the nature and operation of the party system and the funding arrangements that underpinned it. The Italian collapse has no modern precedent and Newell underlines the difficulties inherent in the task of building a new system which commands public and political confidence.

The aim of this volume is to explore different dimensions of the complex interrelationship of party finance and political corruption. The term party finance is used despite the objection that many countries do not have entities that closely resemble the party models familiar to western liberal democracy. The major alternative is the term political finance but if party finance is perhaps too narrow a term, political finance is, for present purposes, far too broad and inclusive. Party finance is intended simply to denote the funds received and expended by political parties. Political corruption is understood as conduct which subverts the declared purposes, principles and policies of political bodies in exchange for personal, private or particularistic advantage.

Parties vary considerably in terms of membership, organization, funding, activity, and electoral salience. Parties may be vehicles for personal ambition or expressions of communal sentiment. They may be strong or 'hollowed out', disciplined or anarchic but, in different degrees, they serve as bridges between society and the political system, between the electorate and the government. The contributors to this volume seek to address three major issues: the current problems of party finance and political corruption in a specific country or region; the nature and impact of previous reform efforts; and the prospects for and obstacles to future reform. Their diagnoses and prognoses vary but they agree on the importance of the issues, and the chapters which follow are intended to illuminate and advance the increasingly important debates about party finance and political corruption.

### Notes

1  Herbert F. Alexander (ed.), *Comparative Political Finance in the 1980s*, Cambridge: Cambridge University Press, 1989, p. 10.
2  Peter Burnell, 'Introduction: money and politics in emerging democracies', in Peter Burnell and Alan Ware (eds), *Funding Democratization*, Manchester: Manchester University Press, 1998, p. 10.
3  Karl von Beyme, *Political Parties in Western Democracies*, Aldershot: Gower, 1985, p. 196.
4  Burnell, p. 9.
5  Robert Williams, *Political Scandals in the USA*, Edinburgh: Keele University Press, 1998, p. 12.

6 Peter Lösche, 'Problems of Party and Campaign Financing in Germany and the United States – Some Comparative Reflections', in Arthur B. Gunlicks (ed.), *Campaign and Party Finance in North America and Western Europe*, Boulder: Westview Press, 1993, p. 225.

7 Karl-Heinz Nassmacher, 'Comparing Party and Campaign Finance in Western Democracies', in Gunlicks (ed.), p. 234.

8 Geoffrey Pridham, 'Political Parties and Their Strategies in the Transition from Authoritarian Rule: the Comparative Perspective', in Gordon Wightman (ed.), *Party Formation in East-Central Europe*, Cheltenham: Edward Elgar, 1995, p. 21.

9 Committee on Standards in Public Life (1998) *The Funding of Political Parties in the United Kingdom*, Cm. 4057.

# 2
# Party Finance and Corruption: Britain

*Justin Fisher*

## Introduction

The British system of party finance is remarkably unregulated. Its development has been characterized by pragmatic evolution and yet the level of scandal and corruption surrounding British party finance has been surprisingly low during the last seventy years. However, a new review seems likely to change the whole face of British party finance. The recommendations by the Committee on Standards in Public Life signal a huge sea change in terms of regulation and established practice. In order to understand the importance of the new proposals, however, it is essential to examine the evolution of party finance and the system currently in operation. This chapter will therefore examine first the development of British party finance, second the scope for corruption which the system has engendered and finally, the attempts at reform which have occurred.

## The evolution of British party finance

In his study of British political finance from the early nineteenth century, Pinto-Duschinsky identifies three phases of development in party fund-raising: the aristocratic era; the plutocratic era and the modern era (Pinto-Duschinsky, 1981:15). Developments in recent years suggest that a new era of political finance may well be upon us – the post-modern era.

## The aristocratic era

The origins of the aristocratic era were in the early stirrings of modern party activity in the first half of the nineteenth century. Elections during much of the nineteenth century were marked by a high degree of corruption, largely through the bribing of voters – an expensive pursuit (Pinto-Duschinsky, 1981:15–20). The result was that though some assistance was provided from central party funds, it was largely only members of the aristocracy who could afford the high costs of bribery, particularly since most evidence of central party fund-raising suggests that it existed only from 1831 onwards (Pinto-Duschinsky, 1981:21).

These electoral practices came under pressure from the growth of the franchise as a result of the 1867 Reform Act, and the Ballot Act of 1872 which introduced secret voting. Not only were there now 2 230 000 voters to bribe, as opposed to 440 000 prior to the 1867 act, but the secret ballot made the transaction potentially unreliable. Moreover, as parties began to take a modern shape, so identification with parties rose and fewer seats in the House of Commons went unchallenged. The likely guarantee of electoral success was therefore put in doubt. Additionally, with the growth of a more disciplined party organization, it became less worthwhile for individuals to invest large sums in an attempt to get elected since independent power in the House (and often therefore the likely material gain arising from the exercise of such power) had declined. Finally, the passing of the Corrupt and Illegal Practices (Prevention) Act of 1883 further limited the scope for local political corruption, since not only did it outlaw bribery, it also placed limits upon local campaign spending. Altogether, the pressures on the old system increased and gave way to the plutocratic era of finance.

## The plutocratic era

Both the Liberal and Conservative Parties were now required to seek alternative means to fund the central party. The landed aristocracy was not a good source for two principal reasons. First, the fall of agricultural prices from the 1870s onwards had undermined landed wealth and, secondly, whilst members of the landed aristocracy had been happy to spend money for a seat which afforded local political influence, they were far less willing to give the money centrally (Pinto-Duschinsky, 1981:28–32).

The alternative to aristocratic funding was that from businessmen. Despite the fact that many were very wealthy, they were not accepted socially. The nouveau riche craved social acceptance. This could be achieved through the award of honours. The Liberals were first to exploit the potential of this situation, prompted in part by the party's financial difficulties in 1886. The crisis had arisen partly because of a split in the party over Irish Home Rule. Many of the party's aristocratic supporters owned land in Ireland and transferred their allegiance to the Conservatives. In addition, the election of 1886, caused by the Liberal government's collapse after winning the election a year earlier, put immense strain upon Liberal finances (Pinto-Duschinsky, 1981:32–3).

Whilst in power, the Conservatives also exploited this situation enthusiastically. The person responsible for recommending honours (the chief whip) was also responsible for the collection of Conservative central party funds and, in effect, donations were solicited and accepted in return for titles (Pinto-Duschinsky, 1981:32–9). It follows that the Conservative Party's removal from office in 1906 presented a problem, since it was no longer in a position to award honours. However, the party still managed to collect money on the basis that honours would be forthcoming when it was returned to power. It was not able to honour the promises, however, until Lloyd George became Prime Minister in 1916. He was dependent upon Conservative support in the House of Commons, and the party was rewarded with a share of the growing honours market which Lloyd George himself had expanded to unprecedented levels (Pinto-Duschinsky, 1981:44). In addition, there was now a new pool of potential donors as the war economy had created many new millionaires who, like others, were keen to gain social acceptance.

These practices continued for some four years after the war and had a strong effect upon the internal structure of the Conservative Party. Despite the widespread practice by both main parties, the effective sale of honours required the details of central party finances to be kept secret, lest confirmation be available that the practice was actually occurring. Secondly, formal party accounts were avoided and contributions were often held by the main party fund-raisers. Finally, the secrecy of the operation meant that the fund-raising was carried out by a small number of people (Pinto-Duschinsky, 1981:55–6). Such secrecy has continued to be a feature of Conservative Party finances.

## The origins of the modern era

The modern era owes its origins in part to the development of trade union funding, first of individual candidates and then of the Labour Party. The earliest was in the election of 1874 (Gwyn, 1962:150). The miners were to set the pattern for future trade union support of candidates, and two candidates (Liberals) were elected to the House of Commons. One had been sponsored by the Northumberland section of the Miners' National Association, whilst the other was funded by the Labour Representation League, a group whose explicit function was to return working men to Parliament (Gwyn, 1962:147–77). Yet, despite these early successes, trade unions were unable effectively to penetrate the established party system and, by the 1880s, the trade union political movement had divided into two groups: those who favoured working with the Liberals, and those who desired the formation of a new party, independent of the Tories and the Liberals.

Thus, in 1900, as is well documented, the Labour Representation Committee (LRC) was set up by the Trades Union Congress, along with the Social Democratic Federation, the Independent Labour Party and the Fabian Society; the trade unions having 94 per cent of the affiliated membership. The trade unions also provided the bulk of the funds and in General Elections between 1906 and 1910, 74 per cent of the Labour Party (so named after 1906) candidates were sponsored by trade unions (Pinto-Duschinsky, 1981:62). In addition, the miners' candidates, who stood as Liberals, were also sponsored.

The money from the trade unions came from parliamentary funds set up by a ballot, or from general funds where balloting was not required. These general funds had been used for political purposes for over 30 years, yet no attack upon this usage occurred until the establishment of the LRC. The first challenge to this broader relationship occurred in 1904 with the registration problem (Ewing, 1982:17–22). This unsettled trade unionists and raised fears that political activity was unlawful. The *Plumbers' Case* in 1905 made the legal position concerning political funds still more vague, especially as the legality of political payments was not tested in the High Court until 1907 (*Steele* v. *South Wales Miners' Federation*) (Ewing, 1982: 18–80). Both judges in this case upheld trade union political payments. However, in 1910, following *Osborne* v. *Amalgamated Society of Railway Servants (ASRS)*, the so-called Osborne judgement was given. W.V. Osborne, a member and branch secretary of the ASRS, sought a court judgement that the parliamentary fund rules were invalid and called for an injunction to restrain the Society from levying and distributing money for political purposes. The Court of Appeal gave judgement and the decision was upheld in the House of Lords. The implications for the Labour Party were serious. It could have been weakened considerably which would have threatened its existence as a major political force. Within a year of the judgement, 25 trade unions had their political activities restrained by injunction. Pinto-Duschinsky is of the opinion that the Osborne judgement did little harm to the Labour Party, since its main burden of expenditure was eliminated with the introduction of MPs' salaries in 1911 (Pinto-Duschinsky, 1981: 66–7). Nevertheless, a challenge to the new pattern of political finance had clearly been posed.

The Liberal Government, elected in December 1910 and dependent upon the Labour Party for its majority, pledged to legislate upon the Osborne judgement. Labour members urged for a simple reversal of Osborne, opposing even any provisions to 'contract out' of political payments by individual trade unionists. The Liberals did not yield to this particular demand though did proceed with legislation, despite fierce resistance from Conservative members. The result was the Trade Union Act of 1913. The Act permitted trade unions to make political contributions provided that certain conditions were observed. First, a separate political fund was required. Political payments could only come from this fund, the Act creating a special category of spending on political objects. Secondly, the political fund could only be established after a successful ballot of unions' members to approve the political objects in question. There was no restriction on the number of ballots. A union could hold elections until it achieved a successful result; and once a ballot had supported its formation, this fund could be maintained indefinitely without further balloting. Finally, once a political fund was in operation, any member of a union could still claim exemption from payment. The member could 'contract out' without any discrimination or removal of rights as a union member. Should he feel that he was suffering discrimination, he could make a complaint to the Certification Officer. The ballots required by the act produced generally low turnouts, but there was a substantial overall majority in favour of holding a political fund. Coupled with the fact that few members bothered to 'contract out' once the political fund was established, the financial result for the Labour Party was excellent. This was compounded by the dramatic rise in trade union membership during the Great War. The beginnings of the *modern era* then lie with the formation of the Labour Party. Yet, one could not argue that the *plutocratic era* had ended until other institutions had become more relevant to political income. The move towards institutional funding by the Conservative Party, though by no means immediate, was largely a response to the growing labour movement and, specifically, the Labour Party. It was also spurred on by a desire within the Conservative Party to distance itself, in image and probably practice,[2] from the dealings in honours practised by Lloyd George and others.

The beginnings of change in Conservative Party income in the 1920s can be attributed to the Party Chairman, J.C.C. Davidson. He sought donations from the business community, concerned with the rise of socialism. The donations were apparently given on grounds of ideology and commercial self-interest rather than for honours. They came from London-based business, in particular the City. The change from *individual* to *institutional* was not, however, swift. Two reasons account for this. Firstly, there were legal problems for some companies in donating to political parties. Consequently, some opted to pacify their auditors and donate to anti-socialist organizations, which was considered acceptable business practice, rather than donate directly to the Conservative Party. Secondly, personal taxation was still sufficiently low to allow personal donations from businessmen without them suffering undue loss from their after-tax profits.

That said, the trend towards institutional giving did grow in the 1920s and 1930s. This can be attributed to a number of major factors. Firstly, certain major family businesses were now adopting a corporate structure. Secondly, the emergence of the Labour Party presented a clear threat to business and gave an incentive for contributions which had not existed before the Great War. Added to that, there was a general fear of organized labour (Pinto-Duschinsky, 1981:112).

The new era of party finance was not immune to threats, at least in the case of the Labour Party. First of all, severe unemployment in the 1920s reduced the number of union members and therefore political levy payers. Secondly, opposition to the 1913 Act remained within the Conservative Party. Conservative backbench Bills were introduced proposing 'contracting in' (rather than 'contracting out') in every Parliamentary session between 1922 and 1925. The Lloyd George cabinet resisted calls for reform, noting that the trade union movement was at a low ebb. Even Baldwin's cabinet was opposed to a change in the law, fearing in 1925 that such a move might endanger industrial peace. Yet only two years later, following the General Strike, the Trades Disputes and Trade Unions Act 1927 was introduced 'by a Conservative government bent on recrimination' (Ewing, 1982: 53).

Section 4 of the 1927 Act altered the provisions relating to political funds, introducing a system of 'contracting in'. This change was potentially very serious, yet in fact the financial damage to the Labour Party was limited. Much of the credit for this must go to the trade unions. The bitterness which followed the 1927 Act prompted intensive campaigns to urge 'contracting in' by members. The success of these campaigns was variable but the unions also tackled the anticipated shortfall of funds by raising affiliation rates in 1931 and imposing a special levy on affiliated unions. In addition, political funds hoarded before 1927 were now used.

Despite Liberal and Conservative Party opposition, 'contracting out' was restored by the post-war Labour government in the form of the Trade Disputes and Trade Unions Act 1946. Institutional funding now also became the mainstay of Conservative Party finance. In essence, a consensus surrounding party finance emerged, such that both sides broadly accepted trade union funding of the Labour Party and corporate funding of the Conservatives. This continued until the election of Margaret Thatcher's Conservative government in 1979. The change of government heralded a dramatic change in policy towards trade unions. The issue of political activity was soon addressed as part of a continuing series of trade union reforms. The relevant legislation was contained within Part III of the Trade Union Act 1984. It required that trade unions hold periodic ballots to determine the continuation of the political fund and extended the definition of political objects set out by the Trade Union Act of 1913. In the event, all unions that were required to hold a ballot returned a positive vote in favour of retaining the fund in both rounds of voting in 1985–6 and 1995–6. Moreover, as an unexpected consequence, the legislation did not reduce trade union political activity. Rather, some unions decided to establish a political fund in the light of the legislation, though this was most probably caused by a desire to avoid illegal activity rather than through a desire to become more politically active.

Overall, in much of the post-war period British party finance was comparable with arrangements in other countries where finance for political parties was not wholly provided by public funds and parties were essentially class based (Heidenheimer, 1970:5–9; Paltiel, 1981:143–7; Ewing, 1992:6–7). However, a number of factors indicate that British party finance may be developing in a different form. First of all, both major parties have suffered fluctuations in their institutional income in the 1990s. Secondly, it seems as though political parties are realising the possible fragility of their income and have looked towards newer forms of fund-raising. Finally, instances in the 1990s of personal donations comparable in size with corporate ones suggest perhaps that a greater mix of funding may be emerging. In short, this may be a post-modern era of party finance.

## The current system of party finance

In both the Conservative and Labour Parties there have been important developments in techniques of party fund-raising which indicate something of a shift away from traditional sources of finance (Fisher, 1996, 1997). In the case of the Conservatives, business donations are under threat from a growing trend of corporate political independence. There is evidence to suggest that companies question the reasons for their political donations as well as their economic utility (Fisher, 1994a:69; 1994b:691). Moreover, changing structures of corporate ownership indicate that there will be more multinational corporations which can pose a threat to donations where there is parent-company disapproval (Ewing, 1992:98; Fisher, 1997). In the case of Labour, much of its income has traditionally been provided by trade unions via affiliation payments, grants and ad hoc donations, sponsorship of candidates and MPs, advertisements in Labour Party publications, stands at Party conferences and a wide range of payments in kind including the provision of both resources and personnel. This variety of techniques is in part explained by the long-term institutional links between the Labour Party and affiliated trade unions. However, the proportion of central income provided by trade unions has declined rapidly since the late 1980s on account of the growth in new forms of income.

In all three main parties, there has been a growth of entrepreneurial forms of income which are comprised largely of commercial activities such as financial services, conferences and sales. These forms of fund-raising all provide a selective benefit for the institution or individual contributing money in these ways. This is opposed to direct donations which are seen as providing collective benefits (Fisher, 1995). In addition, the Conservative Party has also looked to other techniques of fund-raising which provide selective benefits. For example at least two 'clubs' operate: the Premier club and the Millennium club. Membership of these clubs is on a varying financial scale, members being offered benefits accordingly, such as contact with key party figures (Fisher, 1997).

Labour has also been successful in diversifying its fund-raising. Traditionally it has been less successful in attracting large individual donations. Nevertheless, one of the most recent initiatives, the Labour Party Business Plan, has been largely financed by individual donations from members and supporters, or activities, such as high profile dinners, which attract money from individuals rather than institutions.

A third trend has been the reemergence of personal donations to the extent that some individual donations have exceeded any made by a corporation (Pinto-Duschinsky, 1989:210; Fisher, 1994a, 1997). In 1995–6, this meant that contributions from individuals accounted for three quarters of all donations to the Conservative Party. There has also been an apparent growth in donations emanating from individuals abroad (Fisher, 1994a, 1997). Yet for all the diversification, the Conservative Party has faced severe financial difficulties. This has resulted in a growing dependence on loans which have helped finance the central party, secured from both local constituency parties and private sources.

Labour too has benefited from new sources of donations. One of the major new developments in party finance has been the readiness of individuals and businesses to support Labour financially. It has received both corporate and individual donations in the past, although the former have tended to be few in number and of small value, while the latter have not been of anything like the size received by the Conservatives (Fisher, 1997). However, Labour has now been successful in attracting individual donations of significant size. It has also attracted increasing levels of corporate financial support.

British parties have also benefited from an evolving system of limited state support. The earliest example of this was the introduction of the payment of MPs in 1911. Today, parties also receive free mailing, free use of public halls, state security at party conferences and, for the larger parties, free broadcasting air time for a controlled number of party broadcasts. Opposition parties additionally receive resources for their work in Parliament (known as 'Short' money). These subsidies are modest compared with many other Western countries (Nassmacher, 1993). Nevertheless, the significance of free broadcasting for Party Political Broadcasts should not be understated when comparing this with nations where parties must pay for this service. That said, the free broadcasting time in Britain is strictly regulated and parties are not able to purchase advertising time on television or radio.

The absence of regular state assistance to parties has, however, contributed to a funding cycle based around the cycle of British General Elections (Fisher, 2000). This funding cycle leads to two principal problems for parties. First, most expenditure for British political parties is routine rather than being focused only upon campaigning. Thus in order simply to maintain themselves as viable organizations, parties require some consistent financial input. Secondly, the notion of an electoral cycle every four to five years in British politics is something of a misnomer, as far as parties are concerned at least. Whilst parties do concentrate most resources and interest upon General Elections, they also campaign on a national basis in European elections (every five years) and across large proportions of the country in most years for the various staggered local elections, which in recent years have been contested by all parties in a far more 'national' way. The result is that whilst voluntary funds tend to cycle, party expenditures do so to a lesser extent. As a result, parties find themselves routinely in deficit, not necessarily by excessive campaign spending at general elections, but by simply trying to operate upon a routine basis.

Overall, party finance in Britain has evolved into a system which shares many characteristics with comparable democracies, such that the institutions of capital and labour support the two main parties. However, two features distinguish British party finance. First, the level of state support, whilst having grown, is still unusually low. Secondly, British party finance has evolved further, such that parties have become increasingly entrepreneurial and individuals have become more significant in party funding overall.

## Corruption and British party finance

At the heart of any debate regarding the financing of political parties there is one underlying fact which must be borne in mind. *For political parties to exist and perform satisfactorily, they must have income and resources. Therefore, unless the party can generate sufficient income from membership dues and trading or investments there must be alternative sources of income.* Neither the Conservative Party nor the Labour Party have a sufficiently large membership to be self-financing. Current estimates put Conservative Party membership at 350 000 and Labour's at 400 000. Moreover, whilst the two main political parties are becoming more skilled at exploiting the commercial potential of events such as party conferences, they do not generate enough income from these activities to be economically self sufficient. The Liberal Democrats do manage to finance themselves almost self sufficiently, but exercise greater restraint in spending. Consequently, parties must look to a variety of sources to satisfy their financial needs. This might suggest that strict rules are required in order that the process of income generation is not corrupted.

Yet, British party finance is remarkably unregulated. Existing law on British political finance is limited and largely applies at local level. Under the Representation of the People Act there are spending limits imposed on constituency election spending but not at national level. The spirit of this law developed in the nineteenth century when election campaigns were conducted on a more local basis than is the case today (Johnston and Pattie, 1993). Nor are there any limits on income. Any political party may raise as much money as it chooses from as many sources as it can solicit funds. In the case of corporate donations, the only legislation governing political finance is the Companies Act (1985, amended), which states that any donations that exceed £200 defined as being for *political purposes* shall be declared in the directors' report for that year. Foreign companies are not however bound by this legislation.

No such declaration is required for individual donations. Labour voluntarily publishes the names of donors contributing in excess of

£5000 per annum (though not the amounts contributed). The Conservative Party, however, declares neither its corporate nor its individual benefactors. It has been able to avoid giving such details in its accounts because the party is an unincorporated association with no legal status, and as such is subject only to internal rules. The only way in which interested parties can ascertain information regarding corporate donations is by examining the accounts of individual companies. Given that there are around one million companies in Britain this is an impractical task. Declaration is provided in the case of trade union funding of Labour. However, this has not prevented long-term unease regarding relations between trade unions and the Labour Party, principally over the relationship between affiliation and votes at the party conference (see, for example, Pinto-Duschinsky, 1981).

The secrecy surrounding donations has generated much debate, with accusations of the effective purchase of political influence and abuses of the honours system. There is both historical and contemporary precedent for such claims. The sale of honours in return for political funds by Lloyd George prompted The Honours (Prevention of Abuses) Act 1925. Moreover, studies of political finance practice in other countries have thrown up many examples both of corruption and, importantly, assumptions of quid pro quo in legislation. Yet, since the time of Lloyd George there have been no substantiated scandals in the sphere of British party political finance. That is to say, there have been no proven revelations of illegality in terms of selective benefits being acquired in return for party donations. Nevertheless, periodic debate has highlighted a number of episodes which have undermined confidence in the probity of party finance. In the 1990s these have centred largely upon income received from apparently dubious sources and foreign donations which, under the largely unregulated British system, have nevertheless been perfectly legal (Fisher, 1994a, 1997).

Much of the criticism has been focused upon the Conservative Party. Traditionally, donations have attracted criticism because it was claimed that honours were awarded to those who contributed personally or whose companies did so. Indeed, such assertions are almost the stuff of popular folklore. More serious, perhaps, have been claims in the most recent debates about party finance that donations are now being rewarded in financially beneficial ways through membership on QUANGOs. If there is any truth in such claims, this presents a far more serious scenario than patronage through the Honours List, since membership of such agencies is more likely to be able to produce economic benefit (Fisher, 1997).

Donations to the Labour Party have also attracted criticism. In late 1997, it was revealed that the Labour Party had received a donation of £1 million from the Head of Formula 1 Racing, Bernie Ecclestone. The reason this donation was problematic was that the government had excluded Formula 1 from its proposed ban upon tobacco advertising in sport. There were suggestions therefore that the donation, whilst not unique in size, had been reciprocated with a change in policy. Labour immediately sought to limit the political damage by declaring the matter to the chair of the House of Commons Standards Committee and returning the donation to Mr Ecclestone. Moreover, the Prime Minister then instructed the Committee on Standards in Public Life (now chaired by Lord Neill) to examine the whole issue of party finance.

Thus, whilst there have been no substantiated scandals on the scale witnessed in other democracies (or at least, none which have come to light), British party finance has nevertheless come under considerable scrutiny. Parties have needed to respond to increasing financial demands but the secrecy surrounding donations, together with the size of some individual payments, has led to unease both amongst political elites and the broader public. This has presented a serious problem since, as Lösche has observed in Germany, even the *appearance* of corruption leads to negative feelings about parties and the ways those parties finance their organizations (Lösche, 1993). It is for this reason, together with periodic concern regarding the financial health of parties, that reform has been attempted, even though the level of genuine scandal in British party finance has been comparatively low.

## Attempts to reform British party finance

The principal act with regard to party and electoral finance is the Corrupt and Illegal Practices (Prevention) Act 1883. This was designed to limit the scope for local political corruption by outlawing bribery and placing limits upon local campaign spending. It is this act which forms the basis of current party and electoral finance law in the United

Kingdom. The provisions in the act are regularly modified by the Representation of the People Act (Johnston and Pattie, 1993). As we have seen, the system of party finance evolved and a broad, though flawed, consensus emerged. Since the 1970s however, the system has been under strain and subject to periodic examination.

In 1975, financial assistance for parliamentary opposition parties was introduced. Named 'Short' money (after the Labour leader of the Commons), this was (and continues to be) a sum allocated according to the number of seats in the House of Commons, together with a calculation linked to inflation of a sum relative to votes won at the preceding General Election. This form of assistance continues to this day. To that end, in the period from the 1997 election to the end of March 1998, the Conservatives received £986 762 and the Liberal Democrats £371 997. Other opposition parties taking their seats in the House of Commons (that is, excluding Sinn Féin) also receive income. In addition, since 1996 small sums have also been payable to opposition parties working in the House of Lords. This is known as 'Cranborne' money. The total allocation in 1997–8 was £134 000 (Committee on Standards in Public Life, 1998:101).

A desire to examine the possibilities for the state funding of political parties was announced soon after the first election in 1974. The new Labour government announced that it was to appoint an independent committee with Lord Houghton, a former Labour cabinet minister, as Chair. The Committee on Financial Aid to Political Parties (generally known as the Houghton Committee) reported in 1976. The report favoured state subsidies to parties as a means of halting what it saw as the decline in parties' contribution to public life. It argued that membership fees and traditional fund-raising methods were inadequate and meant that parties were frequently operating below minimum levels of required activities and efficiency. Moreover, traditional fund-raising created an unhealthy reliance upon trade union and business support. To counter these problems, the Committee proposed annual grants to central party organizations based upon popular electoral support as well as limited reimbursement at local level of candidates' election expenses for both parliamentary and local elections. The committee was not, however, unanimous in its recommendations. Four of the committee of twelve opposed subsidies in principle and a further member expressed written reservations about the proposed scheme (Pinto-Duschinsky,

1981:2). When the report was published, Labour supported the principle of state subsidy whilst the Conservatives rejected it. After the 1977 Labour Party Conference endorsed the notion of state aid, it was thought that the government would introduce Houghton's proposals in some form. However, they failed to do this before their election defeat in 1979 and the new Conservative government continued the party's opposition to subsidies. The Houghton recommendations were effectively buried.

This opposition continued when the Hansard Commission on the Financing of Political Parties reported in 1981 (*Paying for Politics*). This report proposed state aid on a matching funds basis from a maximum available sum and sought to limit the size of individual donations to £2 (£4.23 at 1997 prices) in the hope that this would encourage a larger number of small donors. There were also proposals to limit campaign expenditure, disclose donations over a certain size and oblige parties to publish full accounts. In the depths of recession and with a government committed to cutting public spending, the recommendations were predictably rejected.

Two further Hansard Society sponsored reports appeared during the next ten years. In 1985, a jointly sponsored report (with the Constitutional Reform Centre) recommended that whilst corporate donations should continue, they should be subject to shareholder approval at least once in the lifetime of each parliament and in advance for specific donations. Moreover, donations should be made directly to a party, rather than through an intermediary body (Constitutional Reform Centre/Hansard Society, 1985). In 1992, the Hansard Society report, *Agenda for Change*, was divided over support for the principles outlined in the Houghton report and recommended only that a tax 'check off' be introduced to encourage small donations. None of these recommendations were implemented.

Despite the Conservative government's continuing opposition to reform, the Select Committee on Home Affairs decided in November 1992 to examine party finance. This occurred after one Conservative member of the committee supported opposition members' calls for an investigation, thereby securing a majority decision in favour. Proceedings began in June 1993. The terms of reference were not to investigate scandals, but to examine the case for and against the state funding of political parties, the methods by which parties are financed and the desirability of controls both on income and expenditure.

It provided a strong focus for the issue of political finance and therefore the impetus for further revelations and claims about Conservative Party income. During the course of the Committee's investigations, a series of revelations appeared regarding donations emanating from foreign and apparently dubious sources (see Fisher, 1994a). Indeed, so much coverage was given to the revelations that proceedings in the Select Committee were frequently dominated by accusations rather than the central theme of the remit, with members attempting to score party political points against each other.

The committee divided along party lines regarding the final report, with the Chair exercising his casting vote. The report itself was very limited in its recommendations. It rejected the extension of state funding, any further disclosure regulation or contribution limits. The only possible changes recommended were the requirement that party accounts contain reasonable levels of detail, including payments in kind, together with the consideration of Civil Service secondment to parties as a form of 'in kind' state funding. Beyond that, the report gave a clean bill of health to British party finance.

## The Neill Committee

However, the election of a Labour government in 1997 meant that some reform was possible, the party having promised to reexamine the issue of party finance in its manifesto. The hand of the new government was forced, however, by the Ecclestone affair. The result was that the Prime Minister instructed the Committee on Standards in Public Life (the Neill Committee) to examine the whole issue of party finance. The committee investigated the issue in the context of three further important developments which were to guide their thinking. The government's constitutional reforms had led to two new scenarios. First, there was the increased use of referendums. Within a year of Labour taking office, referendums on the establishment of new assemblies were held in Scotland, Wales and London. There was also a referendum in Northern Ireland on the terms of the Good Friday Agreement. Secondly, the new government had introduced alternative electoral systems for the 1999 European elections as well as for the future elections in Scotland, Wales and London. Indeed, the electoral systems adopted necessitated the registration of political parties (for the allocation of vote share and top-up seats) and thus, one of the potential obstacles to reform, the legal status of political parties, had already been addressed. Moreover, with the appointment of Lord Jenkins to examine alternative electoral systems for elections to Westminster, the likelihood was that any new recommendations on party finance would need to take new electoral arrangements into account. Finally, the whole question of regulation was thrown into some doubt by the Bowman ruling in the European Court.

Phyllis Bowman was the executive director of the Society for the Protection of the Unborn Child (SPUC). During the period immediately prior to the 1992 General Election, Bowman arranged for 1.5 million leaflets to be distributed throughout Britain. Of particular concern were the 25 000 leaflets distributed in the constituency of Halifax. On that leaflet were details of both embryo development and the relevant views on abortion and embryo experimentation of the three major party candidates contesting the seat. As a consequence, Bowman was charged with an offence under Section 75 of the Representation of the People Act. The act states that campaigning by a 'third party' (not a candidate or his approved campaign organizers) which seeks to promote a candidate and exceeds the aggregate sum of £5 is guilty of a corrupt practice. In fact, the prosecution was dismissed on a technicality (the summons was issued out of time). However, Bowman took the case to the European Court, contesting that Section 75 violated Article 10 of the European Convention on Human Rights which guarantees freedom of expression. Bowman's contention was that she should never have been prosecuted. The European Court, upheld Bowman's contention on the grounds that the limit of £5 was so low as to make third party expenditure effectively illegal and this constituted an unjustifiable restriction on her freedom of expression. Potentially, this could have led to an approach similar to that pursued in the United States (following *Buckley* v. *Valeo*) which would, in effect, have made many proposed reforms unworkable.

The Neill Committee reported in October 1998. Given the nature of the Home Affairs Committee report, the new electoral landscape and the Bowman case, there were fears that the report would not recommend a great deal of reform. Hitherto, those who had emphasized legal loopholes rather than political principles had held sway in the ongoing debate. Indeed, one could have been forgiven for thinking that the regulation of party finance was the most difficult policy area imaginable. As a consequence, some viewed virtually any reform as being unworkable. This was a curious view given that no other areas of electoral law were deemed to be so problematic.

The Neill report is radical, however, and represents proposals for the most fundamental reform in British party finance since the Corrupt and Illegal Practices Act 1883. It is a wide-ranging report which makes no less than 100 proposals for reform. The key ones are outlined below. First, there will be the establishment of an electoral commission to oversee the implementation of the law relevant to party finance as well as for other electoral matters. To that end, parties will be required to submit audited accounts based upon identical time periods in a standard format. Such accounts will be required within three months of the accounting year end. In terms of donations, a number of regulations are proposed. First, donations in excess of £5000 nationally and £1000 locally are to be publicly declared. Importantly, this includes 'in kind' payments.

Second, anonymous donations to parties in excess of £50 will be prohibited. Third, there will be an end to 'blind trusts'. These are trusts set up where the donor's identity is not known to the recipient. Fourth, shareholders are to be balloted prior to political donations being made by companies. This authority will be valid for four years and will provide the board of directors with discretion during that period to make donations up to a prescribed limit. This compares with the ten-yearly ballots required of trade unions holding a political fund. Finally, foreign donations are to be banned, or rather donations will only be permitted from permissible sources, those being individuals entitled to be registered as UK voters; companies incorporated in the United Kingdom; partnerships based in the United Kingdom or who operate principally in the United Kingdom; registered trade unions and other organizations based in the United Kingdom or those parts of organizations whose principal spheres of operation are based in the United Kingdom.

One of the report's most radical suggestions is the limit upon campaign spending at a national level. Hitherto, only local campaign expenditure has been regulated. One of the problems in imposing a national limit is the definition of when a campaign begins. The report acknowledged those difficulties but decided nevertheless to impose a ceiling of £20 million per party on General Election spending. This ceiling would be lowered for parties contesting fewer seats.

This cap was a surprise move given that of all the regulations, this was most likely to attract loophole seeking. However, the committee's approach was one similar to that imposed at local level. The analogy was with speed limits. A 30mph speed limit will not prevent drivers travelling at 35mph, but it is likely to prevent speeds of 50mph. Secondly, the cap of £20 million is actually very high. Given that parties will be campaigning even more regularly in the future with three new large assemblies presently being established in Britain, the parties may face some difficulty actually spending £20 million. This is particularly so since the report pledged support for the continuation of a ban on political advertising on television and radio and a desire that new communication media should also be subject to regulation. As a consequence, the free access to television and radio enjoyed by parties through Party Political Broadcasts looks set to continue.

The committee also avoided the potential problem of the Bowman case by proposing an increase in the sum permitted for third party expenditure to £500 – a one-hundred-fold increase on the previous level. It is hoped that the European Court will accept that this limit no longer breaches freedom of expression and since the Court accepted that some restrictions were required in order that elections are conducted in a free and fair manner, there is a hope that this new limit will prove to be satisfactory. That said, the report also imposed a ceiling of £25 000 on general political campaigns undertaken by non-registered 'third parties' during an election campaign. 'Third parties' registering their campaigns will be permitted to spend up to 5 per cent of the maximum limit set for any political party – in effect £1 million based upon the £20 million ceiling. This restriction goes well beyond what was permissible beforehand.

The report does not explicitly support an extension of public funding to political parties, despite the fact that a number of the initial questions issued for consultation were concerned with this subject. However, there are a number of proposals which do indicate that the principle of increased public funding has been more readily accepted. First, tax relief is to be provided for donations of up to £500. This will result in some state funding by virtue of monies which would normally go to the Treasury. Second, a Policy Development Fund will be established, initially cash limited to £2 million per annum, to assist parties to engage more fully on policy development. Finally, it is proposed that the provision of 'Short' money be increased threefold to represent a cost of around £4.8 million. As a consequence of these proposals, there will in effect be an extension of public funding of parties. Moreover, given the report's view that parties are fundamental to parliamentary democracy, that they should be able to function adequately, and that the importance of parties goes beyond contesting elections, there is the possibility of further state aid should parties find themselves in financial difficulty. Given that parties face increasing campaign costs in uncertain electoral arrangements, it may be pure practicality which ushers in further state aid.

The final principal area of the report is referendums. Whilst not strictly relevant to party finance, the recommendations proposed are nevertheless pertinent to the discussion. First, the desire to regulate is upheld such that campaign groups are registered, disclosure limits are set and campaigning by 'third parties' is restricted. More important is the recommendation that in order that referendum campaigns are fair, registered campaigns may apply for core public funding. The implication here is that the market is insufficient to provide an even political contest – a principle which could theoretically be applied to elections. For all that, however, the most radical proposal is that governments should remain neutral in a referendum and not distribute any literature at the public expense – even factual literature.

## Conclusions

The development of British party finance has been pragmatic, largely unregulated and yet seemingly devoid of the kinds of scandals which have beset other democracies. To be sure there is unease with some practices and this unease has been growing. However, unlike most significant institutional change, there has not been one single incident which has produced the kind of reform now envisaged by the Neill Committee. The Neill recommendations represent a huge break from the past in terms of party finance. Significant reform is proposed and, given that the report has received backing from all three main parties, the reforms stand every chance of becoming law. Perhaps the only exceptions will be the tax check offs and the referendum proposals – the latter of which has attracted most debate. Notwithstanding the success of the 1883 Act, previous attempts at reform have failed. Houghton failed because of a lack of political will to implement it before a change of government. The reforms proposed in various Hansard reports were ignored, much as the support for the status quo in the Home Affairs committee was noted – both suited the interests and ideology of that government. Given the Labour government's commitment to regulate these matters, its broad constitutional programme and not forgetting the huge majority it enjoys, the likelihood is that the most recent reforms will succeed at least in reaching the statute book. British political finance is about to become modern and regulated in ways more akin to most other democracies.

## Notes

1  In the four General Elections prior to the reform act of 1867, between 43 and 60 per cent of seats were uncontested. By 1880, the figure was only 17 per cent (Pinto-Duschinsky, 1981:19–24).
2  There is some debate as to when dealing in honours *actually* ceased, summarized in Pinto-Duschinsky, 1981:104–11.

## Bibliography

Committee on Standards in Public Life (1998), *The Funding of Political Parties in the United Kingdom*, London: Cm 4057.
Constitutional Reform Centre/Hansard Society (1985), *Company Donations: A Suggested Code of Practice*, London.
Ewing, K. (1982), *Trade Unions, The Labour Party and The Law*, Edinburgh: Edinburgh University Press.
Ewing, K. (1992), *Money, Politics and Law*, Oxford: Clarendon Press.
Fisher, J. (1994a), 'Political Donations to the Conservative Party', *Parliamentary Affairs*, 47: 61–72.
Fisher, J. (1994b), 'Why Do Companies Make Donations to Political Parties?', *Political Studies*, 42: 690–9.
Fisher, J. (1995), 'The Institutional Funding of British Political Parties', in D. Broughton *et al.* (eds), *British Elections and Parties Yearbook 1994*, London: Frank Cass.
Fisher, J. (1996), 'Party Finance', in P. Norton (ed.), *The Conservative Party*, Hemel Hempstead: Prentice Hall.
Fisher, J. (1997), 'Donations to Political Parties', *Parliamentary Affairs*, 50: 235–45.
Fisher, J. (2000), 'Financing Party Politics in Britain', in Malamud and Posado-Carbó (eds), *Financing Party Politics in Europe and Latin America*, London: Macmillan, forthcoming.
Gwyn, W.B. (1962), *Democracy and the Cost of Politics*, London: Athlone.

Heidenheimer, A.J. (1970), 'Major Modes of Raising Spending and Controlling Public Funds During and Between Election Campaigns', in Heidenheimer, A.J. (ed.), *Comparative Political Finance*, Massachusetts: Heath.

Hansard Commission (1981), *Paying for Politics*.

Hansard Commission (1992), *Agenda for Change*.

Home Affairs Select Committee (1994), *Funding of Political Parties*, London: HMSO.

Johnston R. and Pattie, C. (1993), 'Great Britain: Twentieth Century Parties Operating Under Nineteenth Century Regulations', in Gunlicks, A.B. (ed.), *Campaign and Party Finance in North America and Western Europe*, Boulder: Westview Press.

Lösche, P. (1993), 'Problems of Party and Campaign Financing in Germany and The United States – Some Comparative Reflections', in Gunlicks, A.B. (ed.), *Campaign and Party Finance in North America and Western Europe*, Boulder: Westview Press.

Nassmacher, K.H. (1993) 'Comparing Party and Campaign Finance in Western Democracies', in Gunlicks, A.B. (ed.), *Campaign and Party Finance in North America and Western Europe*, Boulder: Westview Press.

Paltiel, K.Z. (1981), 'Campaign Finance: Contrasting Practices and Reforms', in Butler, D., Penniman, H.R. and Ranney, A. (eds), *Democracy at the Polls*, Washington: American Enterprise Institute.

Pinto-Duschinsky, M. (1981), *British Political Finance 1830–1980*, Washington DC: American Enterprise Institute.

Pinto-Duschinsky, M. (1989), 'Trends in British Party Funding 1983–1987', *Parliamentary Affairs*, 42: 197–212.

*Report of the Committee on Financial Aid to Political Parties* (1976) (Cmnd 6601).

# 3
# Parties, Corruption and Campaign Finance in America

*Dean McSweeney*

Financing American national elections has several distinctive features: parties raise and spend only a minority of campaign money; individuals and interest groups supply the bulk of money raised; candidates and interest groups spend the majority of campaign money; election finance law limits donations, and requires disclosure of many expenditures and contributions; these laws have proved ineffective in containing costs or preventing wealthy interests from heavily funding elections; concern about corruption centres on the influence derived from legal uses of money. This chapter seeks to explain the formation of the campaign finance system, the forms corruption takes, and the obstacles to reforming the law to penalize and curb corrupt conduct.

## Parties and corruption

Fears about the misuse of office for personal or sectional advantage informed the writing of the Constitution. Assuming human nature to be selfish, the Founders created a system of government designed to allow for the expression of self-interest whilst restraining its pernicious effects. Authority was fragmented between institutions and levels of government to restrict the range of powers any one interest could exercise. Power sharing between the institutions of national government fostered a competitive struggle between conflicting interests. Out of these clashes and compromises the Founders hoped to produce republican government: government in the public interest.

Parties were distrusted as threats to republican government because parties were expressions of partial rather than general interests. Parties (or factions) were always the servants of one interest to the detriment of the interests and liberty of others. Most dangerous of all was a majority faction, empowered by its numbers to promote its interest more effectively than others. A large territory created social impediments to the formation of a majority faction but the Founders also sought to erect institutional barriers to the political influence of such an interest. The battery of checking and balancing mechanisms – fixed terms, staggered elections, different methods of election – were designed to guard against the corrupting effects of majority domination.[1]

Distrust of parties has been a recurrent theme in American political history from the Founders onwards. Favouritism and venality were associated with the parties of the enlarged electorate in the Jacksonian era. The machines of the late nineteenth century used government to benefit their electors, activists and business financiers, contributing further to the odious reputation of parties. Dishonest and incompetent government under machine control became a focus for journalistic exposés, and reforming legislation in the Progressive era.

Reform inaugurated a process which debilitated parties in elections and government. The introduction of primaries, whereby voters rather than party bosses chose candidates, set in motion the separation of candidates from parties, which has become a distinctive feature of American electioneering. Internal party election contests encouraged the formation of personal campaign teams dependent upon non-party sources of funds. Subsequent developments, including the decline of machines and the appearance of capital-intensive forms of electioneering, utilizing technology rather than labour, extended personal organizations into general elections. Writing in the early 1960s, V.O. Key noted the consequences for election finance: 'The problem of raising money to support political activity is not one of party finance but in large measure one of financing individual candidates. ... In substantial degree ... American politics is atomized and each candidate must in some way or other cover his own personal campaign expenses.'[2]

Machines funded party activity through illicit means. They harvested the government. Business exchanged donations to the machine for favourable treatment from government. Public funds were stolen, sinecures in public employment financed full-time party activists and tithes on public employees went into party funds. Funding parties became problematic after machines declined. American parties never had members, and they have therefore lacked regular income from party membership fees. In the absence of membership fees, sources outside the party organizations – individuals and groups – have supplied their funds. But this reliance on external funding has made American parties particularly dependent on 'interested money' seeking returns on investments.

## The legal framework

Reactions to corrupt behaviour or fears of its potential have inspired much of the campaign finance law enacted in the twentieth century. Substantial company donations to the 1904 Republican presidential campaign stimulated attempts to eliminate corporate funding of elections. The 1907 Tillman Act outlawed donations from companies and banks. The Progressive preoccupation with purging business influence from politics was revived in the 1920s by the Teapot Dome scandal. The bribery of officials in the Harding Administration by company officials had been preceded by large donations to the campaign which elected Harding. In response, Congress enacted the Federal Corrupt Practices Act, which limited donations to a campaign committee to $5000. Candidates were required to submit reports of expenditures which took place with their knowledge and consent.

Concern at the political influence of organized labour during the New Deal resulted in the ban on use of union funds to finance elections. Finalized in 1947, the Taft–Hartley Act formed a non-identical twin to the Tillman Act of 40 years before. The 1940 Hatch Act limited spending by any political committee to $3 million per year. The Corrupt Practices Act was superseded by the Federal Election Campaign Act (FECA) of 1971. FECA was a response to a surge in the costs of elections: it capped campaign spending, and expenditures by the candidates and their families.

These enactments failed to extricate organized interests from elections. Business reacted to the new Tillman Act by encouraging company executives to make individual donations which were reimbursed through salary bonuses. Organized labour created political action committees (PACs), separate organizations soliciting funds from union members. Business and labour interests were thus able to retain a legal role in election funding by adjusting the methods they used. These adaptations coincided with the survival of illegal practices, because the legislation lacked effective enforcement. In the 49 years of the Corrupt Practices Act only one case was taken to court and that produced a not-guilty verdict.The early political career of Lyndon Johnson illustrates the inefficacy of federal law. When Johnson first ran for Congress in a special House election in 1937 he submitted a report of expenditures of $2242.74. A campaign aide offered a more realistic estimate of between $75000 and $100000.[3] Key dismissed the restraining impact of the laws as 'purely illusory'.[4]

But the detachment of candidates from parties, which primaries began, was augmented by the ceilings on contributions to, and expenditures by, any one committee. They encouraged the formation of multiple committees each entitled to receive and spend the legal maximum. The proliferation of committees undermined co-ordination of campaigns by a party organization.

Watergate, the most lavish election scandal in American history, inspired a new round of reform which further disconnected candidates from party funding. The abuses of Watergate were the work of a candidate organization, not a party. The Committee to Reelect the President (CRP) was devoted exclusively to the presidential contest in 1972. CRP had a staff, network of state and local organizations and a spectacularly successful fund-raising operation separate from the Republican Party. CRP employees perpetrated the crimes uncovered in Watergate, of sabotage of opposition campaigns, extortion in fund-raising, burglary and the financing of a criminal cover-up.

Watergate exposed the futility of existing law in preventing abuses. Companies such as Goodyear, American Airlines and 3M contributed to CRP, a violation of federal law since 1907. Watergate also exposed the favourable treatment in government towards contributors. Government subsidies of milk prices followed an agreement by Associated Milk Producers, Inc, to donate $2 million to Nixon's campaign. CRP sought company donations accompanied by threats of retaliation for non-payment. Some wealthy backers were rewarded with government appointments despite their dubious credentials. Ambassadorships were allocated by auction. One aspiring appointee questioned the asking price: 'Isn't $250000 an awful amount of money for Costa Rica?'[5]

It was a party organization, the Democratic National Committee, which was the target of the failed burglary in the Watergate complex from which the scandal unravelled. Yet the reforms of election finance law which followed Watergate capped the donations parties could make to candidates. The financial independence of candidates from parties, already well advanced, gained legal authority.

In reaction to Watergate, amendments were made to FECA in 1974 which constituted 'the most sweeping change imposed upon the interaction between money and politics since the creation of the American Republic'.[6] The intention was to eliminate large donations and curb the cost of elections. The methods used to secure these objectives were a mix of the traditional caps on contributions and spending plus disclosure, allied with the more novel public funding, and the inception of a regulatory commission.

Maxima were specified for donations (all amounts are annual ceilings): from an individual to a candidate ($1000 per election); from an individual to all candidates, parties and committee ($25000 in total); $5000 from a political action committee to a candidate; $5000 from national party committees to a candidate ($17500 from Senate party committees). Other attempts to free candidates from dependence on large donations included full public funding for presidential elections and partial public funding for presidential nominations. To ensure enforcement, a Federal Election Commission (FEC) was created to administer the law. Expenditures and donations of $100 were to be reported to the FEC. Spending maxima were also applied. Limits were set on total spending, candidates expenditures on their own behalf and on independent spending (monies spent by individuals or groups on behalf of a candidate without either giving money or liaising about its use).

Attempts to curb candidates' use of their own money and independent expenditure were subsequently invalidated by the Supreme Court in Buckley v. Valeo (1976). Opponents of FECA argued that all limits on expenditures and donations were unconstitutional. A Court majority accepted that only some of the limits on spending were a substantial restraint on the exercise of free expression protected by the First Amendment to the Constitution. The Court recognized the right of Congress to legislate to deter corruption, but it found no such rationale in curbing candidates' use of their own funds or spending on their behalf which they did not control.[7] FECA further distanced candidates from parties. In one respect FECA dealt more severely with parties than individuals or other committees. Candidates were limited in how much they could receive from a particular individual or political action committee but there was no aggregate total for donations from all individuals or committees. But the rules for party committees set aggregate totals ($30000 in House elections, $20000 from national organizations, $10000 from state parties). The maximum donations allowed to parties were substantially below the cost of most campaigns when FECA was written. In 1974 the average House campaign spent $53384. Parties could finance no more than 56 per cent of that total. As those totals have never been adjusted to take account of inflation or the increase in campaign spending, so the legal maximum parties can provide has shrunk. Candidates' dependence on non-party sources was already the norm by the 1970s and FECA accelerated their independence from party funding. In 1972, the first election for which sufficiently reliable data is available, 17 per cent of House campaign receipts derived from parties. In 1976, the first election FECA was in operation, the party share halved to 8 per cent.

For presidential elections, FECA required almost complete candidate financial independence from their parties. Public funding was supplied to major party candidates who agreed to restrict spending. From 1976 all major party candidates have accepted public finance, restricting party contributions to a small fraction of expenditure.

Other forms of party assistance to candidates were permitted under FECA. Co-ordinated expenditures allowed parties to liaise with candidates and spend on their behalf without making donations. Co-ordination can include the party mounting a campaign for a candidate or sharing the results of opinion polls commissioned by the party. Co-ordinated expenditures are adjusted for inflation and they are considerably larger than the maximum donations. In the 1996 elections, co-ordinated expenditures by parties were almost ten times larger than their contributions to candidates.

FECA amendments in 1979 facilitated an exponential increase in party spending. Concerned at the debilitation of traditional grass-roots campaign activity, Congress freed state and local parties from spending limits on electioneering materials such as badges, bumper stickers, yard signs, leaflets, party newspapers, voter registration and get-out-the-vote drives. This relaxation on FECA limits inaugurated what came to be known as 'soft money' (distinct from the 'hard money' subject to spending and donation limits). Soft money allows unlimited donations, and from sources such as union and corporate treasuries barred from contributing to candidates. Only after a further amendment in 1991 were soft money contributions and expenditures subject to FEC reporting requirements. Soft money has to be spent below national level but national party organizations are active in raising and collecting funds which are then disbursed to state and local parties. Some soft money has been deployed for activities outside those defined in the 1979 revision, including television advertising.

Unlimited independent expenditures became available to parties following the 1996 Supreme Court decision in *Colorado Republican Federal Campaign Committee* v. *Federal Election Commission*. The Colorado decision afforded to parties the rights granted to individuals and groups in the Buckley case 20 years earlier. Such spending can be used to promote a candidate without donations or liaison with them in devising how monies will be deployed. In its inaugural campaign in 1996, parties' independent spending was double their contributions to candidates.

FECA exhibited a distinctively American treatment of political parties. The assumption behind contribution caps was that all private sources of money represents vested interests. Parties, like individuals and groups, had to be constrained to allow candidates to serve the public interest. Contribution caps ensured that candidates obtained most of their funds from non-party sources. Like the Founders, President Ford and the 93rd Congress which enacted the FECA revisions, saw parties as partial interests. Unlike the Founders, the FECA amendments' authors were party politicians.

In other democracies a more benign view of parties has prevailed. Campaign finance law has been aimed at protecting parties from special interests rather than treating parties as special interests. Public funding of parties has been adopted to immunize them from partial interests. In the US, however, the immunity was applied to candidates *against* parties. Soft money, coordinated and independent expenditures have allowed parties to raise and spend large sums in elections, but this is achieved by keeping them at arm's length from the candidates who use the party's name (Table 3.1).

*Table 3.1* Party Spending on Federal Elections, 1995–96 (in $ millions)

|  | Democrats | Republicans |
| --- | --- | --- |
| Soft money | 121.8 | 149.7 |
| Candidate contributions | 2.2 | 3.7 |
| Co-ordinated expenditures | 22.6 | 31.0 |
| Independent spending | 1.5 | 10.0 |
| **Total** | **148.1** | **194.4** |

*Source*: Federal Election Commission.

## Campaign finance in practice

The creativity of Congress in prescribing regulation has been matched by the ingenuity of the regulated in inserting their funds into elections in attempts to create obligations amongst officeholders.

Federal law bars donations to candidates from corporations and unions but the political action committee (PAC) form allows organizations connected to companies and unions to fund candidates. By capping the individual contributions company executives could make to a candidate, FECA stimulated corporations to create PACs. Previously the preserve of organized labour, hundreds of corporations created political action committees. Using categories employed by the Federal Election Commission, the corporate sector has the largest number of PACs, 1674 in 1995 compared to 334 union PACs. Another fifth of all PACs, defined by the FEC as 'trade, membership, health', are trade associations such as the National Federation of Independent Business, the US League of Savings Institutions and the American Bankers Association, funded either by firms or individuals. They add several hundred PACs to the representation of business interests. Thus approximately three-quarters of all PACs express the interests of unions or business, which reformers sought to remove from election financing in the first half of this century. The corporate and labour categories supplied 55 per cent of all PAC contributions in the 1996 elections, some $115.8 million.

Funds from corporate and union accounts are paid to parties as soft money. In 1995–6 soft money income for the two parties' national organizations totalled in excess of $250 million, double the sum allocated to their candidates for public financing of the presidential election. No limits apply to soft money donations. The largest donations derive from the unions, corporations and wealthy individuals whose giving has been the target of repeated regulation during the twentieth century. In the 1996 elections the group Common Cause logged 130 soft money donations in excess of $250000. Five contributions exceeded one million dollars. 112 of those donations were made by unions, corporations or their shareholders. Major donors included AT&A, the Walt Disney Company, the News Corporation, the public employees union AFSCME, the Coca Cola Company, the American Federation of Teachers and Glaxo.[8]

Union and corporate treasuries also fund 'issue advocacy' advertising. Judicial interpretations of issue advocacy derived from the Buckley case excluded from limits, spending on election materials provided they do not expressly recommend the election or defeat of a named candidate. Praise or condemnation of a named candidate is permissible provided certain 'magic words' like 'Vote for or against' and 'Defeat' are not used. Although issue advocacy advertising is employed as part of lobbying efforts it escalates at election times, allowing companies and unions to promote candidates by legal means without resort to PACs. In 1996 the AFL–CIO spent $35 million in issue advocacy to unseat Republican members of the House. A counterattack organized by the Chamber of Commerce consumed $7 million.

Nor did FECA depress the election expenditure. Campaign spending continued to rise through to the end of the 1980s, outstripping the general rate of inflation. FECA probably added to the cost of electioneering. Forcing candidates to attract modest sums from large numbers of sources professionalised fund-raising but in so doing required more money to raise money. Informal contacts with wealthy 'fat cats' were no longer sufficient to fund campaigns. Direct mail campaigns became a common means of soliciting large numbers of potential donors but at great cost. Much direct mail spending is wasted in minuscule response rates. The money spent raising money increased as the number of organizations competing for funds multiplied.

## Corruption under FECA

No consensus exists about the definition of political corruption. Three definitions of corruption will be used to provide guides to its incidence under FECA. One equates corruption with illegal abuse of a public role. A second relies on public conceptions to define corruption. A third treats corruption as the use of favours to secure private interests.[9] FECA established a more detailed legal framework for federal campaign finance than ever before. But whilst the law (and subsequent court decisions) limited the scale of donations, subsequent amendments and interpretations by the Court and FEC relaxed previous controls over the forms of contributions and spending. Soft money donations, independent spending and issue advocacy allowed forms of spending by organizations which had been forbidden in earlier legislation. Restrictions on PAC formation were also eased. Thus some legal barriers to the injection of money into elections have been lowered. The increase in legal opportunities for money to be used in campaigns has probably reduced the incidence of illegality in US electioneering.

Deterrents to illegality were increased under FECA with the creation of the Federal Election Commission to provide the monitoring and enforcement of election finance law which had previously been lacking. The FEC's ineffectiveness has been severely criticised.[10] Its lack of rigour is unsurprising in a country where regulatory commissions have frequently been ineffectual in policing industries. The prospects for regulatory rigour from FEC were never high, given that it was designed to regulate its creators in Congress and the executive branch. Insufficient resources, a voluminous workload and partisan deadlock obstructing Commission decision-making have contributed to its ineffectiveness. Far more violations are alleged than are actively investigated. Proven violations usually receive belated, mild penalties. For example, John Glenn's 1984 presidential campaign was found to have obtained a $2 million unsecured bank loan illegal under federal law. Glenn was subsequently fined $2000 in 1987. However, two members of the House have been sentenced to prison terms for FECA violations. George Hansen of Idaho was convicted for failing to make disclosures in his 1972 campaign. Jay Kim of California was convicted in 1998 for taking contributions from companies (including his own) and foreign nationals in his 1992 campaign.

Though the regulation of FECA has been mild, it appears severe in contrast to the virtual irrelevance of election finance controls in earlier times. No one was ever punished for violation of the Corrupt Practices Act. Expenditure reports sometimes owed more to fiction than fact. Some, presumably accurate, reports contained illegal sources and sums but no penalties were imposed. The House Clerk reported 107 campaigns to the Justice Department for violations of campaign laws in 1968 but no action was taken.[11] In the 1962 elections over 50 campaigns for the House failed to submit reports.[12]

Public definitions of corruption extend beyond illegality. Americans see deception, unfairness and the denial of equal opportunity as corrupt.[13] This broad conception allows use to be made of a variety of public opinion data despite the paucity of surveys explicitly addressing questions of corruption and campaign finance.

Trust in government has been in precipitous decline for most of the last generation. By 1992 three-quarters of the American public thought that the government was run by a few big interests rather than for the benefit of all. Close to half thought quite a few of the people running the government were a little crooked. Over half the public believe that half or more of the members of Congress are financially corrupt. Only 7 per cent believe that hardly any members are financially corrupt (see Table 3.2).

*Table 3.2*  Public Confidence in Officeholders, 1992 (in percentages)

| Would you say the government is pretty much run by a few big interests looking out for themselves or that it is run for the benefit of all the people? | |
| --- | --- |
| Few big interests | 74.7 |
| Benefit of all | 20.1 |

| Do you think that quite a few of the people running the government are a little crooked, not very many are, or do you think hardly any of them are crooked at all? | |
| --- | --- |
| Quite a few | 45.4 |
| Not very many | 43.3 |
| Hardly any | 8.8 |

| Now, think about all the members of the House and Senate. How many of them do you think are financially corrupt – most, about half, some or hardly any? | |
| --- | --- |
| Most | 30.0* |
| About half | 28.0 |
| Some | 29.0 |
| Hardly any | 7.0 |

*Figures have been rounded
*Sources*:   American National Election Study; CBS/New York Times.

Attitudes towards campaign finance show broad support for change. In 1998 a Fox News poll found 66 per cent expressing strong support for reform. Informed of the Supreme Court's protection of campaign spending as freedom of expression, 77 per cent still believed reform was needed.[14] Exactly the same figure was recorded in support of limits on campaign spending in a 1993 Greenberg–Lake poll.[15] Support for public funding of elections fluctuates. The principle often evokes more opposition than support. But support rises when possible conditions attached to receipt of public funds are specified. Polls on state election spending limits, equality in campaign funds and prohibitions on private donations show substantial majority support for public funding allied with these provisions.[16]

Initiative votes at state level have frequently demonstrated support for limits to election spending and contributions. Voters in Maine in 1996 backed public funding for candidates who agreed to expenditure limits. Majorities in Oregon and Missouri in 1994 supported contribution limits of $100. Though the limits to donations were subsequently invalidated in court, they show the public prefers contribution limits much lower than those allowed under FECA.[17]

The sum of poll evidence shows a widespread distrust of those in government. Financial dishonesty is considered common amongst office-holders. Campaign finance may have no bearing on these negative judgements. Growth in public distrust began to grow before, and continued after, Watergate. But the reform of campaign finance has done nothing to reverse the deterioration in public confidence.

The existing campaign finance system enjoys little support. It fails to institutionalize Americans' sense of fair play and equality of opportunity. For many, the denial of these values equates with corruption. Reforms to promote fair play and equality of opportunity have widespread support.

A third conception of corruption equates it with government decision-making in which money or other inducement gains influence for private interests. Such influence is corrupt in this conception because service to the public is deflected. This definition resonates with Americans' sense that favouritism and unfair competition constitute corruption. It is also consistent with the Founders, attempts to guard against public office in service to private interests. Such a conception of corruption is difficult to operationalize because it involves the motivations of those in office (or aspiring to it), which are rarely ascertainable. Correspondence between private interests and behaviour is easier to demonstrate than a causal relation between them. But it is such correspondences that have fuelled the campaigns for campaign finance reform conducted by groups such as Common Cause and the Centre for Responsive Politics, and the mass media. Prominent in the reformist critique are the influence of political action committees and soft money.

## Political action committees

Republican Senator Robert Dole articulated a view of PACs consistent with the conception of corruption defined above: 'When these political action committees give money, they expect something in return other than good government.'[18] PACs and PAC money were an unintended outgrowth of the FECA reforms. They flourished when other opportunities for giving were curbed. Limits on individual contributions increased the appeal of PACs, especially for business. PACs also grew because FECA, the courts and the FEC removed previous restrictions on, and deterrents to, their formation. The 1974 amendments removed the bar to federal contractors (organizations undertaking work for the national government) forming PACs. A 1975 FEC ruling allowed companies sponsoring PACs to use corporate funds to solicit contributions. Multiple PACs connected to the same sponsor were also permitted, provided they were separately organized. Unlimited independent spending by PACs was made possible by the Buckley case.

Candidates' dependence on PACs grew progressively for nearly twenty years after the inception of FECA. In 1974 PAC contributions averaged 17 per cent of funds raised in House campaigns, 11 per cent in Senate campaigns. By 1995–6, past the peak of PAC dependency, the average House campaigns' reliance on PACs had doubled to 34 per cent. A substantial increase had also occurred in Senate elections, the average campaign obtaining 19 per cent of funds from political action committees.

Donations are only the most direct and visible evidence of PAC aid to candidates. Some engage in bundling, encouraging individuals to send to the PAC office cheques for up to $1000 made out to named candidates. Bundles of cheques are then rerouted to candidates. In FECA reports, bundles are defined as individual contributions. They do not count against the $5000 maximum a PAC can donate to a candidate but the recipient is aware of the source which stimulated funds far in excess of the PAC contribution limit. Such an example is the $150000 bundle sent in the 1980s to Republican Senator Robert Packwood of Oregon by ALIGNPAC, the Associated Life Insurance Group National Policy Advisory Committee. Packwood chaired the Senate Finance Committee which was considering taxes on the insurance industry.[19]

Independent spending allows PACs to make unlimited expenditures on a candidate's behalf. Few PACs risk the cost of mounting an independent campaign but there have been some lavish, controversial and, possibly, electorally successful examples. The National Conservative Political Action Committee (NCPAC) committed $1 million for the 1980 campaign, and $3 million in 1982. In the former year, six liberal Democrat incumbent senators targeted by NCPAC were defeated. The publicity surrounding the criminal Willie Horton in the 1988 presidential election originated from television commercials funded by political action committees.

Candidates' dependence upon a single PAC can thus incorporate donations, bundling and independent spending worth, in combined value, far in excess of the very modest $5000 FECA donation limit. Moreover the winners who go on to hold office have a much higher dependence on PACs than the losers. Winning House candidates in 1996 averaged 4.75 times more in PAC contributions than their opponents. Of winners, total receipts, 38 per cent derived from political action committees compared to 22 per cent for the candidates they defeated. These candidates did not win because they had the advantage in PAC donations. Part of the attraction for many PACs of funding these candidates was the probability of their winning. PAC pragmatism was a confirmation of election prospects more than a formative influence upon them. But it leaves incumbents with above-average obligations to PACs for funding their campaigns.

PACs are an unrepresentative sample of all interest groups. Surveys of Washington-based national membership organizations – itself an unrepresentative sample – found only a fifth had created political action committees. PACs are usually connected to sponsoring companies, unions, professional bodies and trade associations. PACs concerned with economic policy are the most numerous. These organizations are most able to overcome the free rider problem to spur political activity, at least in making contributions, for they are already organized to engage in the marketplace. The sponsoring body can absorb all the costs of administering the PAC. Citizen groups, on the other hand, will incur costs in running a PAC. Their sources of income – government grants, foundations, religious organizations – may be disbarred by law from use in campaigns.[20] These legal impediments, in addition to the poverty of potential sympathizers, helps to explain why 'There aren't any Poor PACs or Food Stamp PACs or Nutrition PACs or Medicare PACs.'[21]

There are great inequalities of resources between political action committees. In the 1991–2 elections 8 per cent of PACs accounted for three-quarters of total donations. A handful of PACs contributed millions of dollars whilst over half donated no more than $5000 in total.[22] A few groups give to many candidates; most give little to few candidates.

The fear that PAC money 'talks', providing a legal form of bribing public officials, has been discounted by most academic research on the subject. Scholars who have matched votes cast in Congress against PAC donations have found modest relationships between the two. These relationships fade when controls are introduced for party, constituency and the member's ideology.[23] As PACs tend to reward allies rather than attempt to convert opponents it is unsurprising that money has little independent effect.

But PAC money has shown up as an independent effect on members where other influences are weak, the typical condition for interest groups to exert an impact. In the absence of cues from party, constituency, public opinion or the members' ideology, on issues of low visibility, the probability of PAC influence rises.[24] Commenting on the unevenness of PAC influence across issues, Grenzke observes, 'The good news is that most members of Congress do not seem to be influenced by Pac money on issues of major significance and publicity. The bad news is that much legislation is of low visibility and low conflict where money may matter.'[25]

Money may not talk but one study suggests that it activates and amplifies. In committee, Hall and Wayman found members funded by a PAC tended to be more active in its cause than other members. They made speeches, sponsored bills, proposed amendments favourable to their benefactors.[26] Given the deference accorded to most committee recommendations, concentrating contributions on a few members may be sufficient to affect legislative outcomes.

Congressional opponents of PAC interests may modify their opposition to attract donations. Thus conversion may take place over time, effected not by contributions but in anticipation of them in future. This interpretation has been offered for the Democrats, rightward shift in the early 1980s.[27] Democrats, it is argued, adapted to the predominance of business PACs favouring Republicans by redefining themselves to maintain competitiveness in funding. By adjusting positions on issues like defence spending and welfare benefits, Democrats became more attractive to business donors. At the same time, Democrats became more aggressive in exploiting their majority status in appealing for business PAC funds.[28]

Business PAC money did shift its allegiance during the 1980s. During the decade Democratic candidates' share of their donations rose from a third to more than half. Why the change occurred is not necessarily attributable to money. The electoral resurgence of the Republicans in the early Reagan years may have been a sufficient threat. Moreover, the claims of rightward shift have not been systematically demonstrated. There is evidence to the contrary, in votes in Congress showing both a growing divergence between the parties and increased liberalism amongst Democrats.[29] What is undisputed in this debate is that the behaviour of Democrats towards business PACs was changed by the attraction of campaign money. Attempts to achieve a greater rapport were made even if no compromises on policy were involved.

## Soft money

Controls on expenditure, limits on contributions and disclosure have been persistent features of twentieth-century attempts to contain the pernicious features of campaign finance. Soft money is exempt from the first two and has been subject to the third only since 1991. Vast sums of soft money are now donated and spent, exceeding $250 million in 1995–6.

Soft money-raising methods in 1996 awakened fears that funds bought access. The White House, Air Force One and Two were used by the President and Vice President to entertain guests who subsequently made contributions. Over one thousand 'coffees' were held at the White House which raised $27 million. Contributions were made by foreign nationals living outside the US, which is illegal under US law. Millions of dollars were returned to these donors by the Democratic National Committee when the contributions became public.

The right to unlimited donations has allowed the return of giving on the scale uncovered in Watergate. Some sources donate millions of dollars. Company and union treasuries, barred from use for donations to candidates for over half a century, supply most of the largest soft money donations. Some organizations made substantial donations to both parties in 1995–6. AT&T, RJR Nabisco, the Walt Disney Company, Joseph E. Seagram and Sons, Time Warner and the Philip Morris Company gave over a quarter of a million dollars each to the Democrats and Republicans.

Soft money provides contribution loopholes through state laws as well as FECA. Most state laws allow donations from companies or unions. Some do not. Soft money allows monies to be raised from sources illegal in one state to be transferred for use in another.

Suspicions that soft money buys influence have received confirmation from several scandals. The Keating Five episode publicized in 1990 found senators had been active on behalf of the owner of financially troubled Lincoln Savings and Loan which had attracted the interest of the mortgage industry's regulator, the Federal Home Loan Bank. Charles Keating was a substantial campaign money-raiser, donor, and one-man bundler for the savings and loan sector. Five senators interceded with the regulator on Keating's behalf. All were beneficiaries of his funding. The most active on Keating's behalf, Democratic Senator Alan Cranston of California, had obtained $850 000 from Keating and his associates for a voter education project, and $85 000 for the state party's get-out-the-vote effort. Keating was subsequently given a prison sentence for his business wrongdoings but none of his political donations were illegal. Nor were any of the senators deemed to have acted illegally in accepting Keating's money and intervening on his behalf. A Senate investigation reprimanded Cranston on the basis of 'substantial credible evidence [that he] engaged in an impermissible pattern of conduct in which fundraising and official activities were substantially linked'.[30] Keating confessed to the self-interested reasons for his donations, 'One question, among many, has to do with whether my financial support in any way influenced several political figures to take up my cause. I want to say in the most forceful way I can: I certainly hope so.'[31]

The vast soft money donations of 1996 prompted claims that funds were reciprocated with access to, and influence over, the Clinton administration. Johnny Chung, a Taiwanese-born businessman based in California, donated over a quarter of a million dollars of his own and his company's money to the Democratic National Committee. Chung made 50 visits to the White House accompanied by business partners and clients. He was reported as comparing the White House to a subway: 'you have to put coins in to open the gates.'[32] The Indonesian Lippo Group controlled by the Riady family channelled soft money funds worth several hundred thousand dollars to the Democrats. Family members made more than 20 visits to the White House from 1993 onwards. In 1994, regulation of foreign banks like Lippo was eased. Donations to the Democrats worth half a million dollars were made by Pauline Kanchanalak and her family. Kanchanalak was an employee of the Thai conglomerate, the Ban Chang Group. She visited the White House with Thai businessmen, lobbying Clinton to visit Thailand. The President stopped off in Bangkok during his trip to the APEC conference in the Philippines in November 1996.[33]

Soft money donations to the 1992 Democratic campaign have been linked to patronage appointments in the Clinton administration. Donations over twenty thousand dollars were made by ten subsequent ambassadorial appointees. Large donors include K.Terry Dornbush, who gave $253750 prior to being appointed Ambassador to Austria; M. Larry Lawrence (Switzerland), who gave $196304, and the subsequent Ambassador to France, Pamela Harriman, donated $130000. Lawrence was fined by the FEC for exceeding the hard money donation limits.[34] Similar criticisms had surfaced about appointees to the Bush administration. Democratic Senator Paul Sarbanes of Maryland observed that 'the appearances are that they bought their jobs.'[35]

## Reform

Disquiet about the operation of FECA has inspired persistent demands for change. Good government groups like Common Cause, the Centre for Responsive Politics and Public Citizen have exposed the escalating cost of elections, the scale of special-interest funding and evidence purporting to demonstrate the influence exerted by campaign donors. Supporters of reform in government have included presidents Carter, Bush and Clinton, congressional leader Speaker Newt Gingrich, and senators Robert Dole and George Mitchell.

For nearly twenty years, since the 1979 amendments to FECA, there have been attempts in Congress to redesign the campaign finance system. None have succeeded. In 1992 a bill passed both houses of Congress but was vetoed by President Bush. The soft money scandals in 1996 led to prolonged congressional investigations, and reactivation of activity around legislative reform. Some 85 bills were introduced in Congress designed to reform campaign finance. A bill to curb soft money passed the House in August 1998 but was then stalled by a Republican filibuster in the Senate.

Discontent with the existing financing regime is broader than agreement on how to remedy it. Reform is on the agenda but action to legislate correctives is stalled by disunity. Durable fault lines over reform divide conservatives from liberals, Republicans from Democrats, senators from representatives. The conservative–liberal divide pivots on ideological differences about the use of government. Partisan and inter-chamber conflicts turn on different conceptions of electoral self-interest. Every major reform model founders on one or more of these divisions over ideology and electoral self-protection.

Public finance for congressional elections promises an escape from the dependence on special-interest money which creates the potential for corruption. Public finance would also allow campaign costs to be restricted in a manner acceptable to the courts. Despite appearing to solve simultaneously two of the severest problems in the FECA system, public finance has repeatedly failed in Congress. Public funding for elections to Congress was contained in the 1974 Senate version of FECA but the provision was dropped in conference under pressure from the House side. Public funding was backed by President Carter but was deleted from a bill which passed the House in 1979. Public payment for in-kind services like television commercials and reduced-rate postage were contained in the bill Bush vetoed in 1992.

Conservatives oppose public funding as an inappropriate use of taxpayers' money, condemning it as a raid on the public treasury and food stamps for politicians. Antagonism in the House reflects the self-interest of incumbents in preserving funding advantages over their opponents which would be curbed by the equal allocations of public funding schemes. Senate elections are characterized by greater equality in funding, giving incumbents less interest in averting well-funded challengers dependent upon public funds.

Limiting spending has attracted more support from Democrats than Republicans. For so long the majority party in Congress, Democrats were predominantly the beneficiaries of incumbency, building name recognition and reputations in office to convert into support in elections. Overcoming such assets is improbable, impossible without large expenditures. Republicans saw spending caps as a means of conserving incumbent electoral advantage against effective challenge. Republican senators rallied against the Boren bill of the 1980s as a guarantor of permanent Democratic majorities. A proposed constitutional amendment to limit election spending produced party-line voting in the Senate in 1988. Democrats divided 48–1 in favour, Republicans voted 41–4 against.

Raising the legal limits on party funding would diminish candidates' dependence on the self-interested money of PACs and individual donors. Schemes to increase party spending are usually sponsored by Republicans and resisted by Democrats. Articulated here is the superiority of the Republican Party in both hard and soft money-raising efforts. Attributable to the greater wealth of Republican supporters, and the greater organizational effectiveness of Republican fund-raising campaigns, an expanded role for parties promises to work to the detriment of Democrats.

President Bush proposed in 1989 a 250 per cent increase in parties' co-ordinated expenditures. That year a House Republican proposal advocated the removal of limits to party co-ordinated expenditures and candidate contributions. Bush's veto of the bill Congress passed faulted its failure to restore the influence of parties in fund-raising. The focus of reform efforts in the Senate after the 1996 elections, the McCain–Feingold bill, proposes the abolition of soft money. Active opposition has been mounted by Republican senators who have successfully filibustered it on several occasions.

Curbing PAC donations would ease candidates' dependence on the money of special interests. Reforms to curtail PAC funding have been favoured more by Republicans than Democrats. Democrats have had the greater dependence on PACs for most of the FECA era, reflecting the funding advantages which accrue to the majority. (Republican candidates obtained over half of all PAC donations in 1996, the first election they had fought as the congressional majority since the inception of FECA.) The highest average donations from any FEC category of PAC derive from organized labour, almost exclusively a financier of Democrats.

In 1987 House Republicans called for lower limits and a ban on bundling. Bush's proposal contained a ban on donations from connected PACs, and a lowering of donation limits on the non-connected. Exemplifying the partisanship around the issue, Democratic Senate leader George Mitchell condemned Bush's proposal for aiming to secure Republican advantage.

In addition to the three sources of disunity, a fourth force for inertia over campaign finance reform is the incumbency advantage. All those involved in deciding policy are beneficiaries of existing campaign finance law. Whilst the minority Republicans resisted enlarging incumbent advantage, they have shown little enthusiasm for any reductions. Winners under the existing system, incumbents have little incentive for change.

The repeated failure to enact reform is therefore bearable for the incumbents who have won under the FECA rules. Considering reform without effecting it may go some way to assuage the minority of the attentive public concerned about the issue whilst simultaneously preserving existing advantages for present office-holders. Appearance has prevailed over substance during legislative struggles over reform. A lopsided Senate vote of 84–7 on Boren's bill in 1985, for example, was facilitated by the recognition that it would not be passed.

Differences are often compromised in the legislative process. But the obstacles to compromise over campaign finance serve to perpetuate the current rules which favour incumbents. Uncompromising stances promote the appearance of a clash over principles whilst inertia contributes to electoral security of those striking poses. This was evident in shaping the final version of the bill which Bush had threatened to veto if it contained public finance and spending limits. The final version contained both. Alexander and Corrado observed that each party seemed 'purposefully to craft its proposals for rejection by the other side'.[36]

Campaign finance exhibits the dilemmas of devising procedures for contests in which the rule-makers are already contestants. No veil of ignorance about the participants' attributes inspires a search for impartial procedures. Redistricting decisions in the states exhibits the same self-interested behaviour by legislators seeking electoral security. Where unavoidable, unpalatable decisions are required, members of Congress have been prepared to defer decisions to the executive and judicial branches. Reforming campaign finance, however, has proved avoidable. Nor have members been prepared to devolve responsibility elsewhere on a matter which bears so strongly on their own career prospects. Bipartisan congressional task forces have been created on several occasions to forge a legislative consensus but all have failed to reach agreement. In 1990 Senate leaders appointed a six-member panel of outside experts to recommend reforms. Its report – advocating generous expenditure limits, enlarging contributions from parties and individual constituents – received a respectful reception. Yet it was not acted upon. Rather, 'political posturing' overrode the report's recommendations, according to Herbert Alexander, a disappointed panel member.[37] President Clinton and House Speaker Gingrich agreed in 1995 to create a committee of experts to devise election finance reforms. No such committee has been appointed.

The conditions which can relieve policy deadlocks in American government – electoral mandates, popular pressure, unified government, decisive presidential leadership – are unlikely to apply to campaign finance. Campaign finance is not an election issue or a priority for many voters. In the absence of some collective embarrassment within Congress over impropriety, as occurred over the House bank, public disapproval of the existing system will not activate reform. On matters which could adversely affect the electoral self-interest of members, responsiveness to presidential leadership is improbable. Divisions between House and Senate elections impair agreement within parties across the bicameral divide. Senate procedures are also conducive to resistance by a minority who perceive their interests threatened by reform.

The history of American campaign finance law also warrants suspicion about the efficacy of any reform which might be enacted. Unintended consequences, and effective, legal evasion have frequently occurred. Nearly a century after reforms began, the costs of elections continue to escalate. Special interests, particularly business and labour, provide substantial funds to candidates and parties. Legislative creativity has been more than matched by the ingenuity of moneyed sources to find legal uses for funds. Corruption in the form of illegality has probably declined. But corruption as service to moneyed special interests within the law survives. Past experience suggests legal reforms do more to change the way corrupt influence is exerted than to reduce its incidence.

## Notes

1 Alexander Hamilton, James Madison and John Jay,*The Federalist Papers*, edited and Introduction by Clinton Rossiter, New York: New American Library, 1961; Richard Hofstadter, *The Idea of a Party System: The Rise of Legitimate Opposition in the United States, 1780–1840*, Berkeley: University of California Press, 1969; Austin Ranney, *Curing the Mischiefs of Faction: Party Reform in America*, Berkeley: University of California Press, 1975.

2 V.O.Key, Jr., *Politics, Parties and Pressure Groups*, 5th ed., New York: Crowell, 1964, p. 494.

3 Robert Caro, *The Path to Power*, New York: Vintage, 1983, pp. 408–9.

4 Key, *Politics, Parties and Pressure Groups*, p. 513.

5 Quoted in Herbert Alexander, *Financing Politics*, 4th ed., Washington, DC: Congressional Quarterly Press, 1992, p. 70.

6 Alexander, *Financing Politics*, p. 32.

7 Buckley *v* Valeo, 1976. 424. US. 1.

8 Common Cause, 'The Soft Money Laundromat', http://www.common-cause.org./soft_money/topgop.htm.

9 These are modifications of definitions in Michael Johnston, *Political Corruption and Public Policy in America*, Monterey, Ca.: Brooks/Cole, 1982, pp. 3–9.

10 Brooks Jackson, *Broken Promise: Why the Federal Election Commission Failed*, New York: Priority Press, 1990; Robert E. Mutch, *Campaigns, Congress and Courts: The Making of Federal Election Law*, New York: Praeger, 1988, ch. 4.

11 Mutch, *Campaigns, Congress and Courts*, p. 28.

12 Alexander,*Financing Politics*, p. 26.

13 Michael Johnston, 'Right and Wrong in American Politics: Popular Conceptions of Corruption', in Arnold J.Heidenheimer, Michael Johnston and Victor T. LeVine (eds), *Political Corruption*, New Brunswick, N.J.: Transaction Publishers, 1989, pp. 743–61.

14 'When Liberty is not so sweet', *The Economist*, 4 April 1998, pp. 56–7.

15 David Magleby and Kelly D. Patterson, 'The Polls-Poll Trends: Congressional Reform', *Public Opinion Quarterly* 58, 1994, pp. 419–27.

16 Public Campaign, 'Five Surveys Reveal Strong Support for Clean Money Reform'/, May 1997, http://www.pulicampaign.org/stpoll.html.

17 Carroll J. Doherty, 'Overload Gridlock on the Hill Contrasts with Action in States', *Congressional Quarterly Weekly Report*, 28 February 1998, pp. 465–8.

18 'Quoted in Larry J. Sabato, *PAC Power: Inside the world of political action committees*, New York: Norton, 1984, p. xii.

19   Alexander, *Financing Politics*, pp. 57–8.
20   Thomas Gais, *Improper Influence: Campaign Finance Law, Political Interest Groups, and the Problem of Equality*, Ann Arbor: University of Michigan Press, 1996.
21   Robert Dole, quoted in Kenneth Janda, Jeffrey M. Berry and Jerry Goldman, *The Challenge of Democracy: Government in America*, 4th ed., Boston: Houghton Mifflin, 1995, p. 344.
22   Paul S. Herrnson, *Congressional Elections: Campaigning at Home and in Washington*, Washington, DC: Congressional Quarterly Press, 1995, p. 108.
23   For a survey of this literature see Gais, *Improper Influence*, pp. 7–15.
24   Frank Davis, 'Balancing the perspective on PAC contribution: in search of an impact on roll calls', *American Politics Quarterly* 21, 1993, pp. 205–22.
25   Janet Grenzke, 'Money and Congressional Behaviour', in Margaret Latus Nugent and John R. Johannes, (eds), *Money, Elections and Democracy*, Boulder: Westview, 1990, p. 152.
26   Richard L. Hall and Frank W. Wayman, 'Buying Time: Moneyed Interests and The Mobilization of Bias in Congressional Committees', *American Political Science Review* 84, 1990, pp. 797–820.
27   Joel Rogers and Thomas Ferguson, *Right Turn:The Decline of the Democrats and the Future of American Politics*, New York: Hill and Wang, 1986; Thomas Byrne Edsall, *The New Politics of Inequality*, New York: Norton, 1984; Robert Kuttner, *The Life of the Party: Democratic Prospects in 1988 and Beyond*, New York: Viking, 1987.
28   Brooks Jackson, *Honest Graft: Big Money and the American Political Process*, New York: Knopf, 1988.
29   Sorauf, *Inside Campaign Finance*, p. 173; David W. Rohde, *Parties and Leaders in the Post-reform House*, Chicago: Chicago University Press, 1991.
30   Quoted in Alexander, *Financing Politics*, p. 68.
31   Quoted in Alexander, *Financing Politics*, p. 68.
32   Quoted in Rebecca Carr, 'White House Videotapes: Focus Turns to Content', *Congressional Quarterly Weekly Report*, 18 October 1997, p. 2531.
33   Material in this paragraph draws heavily on Common Cause, 'Faces in the Crowd', http://www.commoncause.org./publications/subpoenaed.htm.
34   Herbert E. Alexander and Anthony Corrado, *Financing the 1992 Election*, Armonk, NY: M.E.Sharpe, 1995, pp. 292–4.
35   Quoted in Alexander, *Financing Politics*, p. 69.
36   Alexander and Corrado, p. 259.
37   Alexander, *Financing Politics*, p. 155.

# 4
# Party Finance and Corruption: Italy

*James Newell*

## Introduction

Party funding in Italy has only been regulated by law since 1974 (Bull, 1997; Ciaurro, 1989; Rhodes, 1997). The previous system was characterized by multiple sources of private finance, but its most striking feature was corrupt funding of a routinized and institutionalized nature – a system which, in turn, was informed by the informal and often illegal rules of operation of a second, hidden, dimension of power, which lay beneath the veneer provided by the rules of law and the formalities of democracy (Rhodes, 1997:55)[1]. The *modus operandi* of parties in this second dimension rested on the 'partitocratic' nature of the Italian polity – a characterization widely used to refer to the parties' penetration of vast areas of the state and society. As the *basso profondo* underlying the system of corrupt political funding, the organization and mechanics of *partitocrazia* ('partyocracy') will be examined first. While the latter was given a strong underpinning in the post-war period by the nature of the party system – based as it was on the permanent exclusion from office of the main party of opposition, the Communist Party (PCI), and the permanence in office of the Christian Democrats (DC) at the head of unstable coalitions – *partitocrazia* owed its origins to factors whose deepest roots extended as far back as the birth of the Italian state itself. These included a weak state whose low levels of legitimacy would, after the fascist interlude, be perpetuated in the post-war period by the continuing recourse to clientelistic means of managing power relationships.

Part two examines the causal connection between clientelism and corruption and explores the self-generating mechanism involved in the corrupt funding of parties. If this mechanism ensured that corruption would become increasingly well established with the passage of time, it thereby laid the ground for the explosion of the *Tangentopoli* ('Bribe City') scandals beginning in early 1992. Corruption scandals were not, of course, new; what *was* new about *Tangentopoli* was the sheer extent of the revelations, something which appears to have been a consequence both of the original decision of Mario Chiesa, the first defendant, to confess (since his confession implicated subsequent defendants whose confessions in their turn implicated still others), and of an unusually high level of judicial activism. The latter seems, in its turn, to have been at least partly due to the resolution of the 'communist question' (brought about by the collapse of the Berlin Wall and by the decision of the PCI to transform itself into a non-communist party with a new name, the Democratic Part of the Left – the PDS). With the elimination of any residual need to be lenient towards the more dubious practices of the governing class, the judiciary became even keener than it had sometimes shown itself to be in the past to use its powers as the champions of a campaign to moralise public life.

Part three examines the evolution of the system of legal regulation of party finance that was initiated with law number 195 of 2 May 1974. Though the latter provided for a public contribution both to parties' election expenses and to their regular, organizational expenditures, it did little or nothing to stem the continuing proliferation of corrupt party funding, mainly because most corrupt transactions were designed to service the power ambitions of individuals and groups *within* the parties rather than the organizational needs of the formal party apparatuses. While an attempt to secure the abolition of public funding by means of a referendum failed in 1978, the explosion of the *Tangentopoli* investigations later paved the way for the initiation of a number of changes to the regulatory framework. The investigations themselves had been preceded by the emergence of a 'referendum movement' which aimed to strike at the heart of *partitocrazia* through the imposition of institutional reform, to be won by exploiting the Constitutional provision whereby laws and parts of laws can be made the subject of referenda when requested by 500 000 citizens. Thus *Tangentopoli*, besides leading to the disintegration of the main parties of government, also helped to ensure an overwhelming vote to abolish public financial support for party organizations in the referendum held (along with seven others, including one aimed at changing the electoral law) in April 1993. The referendum outcome was followed by fresh party funding legislation in the form of law number 515 of 10 December 1993. The current framework is provided essentially by the latter piece of legislation, which regulates parties' *election* income and expenditure, and by law number 2 of 2 January 1997, which regulates the financing of parties' *organizations*. It is unlikely that either law will make a significant contribution to reducing political corruption because, as we shall see, so much corruption in Italy is generated by pressures greater than those deriving from the parties' functions as interest aggregators.

## *Partitocrazia*

Economic and cultural diversity, and the hostility of the Catholic Church, meant that the Italian state from the outset suffered from low levels of legitimacy and had difficulty in asserting its authority against alternative, unofficial, power centres organized on a clientelistic basis around local elites (and in extreme cases, around organizations such as the Mafia). Under these circumstances, unification failed to produce a national, integrative, ideology. The state's weakness allowed local notables to turn the state to their own interest, structuring the system around networks of personal relationships based on particularistic exchanges of favours. Such activities, by virtue of their tendency to create a large number of vested interests, each of which had a power of veto whenever policy change was considered (Tarrow, 1977:197), made for a deep-seated policy ineffectiveness, thus undermining the legitimacy of the state still further.

If this ensured that 'colonisation' by the parties of vast sectors of the state and society would be particularly easy once the fascist interlude had come to an end, the process was also facilitated by the particular circumstances surrounding fascism's fall. First, the collapse of Mussolini's regime created a power vacuum in which almost the only available points of reference for ordinary people were the Church, with its deep roots in civil society created by its parishes and collateral associations, and the Resistance movement dominated by the PCI (Ginsborg, 1990). If this gave particular legitimacy to the two largest parties, the DC and the PCI, it also ensured that mass loyalties to the new state institutions would be slow to develop, for neither the Communists, nor the Christian Democrats (bearing in mind the Church's original hostility to the unified state) felt themselves to be heirs to the liberal tradition of the *Risorgimento* which had given the Italian state, up until the advent of fascism, what legitimacy it had had (Bourricaud, 1974:90). Second, the growth of political participation which arose from the Resistance 'turned the Communists, Socialists and Christian Democrats into mass-based organizations enrolling between them by 1947 over 3 million members'. This allowed the parties, through their flanking organizations, to penetrate down to the grassroots level throughout the country, and thus to exercise 'a profound influence over the reconstruction of social organizations and interest groups. Many such groups were in effect captured by the parties and subordinated to the dictates of their political controllers' (Hine, 1990:68). The consequence of this was that the parties became the principal channels of access to the bureaucracy and the principal transmission belts in the allocation of resources from centre to periphery; for if government instability meant that the system found it very difficult to take major programmatic decisions, demands for change became 'transformed into appeals for the distribution of resources through existing mechanisms and procedures' (Tarrow, 1977:194). In this way, 'the clientele chains that had sprung up during the pre-Fascist period and stayed alive under Fascism were re-created after World War II with a partisan overlay' (Tarrow, 1977:69).[2]

Finally, the DC was encouraged to colonize the non-civil-service public administration for patronage purposes by the electoral imperatives of the Cold War. A wide range of influential actors both within and beyond Italy looked to the DC to act as the main bulwark against Communism; yet in order to play this role successfully the party had to broaden its appeal far beyond the ranks of the Catholic faithful. This in its turn meant that it had to escape from the Church dominance to which its early reliance on groups such as Catholic Action had tended to subject it. By occupying a wide range of public sector institutions, the DC was able to tap a rich seam of public resources whose exploitation through a continuous flow of clientelistic exchanges not only gave it autonomy but also gave it a strong hold in areas such as the *Mezzogiorno*, where the absence of associational energy meant that attempts at ideological mobilization through the expansion of party organization could meet with only limited success. Access to public institutions could then be extended to other governing parties and most significantly, from 1963, to the Socialists (PSI), as and when coalition negotiations might require.

*Partitocrazia*, then, constituted a complete system of power relations based on a close association between the parties on the one hand and public institutions and interest groups on the other. The public institutions in question were of three basic kinds: the *amministrazioni autonome*, responsible to given ministries and somewhat akin to the former public corporations in Britain; the state holding companies, and the *enti pubblici*. The latter are virtually impossible to define, though a feel for their nature and purpose can be had by noting that over 54 000 of them have been counted; many are organised on a local level; and most are bodies providing, in a piecemeal fashion, services associated with the growth of the welfare state from the 1920s on. What gave them their weight and significance in the operation of *partitocrazia* was the sheer numbers of people they employed, estimated at about 2.5 million by the early eighties (Cassese, 1983:263), and the fact that since powers of nomination to their governing boards typically lie in the hands of one or more elected politicians, such as a minister or a local council, such positions could be filled with political placemen, with the partisan credentials of candidates counting as much as, if not more than, their certified ability to perform the jobs in question. Indeed, by being used to provide jobs, and therefore remuneration, to party officials, partisan appointments to public agencies were *themselves* a covert form of party funding.

The close association between parties and interest groups was of a not dissimilar nature. It tended to undermine the capacity of parties to filter and aggregate demands, leading them instead to function as instruments of the groups, transmitting to governmental structures demands that were narrow and indicative of an unwillingness to compromise (LaPalombara, 1964:8). If this in turn led to the diffusion, or perpetuation, of a view of the state as something to be conquered by one's own group to the disadvantage of others, rather than as an entity that could reasonably be relied upon to further the general interest, so again was the state weakened through the subversion of its standing among the mass public. Thus it is that one arrives at what was the essence of *partitocrazia*: a weak state allowing for considerable overlap between the personnel of the parties on the one hand, and interest groups and administrative positions on the other, making it difficult to draw clear boundaries between these entities and to know in any given case in what capacity individuals were acting.

The informal and particularistic – that is, a clientelistic – management of power relationships which this encouraged was practised in a variety of concrete ways. Sometimes, it was of a repressive, bureaucratic kind. For example, LaPalombara (1964) describes how the small landowners' association, *Coldiretti*, managed to get a number of its officials elected as Christian Democratic deputies. Once elected, such deputies could secure the passage of *leggine* (literally, 'little laws') of interest to the association by taking advantage of the power of parliamentary committees to act in *sede deliberante*, that is, to enact laws on behalf of the legislature as a whole in relative isolation from public gaze. Election of *Coldiretti* officials was normally secured by making use of the preference vote, that is, the option made available to each elector, once having selected a party, then to express three or four preferences among the names making up the party's list of candidates for the given area. *Coldiretti* members in each area would be told what combination of preference-vote numbers to cast – a method which, while not completely destroying the secrecy of the ballot, did allow the leadership to gauge how closely each district adhered to the line established by the leaders. Where deviation was too pronounced, retaliatory measures could be taken, for

> [w]hen an association such as the Coltivatori Diretti establishes close ties with the government and is directly involved in the administration of certain social welfare activities through control of the *mutue* (social welfare agencies) and close ties with agencies of social insurance, the individual farmer refuses to join the organisation at his great peril (LaPalombara, 1964:149).

In other cases, the exchanges involved could be of a more personalistic kind. For example, the politician in charge of a public agency typically acted as an intermediary, exchanging resources both 'downwards' and 'upwards'. Downwards, for example, he was able to influence the placement of workers within the agency itself and perhaps, too, in private companies (if, for instance, the agency had a role in public works and urban planning matters). The resources provided in exchange for these favours were, of course, votes – which would have been channelled 'upwards' in favour of the higher-level politicians to whom the agency boss owed his position and with whom he could exchange votes for further funding for the agency. Meanwhile, he could use these very same connections on behalf of local people to obtain the intervention of powerful political figures in Rome for the solution of their problems (Graziano 1973:22).

## The spread of corruption

Although the terms 'clientelism' and 'political corruption'[3] are manifestly not synonymous, there have been clear causal connections between them in post-war Italy. Graziano points out that one of the most striking features of clientelism, as practised in southern Italy until recent decades, was that it embodied a 'totalitarian' exercise of power – in other words, one not limited by the enforcement of commonly accepted rules:

> it was not only the heaviness of the burden which was resented by the peasant, but 'the incertitude, variety and continuous mutability of these rights' – in a word, the arbitrary way of their imposition. (Graziano, 1973:9)

This is significant, for in many respects arbitrariness would seem to be inherent in the nature of clientelism itself: it entails particularistic treatment which, by definition, is treatment not sanctioned by the rules otherwise applied to members of the category to which the person in question belongs. Those whose power rests on clientelism cannot tolerate competitors since its arbitrary character makes it the negation of open, institutionalized competition. Hence, where clientelism is the predominant form of the management of power relations, the appearance of competitors leads established politicians, irrespective of formal rules, to do whatever is necessary to weaken such competitors – including having recourse to corruption.[4]

Della Porta and Vannucci's (1994) penetrating analysis of the logic by which the system of corrupt political financing operated makes clear that there was a self-generating mechanism involved in it so that once underway, it was likely to spread because of the attempts of the politicians involved to meet a number of the conditions necessary to successful corrupt transactions. In order to be in a position to enter into corrupt exchanges, the politician has to satisfy three needs: the need to gain access to positions which will allow him to influence public decisions in the first place; the need to ensure that the third parties for whom he acts respect their side of any agreements; and the need to secure the silence of those who might otherwise report him to the authorities. The first need was normally met by building up a personal following, measurable in terms of the number of party cards and preference votes the politician was able to control, within the party of which he was a member. Such following could then be traded with faction leaders for appointment to public positions which could be exploited by exchanging bribes for public works contracts and other abuses of responsibility and discretion. Part of the illicit proceeds could then be invested in the acquisition of even larger followings (for example, by paying the subscription fees of party members) which in turn could be traded for still further positions. Thus the power of the corrupt politician was self-reinforcing.

The second need arises from the illegality of the corrupt exchange, a circumstance which makes it impossible for the politician to use the authorities to force his client to pay, should the latter decide to cheat. Though the coercive power of the state is unavailable, the coercion offered by organized crime may be. This was a significant feature of corruption in southern Italy. In a context characterized by low levels of trust and where the state's protection either is, or is perceived to be, weak, organized crime was able to produce and sell private protection as a black-market good to be used to underpin transactions by discouraging cheating, and to provide a means of settling disputes. In such circumstances, the corrupt politician would receive from organized crime the services of the threat of physical violence, in exchange for which he would provide protection from the threat of intervention by the judicial authorities.

The third need – to obtain the silence of outsiders to the corrupt transaction – may be met either by the exchange of silence for the provision of a legal or illegal benefit (such as a cut of the bribe itself), or else through fear on the part of the outsider of the consequences of a failure to keep silent (a fear which might, for example, be induced by using organized-crime connections to establish a semi-public reputation for being 'dangerous'). Once corruption has spread to a certain point, little of a specific nature may need to be done to induce such fear: a general climate of intimidation will be sufficient. Thus it is that corruption is self-generating. The more it spreads the less willing people are to report it to the authorities; the less willing people are to report it, the fewer the risks it involves, the fewer the risks it involves, the less likely it is that the anticipated costs will outweigh the anticipated benefits for subsequent individuals contemplating corrupt exchanges. As these individuals too are thus drawn into networks of corrupt exchange, so it becomes more difficult to eliminate the phenomenon, this by virtue of the need to deploy more thinly the resources available to investigate it. This thus lowers the moral and material costs of corruption even more, and so the phenomenon spreads still further. Not surprisingly then, by the time the *Tangentopoli* scandals first exploded in February 1992 (and as the investigations appeared subsequently to confirm), political corruption seemed to have spread to reach a point where Ginsborg (1995:3) could express the view that Italy was 'one of the most corrupt democracies in Europe'.

The spread of corruption was accompanied by the growth, within the parties, of informal networks and power structures. Since it was through these, and not the formal structures, that illicit funding flowed, and since the purposes of this funding had less to do with 'official' party functions, such as propaganda or the development of policy, than with the simple maintenance and acquisition of power by those directly involved, parties' formal organizations were correspondingly weakened. Signs that the parties were becoming little more than the sum of the interests of the specific power-brokers that composed them had begun to emerge several years before *Tangentopoli* and its aftermath provided conclusive evidence of it. The DC had long been recognized by analysts as being more akin to a federation of factions articulating a series of particularistic demands than an organization capable of aggregating demands in the light of any minimally coherent vision for society as a whole; of the PSI, Pasquino (1986:125) had written bluntly in the mid-eighties: 'The party as such no longer exists.' In effect, as ideology and programmes became less salient features of the internal life of parties, this affected the motives for joining them in the first place, creating a vicious circle whereby a gradual decline in the numbers of ideologically committed members tended to reduce the attractiveness of membership for those with ideological commitments. On the other hand the growth in the number of members whose motives were venal tended to increase the attractiveness of membership for those whose motives were also venal. This, however, brought with it a corresponding decline in the reserves of loyalty and commitment of the membership and was precisely why so many of the major parties collapsed so rapidly and dramatically once the *Tangentopoli* scandals broke. *Tangentopoli* destroyed the parties not only through its impact on their electoral following, because it cut off a major source of funding, or because it led to splits between those directly compromised by the investigations and those who, though uninvolved, still had to bear the political costs of the crisis; it also destroyed the parties because, with venality having almost entirely displaced policy as the main motive for membership, corruption had fatally undermined the parties' organizational structures.

Perhaps the best-known attempt at an empirical measurement of the spread of political corruption in post-war Italy has been that of Cazzola (1988). He is, of course, unable to measure the incidence of political corruption *as such* and is instead forced to rely on measures of the numbers of cases that have come to the attention of the judicial authorities and of numbers of cases reported in the press. Used to assess change over time, such indicators suffer from well-known drawbacks;[5] nevertheless, Cazzola's results are illuminating. From the mid-seventies, reported crimes of corruption and embezzlement involving the public administration rose significantly, going from 412 in 1975 to 1065 in 1985. Meanwhile annual averages rose from 514 for 1963–75 to 681 for 1976–8, to 808 for 1979–86. As regards press reports of corruption, the influential national daily, *la Repubblica*, carried reports of 117 separate cases of political corruption between 1976 and 1979; 110 between 1979 and 1983; and 208 between 1983 and 1986 (Cazzola, 1988:67). Of the 272 cases of parliamentarians accused of political corruption and against whom the judicial authorities moved requests for the lifting of parliamentary immunity between 1945 and 1987, there were 101 cases involving a total of 619 billion lire at 1986 values. If this left 171 cases for which the relevant figures were unavailable, then this in all probability suggests, as Cazzola himself notes, that the foregoing sum constituted not even the visible part of the corruption iceberg but only a very small portion of that part (Cazzola, 1988:138).

The description of some celebrated instances of the system of corrupt party finance at work, while side–stepping the difficulties of scientific measurement, arguably has the merit of offering a more accurate *feel* for the scale of the phenomenon:

- From the late forties, the housing shortage created by war damage gave rise in many places to unauthorized construction work, either because of a failure of local councils to produce town plans in good time or because of a failure properly to apply the law on planning permissions. However, such councils, effectively presented with a *fait accompli* once the work had been completed, then had to provide water, gas, electricity, roads, and other amenities to serve the new dwellings. In most cases, this resulted in enormous increases in the value of surrounding land, a situation which then tended to give rise to considerable land speculation with corruption being used as a means of inducing councils to fail to apply town plans, planning legislation and so forth. Perhaps the most famous of these speculators were the Caltagirone brothers who, in 1975, managed to persuade Italcasse, the publicly owned merchant bank presided over by the DC, to lend them 209 billion lire to finance their activities. In 1978, a Bank of Italy investigating team found that only five billion lire had been repaid and that no proper records of the loan had been maintained by the Caltagirone companies (Galli, 1991:111).
- Between 1968 and 1971, a series of rigged tenders for the construction of roads and motorways allowed the director general, Ennio Chiatante, and other officials of Anas (the road building and maintenance agency tied to the Ministry of Public Works) to collect bribes totalling between 25 and 30 billion lire. Since the procedure for tendering was that contracts were to be awarded to those firms that succeeded in quoting figures which came closest to the secret sums established by the ministry for the realization of the projects in question, it was a simple matter to divulge such sums in exchange for kickbacks (which varied between 5 and 8 per cent of the projects' values). It was widely believed that three successive Ministers of Public Works (Mancini and Lauricella of the PSI and Natali of the DC) were aware of what was happening and that therefore a part of the kickbacks probably ended up in the coffers of their respective parties.
- Finally, in November 1973, it came to light that the oil producers' cartel, the *Unione petrolifera italiana* and its president, Vincenzo Cazzaniga, had been involved in the transfer of a billion lire belonging to the state-owned electricity company, Enel, to the DC, the

Republican Party and the Social Democrats. The operation had been effected by means of a payment by the *Unione petrolifera* to Enel which had then passed the money directly to the parties. Later, the oil producers had effectively been reimbursed by means of an increase in the price paid by Enel for oil consignments. In this way, it had been possible to deny the involvement of both Enel and the oil producers in any illicit transactions: oil prices had always been fixed according to highly complex and obscure criteria, while both Enel and the oil producers could claim that the money passed through Enel to the parties amounted to freely given contributions not subject to any specific actions being carried out in return. However, at the same time, it also came to light that the oil producers had made a series of contributions to the parties since 1967 in exchange for a number of measures ranging from provision for the deferral of tax payments to the granting of public subsidies to cover increased costs borne by the companies as a result of the closure of the Suez Canal in 1967.

## The evolution of party-finance law

The most immediate effect of the oil scandal was to precipitate the passage of law number 195 of 2 May 1974 on the public funding of parties – to which, along with subsequent developments, attention therefore now turns. The purpose of law 195/74 was apparently 'to absolve those implicated in the "oil scandal" and provide a screen behind which corrupt financing could proceed' (Rhodes, 1997:58). However, the foregoing descriptions of given instances of the phenomenon suggest that illegal financing was well established by the mid sixties. This in turn suggests that if the 1974 party finance law was a 'hasty response' to the previous year's oil scandal, the latter had the effect which it did only because it stood at the end of a long line of abuses.[6]

Law 195/74 on 'State Contributions to the Financing of Political Parties' had four basic features.

- First, it provided for reimbursement of the expenditures on elections to the two houses of Parliament (the Chamber of Deputies and Senate) of all parties which fielded candidates in at least two-thirds of the electoral colleges of the Chamber of Deputies, and which obtained *either* one electoral quotient and 300 000 votes at national level, *or* at least 2 per cent of valid votes cast. Reimbursement was also available for parties obtaining at least one electoral quotient in regions whose special statutes provided for the protection of linguistic minorities. The total to be reimbursed was subject to a maximum of 15 billion lire (raised to 30 billion in 1985) to be distributed according to the following formula: 15 per cent to be divided among all eligible parties equally; 85 per cent to be divided in proportion to the parties' vote shares in the election for the Chamber of Deputies (proportions that were changed to 20 per cent and 80 per cent by law number 659 of 18 November 1981). Similar provisions were made in 1980 (law 422/80) and 1981 (law 659/81) for the reimbursement of expenditures on regional elections and elections to the European parliament.[7]

- Second, the law provided for a public contribution to the parties' regular, organizational costs. The total amount was fixed at 45 billion lire (raised to 72.63 billion in 1980 and to 82.886 billion in 1981), to be paid to the parliamentary groups according to the following formula: 2 per cent to be divided among the parliamentary groups equally; 75 per cent to be divided among the parliamentary groups according to their size; the remaining 23 per cent to be divided according to a mixed system. Presidents of parliamentary groups were required to turn over at least 95 per cent of the total sums they received to their party organizations (a proportion that was reduced to 90 per cent by law number 659 of 18 November 1981).

- Third, article 7 of the law placed a ban on any kind of contribution to the parties, their organizations or parliamentary groups, from any branch of the public administration, from any public agency, or from any company, including subsidiaries, in which the state had a shareholding of over 20 per cent.

- Fourth, the law obliged parties to publish regular accounts showing income and expenditure under a variety of headings according to a model balance sheet stipulated by the law itself.

Since all the evidence suggests that illicit party funding in fact continued and expanded during the period following 1974, it may be, as Rhodes (1997:62–4) suggests, that the law had a masking effect by sanctifying party balance sheets whose content was unverifiable (since the categories the parties were to use were not well defined)

and by failing to establish rules to ensure that the income and expenditure of parties' local bodies would be properly accounted for in balance
sheets. However, in view of the extent to which the market for corrupt
transactions had become established by the mid seventies, it is also
fair to suggest that, even had the legislation dealt more adequately
with these points, its impact would still have been slight. True, the
procedure for revising the public contribution was cumbersome (it
could only be changed by law) and this was likely to detract from the
law's effectiveness in curbing a hunger for illegal funds in years of
high inflation and in the face of the increasing costs of politics
(Rhodes, 1997:64–5). It can also be convincingly argued that the
pressures for illegal funding might have been somewhat less intense
had the state financed, not party *organizations*, but the *functioning* of
parties, and had it imposed rigorous spending limits (Pasquino,
1985:125). However, as suggested above, much political corruption
in fact had little to do with official party functions or organization
and everything to do with the fact that the parties had become sites
for the emergence and growth of unofficial networks and power
structures through which individuals and groups sought to realize
personal and material, as opposed to ideological and policy, ambitions. Therefore, much of the political corruption in Italy was effectively beyond the reach of party finance legislation, for the most that
such legislation could do was to place legal boundaries around the
size, the sources, and the nature of *official* party income, while specifying the purposes for which such income could legitimately be
spent. What it could not do was to prevent the proliferation, within
the parties, of individuals and *unofficial* groups for whom power and
resources were an end rather than a means, and for whom, owing to
the inflationary dynamic involved in competition between them,
the pressure to obtain higher and higher amounts of illicit funding
was, as a result, unremitting. Perhaps the best supporting evidence of
this point is given by the fact that corrupt party funding is widely
regarded as having become 'systemic' by the 1980s, this in spite of
the fact that the rules on private contributions to parties and on financial accounting were greatly extended after 1974 and give every
appearance of representing a considerable tightening of the rules laid
down by law 195/74.[8]

In the late seventies, the Radical Party was successful in gathering
the 500 000 signatures necessary to request a referendum aimed at

abolishing public funding. This was, arguably, a further indicator of the way in which the funds made available by law 195/74 became additional to, rather than substitutive of, illicit contributions (Pasquino, 1974:234). This in turn explains the seeming paradox whereby the Radicals, while declaring themselves to be implacable opponents of *partitocrazia* and its corrupt practices, could nevertheless sponsor an initiative designed to eliminate a system which, in theory at least, was aimed at combating the worst features of political corruption. However, if their initiative was also the consequence of an attempt to apply the theory that the referendum instrument could be used to bring together coalitions of forces opposed to the DC (and thereby create pressure for a change in the mechanics of the party system in a bi-polar, left–right, direction) it conflicted with the PCI's 'historic compromise' strategy which aimed at collaboration in government with the DC (Uleri, 1994:9). Thus when the party finance referendum was eventually held (on 11 June 1978), the PCI lined up alongside the DC and almost all the other traditional parties of government in opposing abolition of the law. As a consequence, bearing in mind that most voters in referenda follow the line espoused by their preferred parties, the vote for abolition was lost (by 43.6 to 56.4 per cent).

The 1978 vote made clear that the *political* significance of referenda could often go well beyond the significance of referenda questions *formally* considered (Modona, 1995:243). The PCI dubbed the campaign for abolition an attack 'on the difficult process of democratic advance of the country'. For Scalfari, editor of *la Repubblica*, the vote had been one 'for or against the political system which, for better or worse, had governed for thirty years' (Pasquino, 1978:551). The vote also made clear that the loyalties of a significant proportion of voters, if not to the entire political system, certainly to the established parties, were indeed wearing thin: while the parties opposed to abolition had been able to count on the support of 95.4 per cent of voters at the previous general election, only 56.4 per cent of those casting valid referendum votes had been willing to heed their call. Consequently when, 15 years later, the issue of public financing was again the subject of a referendum sponsored by the Radicals, the changed political context ensured that the outcome would be very different. Once again, the occasion was cast as a plebiscite on 'the System' and on the members of the political class who were its bearers.[9] This time, however, it was clear to all concerned that the chances of containing public hostility by means of the united front tactic used on the previous occasion were non-existent; the period since 1978 had seen the transformation of the PCI into the non-communist PDS, so that (at the end of a period when the electorate had already shown ample signs of growing volatility) long-standing assumptions about the need to support the traditional parties of government at all costs no longer applied. Meanwhile, the fact that transformation of the PCI had been accompanied by a major crisis of the party itself had led the leaders of the governing parties to believe that they could postpone reform of those 'partitocratic' practices which, by undermining public confidence that policy-making was informed by a search for the public good, weakened their own support bases. Finally, by the time the referendum took place, it was clear that the *Tangentopoli* investigations, whose results had begun to emerge in early 1992, were in process of uncovering the most extensive networks of political corruption ever to come to light in post-war Italy. Confirming what had become a frequent practice, namely, altering policy stands to conform to majority opinion on the occasion of referenda, every single party represented in Parliament came out in favour of abolishing public financing. The result was a vote of 90.3 per cent in favour of abolition with 9.7 per cent against.

The context which thus came to be created – one in which all of the referenda aiming to strike at *partitocrazia* were passed; in which, with the sudden end to illicit funding, many of the traditional governing parties went bankrupt; and in which, under the weight of the continuing *Tangentopoli* investigations, they began to disintegrate – was one giving rise to pressure for a new system of party financing as part of an overall package of reforms including a new electoral law. Such a new system took the form of law 515 of 10 December 1993. Technically, the referendum vote had struck down, not all public funding for parties, but only articles 3 and 9 of law 195/74 which provided for a public contribution to the parties' regular, organizational expenses. Reimbursement of the parties' *election campaign* expenditures therefore remained. Law 515 in essence modifies the system of reimbursement of electoral expenses to take account of the new reality created by the changed electoral law (passed in August 1993), while introducing some new features to the regulatory framework.[10]

While the law embraces a number of issues related to the conduct of election campaigns (from access to the media to the use of opinion polls), its provisions with regard to funding and spending fall essentially into four parts:

- First, it establishes new criteria for the fund for the reimbursement of electoral expenditures, while providing for in-kind contributions to parties' campaigns. The fund is set at a figure equal to the sum of 1600 lire multiplied by the total number of inhabitants of Italy, according to the latest census. Half this total is used to reimburse candidates for election to the Senate, the other half to reimburse candidates for election to the Chamber of Deputies. The Senate fund is divided among the 20 regions according to their populations and then among candidates and groups of candidates in proportion to their regional vote totals. To be entitled to a share of the fund, groups of candidates must succeed in getting at least one of their number elected, or in winning at least 5 per cent of the vote in the region in question, while independent candidates must succeed either in getting elected or in winning at least 15 per cent of the votes cast in their single-member constituency. The Chamber of Deputies' fund is distributed, in proportion to parties' list-vote totals, among those parties that have superseded the 4 per cent vote threshold or elected a deputy in at least one single-member constituency and won at least 3 per cent of the vote at national level. In-kind contributions consist of: a reduced rate of postage for the delivery of one election address to every elector registered in the candidate's constituency or electoral district; a reduced rate of Value Added Tax on printed election material; and an obligation on local councils to make available, to parties and candidates, council-owned premises for conferences and debates.
- For the first time, limits on campaign expenditure are imposed. Spending by *both* parties *and* individual candidates is limited. No party can spend more than the sum of 200 lire multiplied by the number of inhabitants of the Chamber-of-Deputies electoral districts and of the Senate constituencies in which the party fields candidates. No individual candidate can spend more than the sum of 80 million lire, plus 100 lire multiplied by the number of citizens resident in the candidate's single-member constituency, or (if the candidate is competing for one of the seats distributed on the basis of the

Chamber-of-Deputies list vote) 10 lire multiplied by the number of citizens resident in the electoral district in question.

- Third, the law places a limit of 20 million lire on contributions to candidates' campaign funds by individuals or organizations.
- Fourth, the law establishes novel procedures for verifying and accounting for campaign income and expenditure, together with a series of fines which can be applied in cases of non-compliance with such procedures. Funds for a candidate's election campaign may only be raised by an election agent, appointed by the candidate him – or herself, and who is responsible for keeping a record of all income and expenditure and for managing the bank account in which the funds are held. Candidates and their agents are required to lodge statements of their election income and expenditures with new regional *Collegi di garanzia elettorale*, composed of judges and experts in administrative and commercial law, whose role is to scrutinize the statements so presented. Members of the public can challenge the legal regularity of any of these statements, which are made available for public consultation at the offices of each *Collegio*. Parties and groups of candidates are required to lodge statements of their election income and expenditure with the presidents of the Chamber and the Senate who must then pass them to the Court of Accounts. Here the statements are examined and a report on their legal regularity made to the presidents within six months.

Looking back over the two general elections that have taken place since law 515/93 came into force (the one held in 1994 and the one held in 1996), the new accounting and verification procedures appear, from one point of view at least, to have been rather effective. One of the main ways in which they innovate as compared to the past is that, since the *Collegi di garanzia* and the Court of Accounts are invested with judicial authority, these bodies thereby have the power *themselves* to apply the penalties provided for by the law – with the result that sanctions can be imposed immediately upon discovery of any irregularity without the need for further lengthy legal investigations. Moreover, Rhodes' (1997:76) judgement, that the Court of Accounts had been assiduous in monitoring party income and expenditure in the wake of the 1994 election, also appears valid for the 1996 election; it is clear that the Court has interpreted its role as being to use its powers to act as an arbiter of 'fair play' (albeit, 'after the event').[11] In 1994, the Court had imposed sanctions against a number of the major parties which had been found variously guilty of exceeding campaign spending limits, of failing fully to reveal the sources of funds, or of irregularities in the documentation relating to certain items of expenditure. In addition, investigations had been initiated to discover whether *Forza Italia* had benefited from covert funding via illegal discounts applied to services furnished by Berlusconi's advertising company, Publitalia (Corte dei Conti, 1995). By contrast, when in August 1997 the Court of Accounts produced its report on the parties' balance sheets for the 1996 election, it emerged that only five minor formations had been found to be in breach of the law (all for failing to supply their statements of income and expenditure).[12] What appears on the face of it to have happened, then, is that, having become aware, the first time round, that there was a very high probability of the application of sanctions in cases of impropriety, the parties then went out of their way to ensure that their houses could not be found to be in disorder at the elections held two years later.

On the other hand, the Court has also in its reports drawn attention to a number of weaknesses which would seem to detract from the law's effectiveness. One of these concerns the definition of what counts as electoral expenditure. Article 11 of the law lists types of expenditure that are to be regarded as belonging to this category; however, for the purposes of enforcing the *limits* on election spending, it is unclear whether what is intended is that parties' expenditure be *confined* to these activities, or whether, of the activities on which they do spend money, only these are to count as *election spending*. The Court has rejected the first interpretation on the grounds that 'its effect would be to exclude, inexplicably, a whole range of legitimate activities in society' (Corte dei Conti, 1997:250). On the other hand, the second interpretation effectively exonerates the parties from having to provide documentation for spending on any activities not listed in article 11 – with the consequence that it undermines the 'moral enhancement' effects of the limit on spending, if not the notion of a spending limit itself. Second, it is not clear *whose* spending is to be limited. Article 10 of the law indicates that the entities concerned are 'each party, movement, list or group of candidates taking part in the election'. But the fact that many parties have legally autonomous local and flanking organizations, which nevertheless openly engage in activities in support of their parties, poses difficult questions about just where to draw the line among these activities in order to be able to decide whether the limit has been respected or not. Third, the law does not give any indication of the headings or categories parties are to use in their statements. This, arguably, weakens the control on income and expenditure by allowing too wide a margin of interpretation of the law's requirements to those who are expected to comply with it. If, therefore, law 515/93 places significant powers of direct control over the parties in the hands of an independent body which can be expected to fulfil its remit meticulously, it also has several weaknesses over which the Court of Accounts has no control. This creates the risk, similar to that associated with law 195/74, that, despite itself, the Court ends up giving 'official sanction' to practices which are in fact of dubious propriety.

While it covered election income and expenditure, law 515/93 was completely silent on the question of the financing of parties' regular activities (for which the April 1993 referendum had abolished *public* funding). It was partly in order to fill this gap at a time when the parties were facing continuing financial crisis that, during the course of 1996, Parliament considered new draft legislation on funding, both public and private – legislation which eventually emerged as law number 2 of 2 January 1997, 'Regulations governing voluntary contributions to movements and political parties'. In essence the law does two things (besides introducing new, tighter accounting and verification procedures to replace those laid down by law 659/81)[13]. First, it gives income-tax payers the option of specifying on their annual tax returns that 0.4 per cent of their tax payments are to be used to finance the parties. The fund so created (which may not exceed an annual total of 110 billion lire) is then to be divided, each year, among all parties with at least one member of Parliament, in proportion to their list-vote totals at the last Chamber of Deputies election. Second, it makes party donations of between 500 000 lire and 50 million lire, on the part of individuals and companies, tax deductible.

To a considerable extent the law belies its name, and for this reason it provoked some of the more picturesque forms of political protest to have been seen in post-war Italy, with the Radicals' charismatic leader, Marco Pannella, on more than one occasion during the course of 1997, taking to the streets to give away to grateful passersby his party's share of the money made available under the new law! The Radicals' anger was understandable, for the new law can be seen as amounting to a rather clever subterfuge. Although citizens' tax contributions to the financing of parties are in theory voluntary, the law also contained a clause providing for an initial 160 billion lire to be distributed among the parties, in advance of the completion of any tax returns, for the financial year 1997. Even more cleverly, the law manages to make appear voluntary what is in fact an obligatory tax contribution to the parties: it requires only a small proportion of tax payers to agree to the 0.4 per cent contribution for the 110 billion lire total to be reached, and yet the real effect of the contribution is of course to reduce by a corresponding amount the *general* tax yield (and therefore the sum available for other public spending) to which *all* taxpayers contribute. For this reason the law can be seen as a straightforward contradiction of the 1993 referendum outcome.

The months following its passage saw what appeared to be mass rejection of the new law with well below 15 per cent of taxpayers agreeing to subscribe their tax contributions to the parties (15 per cent being the proportion which, it was estimated, was necessary for the 110 billion lire figure to be reached). After a television advertising campaign at the end of May 1997, aimed at increasing the numbers of subscribers, the period available to citizens to make their subscriptions was extended until the end of December. According to the law, the sums raised in any one year were to be distributed to the parties by 31 January of the following year. However, owing to the aforementioned extension, by 31 January 1998 it was still not known how much would actually be available for distribution that year. The following month, proposals were being discussed in Parliament whereby the parties would receive the 110 billion lire funding 'on account', with balances being settled at a later stage once all the relevant tax returns had been examined. It really did appear, then, as though public funding for parties' regular activities had been reintroduced 'by the back door'.

## Outlook

Organizationally, Italian parties currently appear weaker than at any time in the post-war period, a weakness that can be seen from several angles. On the one hand, popular discontent with the traditional governing parties, discontent which reached its culmination with the *Tangentopoli* scandals, seems to have accentuated distrust of parties *per se*, with overall membership levels continuing to decline – from 3 804 000 in 1991 to 2 183 000 in 1996, after reaching a low of 1 330 000 in 1993, according to one estimate (Follini, 1997:250). On the other hand, born as a result of the break-up of traditional formations, a number of parties remain 'top heavy', with high levels of co-optation of leadership groups, while others, most notably Berlusconi's *Forza Italia*, having been born as vehicles for the political ambitions of their leaders, remain almost indistinguishable from them. If low levels of membership create pressure for public funding, the fact that many parties are sustained by organizations of a highly oligarchic, personalistic character makes it seem quite unsurprising that they should reach an agreement on funding arrangements whose disregard of the 1993 referendum gives the agreement all the characteristics of a traditional division of spoils. In many respects, therefore, the passage of law 2/97 symbolizes both the continuing crisis of Italian parties and the persistence of those 'partitocratic' practices which had fuelled corruption in the past.

There are few grounds for optimism then about the likely elimination of political corruption in the immediate term. For one thing, the above suggests the persistence of that dilemma whereby, if certain practices require reform, only those parties who engage in such practices are in a position to deliver the reforms in question. For another thing, it is difficult to envisage changes in the party-finance laws in themselves having much of an impact in a context in which the roots of political corruption are so multiform. As we have suggested, there are any number of reforms that might reasonably be expected to reduce some of the potential pressures to obtain illegal funding which are inherent in the parties' function of providing political intermediation between civil society and the state. Yet, it is difficult to envisage them being particularly effective against that part of political corruption which arises when the corruption becomes more or less routine, and thus gives rise to a proliferation of individuals and groups with few if any ideological concerns, but who are dedicated to exploiting party connections in the pursuit of power and resources *as ends in themselves*. This type of corruption, besides being self-generating as we have seen, was and is also fuelled by specific economic and social conditions lying well beyond the purely politico-institutional sphere. As Magatti (1996) has argued, the heightened individualism of the 1980s in a context of renewed economic growth; increasing secularization and 'deideologization'; the decline of Italy's two political subcultures, the Catholic and the Marxist; and the continuing weakness of the state – all served to weaken the normative constraints on individual action, with the result of creating an environment favouring 'the spread of those illicit behaviours which find in corruption, and more generally in clientelism, the two principal ambits of their manifestation' (Magatti, 1996:1064). It is by no means obvious that these social and economic conditions have become any less marked in the nineties.

Not surprisingly, therefore, stories of corruption continue to be daily fare for consumers of the Italian print and broadcast media. Though many relate to offences allegedly committed before the outbreak of *Tangentopoli* (Rhodes, 1997:77), it is indicative of concern about a continuation of corrupt practices that, in October 1996, magistrates based in Milan publicly accused the government of failing to do enough to support them in their efforts to combat corruption in public life, and that similar allegations were again made in February 1998. Such complaints and the sense of public outrage which corruption scandals continue to provoke are, however, reasons for optimism, for they point to the continuing vitality of what Ginsborg has called the 'official morality to which, in the last analysis, everyday morality remains subordinate' (Ginsborg, 1996:24). In a sense, then, they also point to this paradox: that owing to the strong sense of impropriety which continues to be attached to acts of corruption in Italy, such acts themselves may in the long run serve to improve the functioning of democracy in that country rather than to undermine it.

## Notes

1  Ciaurro (1989:153) lists five main sources of party finance, of which the second and third clearly involved corruption on most commonly accepted understandings of the term: contributions from members and supporters; subsidies from private organizations including kickbacks on contracts and supplies to public agencies controlled by the parties; diversion of public money into party coffers through 'creative accounting'; income from party-sponsored commercial activities; donations from abroad.

2  For an analysis of how the transition from clientelism of the notables to party-directed patronage took place, see Graziano (1973).

3  James C. Scott (1972) defines clientelism as 'a largely instrumental friendship in which an individual of higher socio-economic status (patron) uses

his own influence and resources to provide protection and/or benefits for a person of lower status (client) who ... reciprocates by offering general support and assistance.' Following Della Porta and Vannucci (1997:231–2), the term 'political corruption' is here understood as the secret violation of a contract involving the delegation of responsibility and the exercise of some discretionary power by an agent who, against the interests or preferences of the principal, acts in favour of a third party from whom he receives a reward, and where the principal is the state or the citizenry.

4  As Graziano (1973:26) puts it: 'Whenever a new actor appears in the political market of the South and is provided with a sufficiently threatening bargaining power, the ruling party has the instinctive reaction of a monopolist: first it tries to intimidate the newcomer and if unsuccessful to corrupt him.'

5  Movements up or down in either of these indicators may reflect not increases or decreases in the underlying phenomenon, but changes in legal norms; changes in the factors influencing the likelihood that, once discovered, given acts are brought to official notice; changes in the factors influencing the likelihood that, once brought to official notice, the acts are defined and recorded as legal violations that fit the researcher's definition of 'political corruption'; and – in the case of the second indicator – changes in the reporting practices of the press.

6  If previous scandals had been under-reported and investigations often subverted (Rhodes, 1997:56), it is fair to suggest that the public nevertheless had a general awareness of corruption's constant presence as a 'background feature' of the Italian political system. As Giorgio Galli (1991:41) observes: 'At the end of the first legislature, there was a widespread feeling that corruption was a not insignificant characteristic of [the Italian] political system.'

7  For details see Bardi and Morlino (1992) and Rhodes (1997).

8  Thus, laws 659/81 and 22/82 extend article 7 of law 195/74 to include payments made to individual members of Parliament; regional, provincial or local councillors; candidates; party functionaries and internal party groups. Second, laws 659/81 and 515/93 require contributions totalling over five million lire in any one year (a figure to be understood as having been revised over time in line with the official price index) to be accompanied by a declaration signed by donor and recipient and deposited with the office of the President of the Chamber of Deputies. Third, law 659/81 stipulated that parties' accounts were to be accompanied by an auditor's report and deposited every year with the president of the Chamber of Deputies, and that the president in his turn was then to supervise a further examination of the parties' accounts by auditors.

9  This was largely because, as noted earlier, the vote was held concomitantly with seven other referenda, and of these, the one aimed at changing the electoral system had been explicitly promoted as a means of undermining the established political class. Indeed, part of the Radicals' strategy had been to take advantage of the traction which the vote on the electoral law was bound to exert (Uleri, 1994:9).

10 For an explanation of how the new electoral law operates see, for example, Katz (1995).
11 In its report on the 1996 election, the Court defines its tasks as consisting 'in application of the principle of *par condicio* to the electoral competition, and concomitantly, in the prevention, by means of appropriate sanctions, of competition that is corrupt or distorted by improper or compromising financial transactions' (Corte dei Conti, 1997:4).
12 The parties, all virtually unknown, were: *Noi Siciliani* (We Sicilians), *Colpisci il Centro* (Hit the Centre), *Federalisti Liberali* (Liberal Federalists), *Patto Donne Trieste* (Pact of the Women of Trieste), and *Partito Socialista della Toscana* (Socialist Party of Tuscany) (Corte dei Conti, 1997:65).
13 (Law 659/81: see note 10). In introducing the new procedures law 2/97 goes some way to meeting Pasquino's (1985:125) objection to law 659/81, that it failed to require parties properly to account for the spending of their individual candidates or of their sub-national bodies. It does so by obliging parties (starting four years after enactment of the law) to distribute at least 30 per cent of the public funding which it makes available to those of their sub-national organizations that have financial autonomy – while at the same time obliging these organizations to file accounts according to the same terms that apply to the national-level parent party.

## Bibliography

Bourricaud, François (1974) 'Partitocrazia: consolidamento o rottura?', pp. 81–123 in: Fabio Luca Cavazza and Stephen R. Graubard, *Il caso italiano* (Milano: Garzanti).
Bardi, Luciano and Leonardo Morlino (1992) 'Italy', pp. 458–618 in Richard Katz and Peter Mair (eds) *Party Organizations: A Data Handbook* (London: Sage).
Bull Linda (1997) 'Public Money, Political Parties and Corruption: The Italian Case', *Italian Politics and Society*, No. 48, Autumn, pp. 50–60.
Cassese, Sabino (1983) *Il sistema amministrativo italiano* (Bologna: il Mulino).
Cazzola, Franco (1988) *Della Corruzione: Fisiologia e patologia di un sistema politico*, (Bologna: il Mulino).
Ciaurro, Gian Franco (1989) 'Public financing of parties in Italy', pp. 153–71 in: Herbert E. Alexander (ed.), *Comparative Political Finance in the 1980s* (Cambridge: Cambridge University Press).
Corte dei Conti, Collegio di Controllo sulle Spese Elettorali (1995) 'Referto ai Presidenti delle Camere sui consuntivi delle spese e dei finanziameni delle formazioni politiche presenti alla campagna elettorale del 27–28 marzo 1994 per il rinnovo della Camera dei Deputati e del Seanato della Repubblica' (Roma: Istituto Poligrafico e Zecca dello Sato).
Corte dei Conti, Collegio di Controllo sulle Spese Elettorali (1997) 'Referto ai Presidenti delle Camere sui consuntivi delle spese e dei finanziameni delle formazioni politiche presenti alla campagna elettorale del 21 aprile 1996 per il rinnovo della Camera dei Deputati e del Seanato della Repubblica', (Corte dei Conti, Centro Fotolitografico).

Della Porta, Donatella and Alberto Vannucci (1994) *Corruzzione Politica e Amministrazione Pubblica: Risorse, Meccanismi, Attori* (Bologna: il Mulino).

Della Porta, Donatella and Alberto Vannucci (1997) 'The resources of corruption: Some reflections from the Italian case', *Crime, Law and Social Change*, Vol. 27, No. 3–4, pp. 231–54.

Follini, Marco, 'Il ritorno dei partiti' (1997) *il Mulino*, 370, March/April, pp. 242–51.

Galli, Giorgio (1991) *Affari di Stato: L'Italia sotteranea 1943–1990* (Milano: Kaos Edizioni).

Ginsborg, Paul (1990) *A History of Contemporary Italy: Society and Politics 1943– 1988* (London: Penguin).

Ginsborg, Paul (1995) 'Italian Political Culture in Historical Perspective', *Modern Italy*, Vol. 1, No.1, Autumn, pp. 3–17.

Ginsborg, Paul (1996) 'Explaining Italy's crisis', pp. 19–39 in: Stephen Gundle and Simon Parker, (eds), *The New Italian Republic: From the Fall of the Berlin Wall to Berlusconi* (London & New York: Routledge).

Graziano, Luigi (1973) 'Patron–Client' Relationship in Southern Italy, *European Journal of Political Research*, Vol. 1, pp. 3–34.

Hine, David (1990) 'The Consolidation of democracy in post-war Italy', pp. 62–83 in: Geoffrey Pridham, (ed.), *Securing Democracy: Political Parties and Democratic Consolidation in Southern Europe*, (London & New York: Routledge).

Katz, Richard (1996) 'Electoral Reform and the Transformation of Party Politics in Italy', Party Politics, Vol. 2, No. 1, pp. 31–53.

La Palombara. Joseph (1964) *Interest Groups in Italian Politics* (Princeton N.J.: Princeton University Press).

Magatti Mauro (1996) 'Tangentopoli, una questione sociale', *il Mulino*, 368, November/December, pp. 1058–69.

Modona, Guido Neppi, *et al.* (1995) *Stato della Constituzione: Principi, regole, equilibri. Le ragioni della storia, i compiti di oggi* (Milano: Il Saggiatore).

Pasquino, Gianfranco (1974) 'Contro il finanziamento pubblico di questi partiti', *il Mulino* , 23, pp. 233–55.

Pasquino, Gianfranco (1978) 'Con i partiti, oltre i partiti', *il Mulino*, 258, pp. 548–65.

Pasquino, Gianfranco (1985) *Restituire lo scettro al principe: Proposte di riforma istituzionale* (Roma & Bari: Laterza).

Pasquino, Gianfranco (1986) 'Modernity and Reforms: The PSI between Political Entrepreneurs and Gamblers', *West European Politics*, Vol. 9, No. 1, pp. 120–41.

Rhodes, Martin (1997) 'Financing Party Politics in Italy: A Case of Systemic Corruption', pp. 54–80 in: Martin Bull and Martin Rhodes (eds), *Crisis and Transition in Italian Politics* (London & Portland OR: Frank Cass).

Tarrow, Sidney (1977) *Between Center and Periphery: Grassroots Politicians in Italy and France* (New Haven & London: Yale University Press).

Scott, James C. (1972) 'Patron–Client Politics and Political Change in Southeast Asia', *American Political Science Review*, March.

Uleri, Pier Vincenzo (1994) 'The referendum phenomenon in Italy: from the beginnings to the crisis of a democratic system (1946–1993)', paper presented to the workshop on the Referendum Experience in Europe of the Joint Sessions of Workshops of the European Consortium for Political Research. Madrid, 17–22 April.

# 5

# Court and Parties: Evolution and Problems of Political Funding in Germany

*Thomas Saalfeld*

## Introduction

In the 1980s and 1990s the funding of (West) German political parties has attracted considerable public and scholarly attention.[1] To some extent, this is a result of the nature of the topic and a number of highly publicized scandals including allegations of serious corruption. As Peter Lösche puts it, '[p]olitical finance is a fascinating subject. It contains the stuff of detective stories. It smells of corruption – individuals or interest groups buying access of favorable legislation, perhaps bribery of a member of parliament or even of a small party.'[2] From the 1950s to the 1970s, 'high-level' political corruption[3] was not an important issue on the Federal Republic's political agenda. Compared to the scandals elsewhere in the Western world, 'the mostly local scandals in West German construction industries and city authorities seemed of minor magnitude.'[4] Since the 1980s, it has been argued, 'the self-image of legality and propriety has been tarnished. Scandals over party financing and over business failures connected to the political parties have followed one another.'[5] It is difficult to establish whether high-level corruption has become more widespread since the 1970s, whether there is just greater public awareness and sensitivity, or both. Definitions of the 'acceptable' and 'corrupt' may vary considerably across countries and time. Given the 'normalization' of (West) Germany's democracy, which has generally resulted in a more critical attitude towards politicians,[6] a related redefinition and reduced tolerance of corrupt practices is not an implausible proposition.

Not all scandals that affected (West) German political parties during the 1980s and 1990s involved allegations of outright political corruption in a strictly defined sense.[7] The 'Barschel affair' mainly involved 'dirty tricks' during the campaign preceding the 1987 elections to the Schleswig-Holstein state parliament and the mysterious death of the federal state's premier, Uwe Barschel. The scandalization of Cornelia Yzer's change from a government post to a senior management post in a pharmaceutical interest group (1997) reflected Mrs Yzer's lawful but politically ill-judged claim of a transitional allowance paid to former civil servants and certain pension rights. Yet, the 'Flick affair' of the early 1980s and the Bavarian 'Amigo affair' of the early 1990s did involve allegations of corruption in a strict sense. In 1999, the former leader of the Christian Democratic Union (CDU) and the former Federal Chancellor, Helmut Kohl, had to admit having received up to two million Deutsche Mark in undeclared, and therefore illegal, donations for the CDU between 1993 and 1998, which he claimed were used to support the party organization in eastern Germany.[8] Allegations made in this context were investigated by a parliamentary committee of the Bundestag as well as state prosecutors. Such scandals have arguably contributed to what in German is often termed *Parteienverdrossenheit* (disaffection with political parties) or even *Politikverdrossenheit* (disaffection with the political process at large). The Flick affair was directly linked to issues of state funding of political parties and donations. Therefore, and due to the relatively rich material which is in the public domain about this scandal, we shall use it as an illustration of some of the problems of German party finance. Such scandals have arguably contributed to what in German is often termed *Parteienverdrossenheit* (disaffection with political parties) or even *Politikverdrossenheit* (disaffection with the political process at large).

Despite such scandals there is little doubt in the German debate that political parties need resources to perform their legitimate democratic functions and that the costs of political competition have risen dramatically in all modern democracies as a result of technological and organizational changes.[9] Given their crucial role in the political process, the nature of party funding has a considerable impact on the legitimacy of the political process itself, the character of party competition and party systems, and the equality of access to the political decision-making process. Not least, it has an impact on the structure of the political parties themselves. The parties responded to this dilemma (growing financial needs which are, however, unpopular with the electorate) by 'depoliticizing' reforms of party finance and handing over such deliberations to commissions of non-political experts appointed by the Federal President on an *ad hoc* basis. There have been two such commissions which presented their final reports in 1983 and 1994.[10] These experts were called upon by, and reported to, the Federal President, because he is considered to be above the fray of party politics.

The aim of this chapter is to give a descriptive account of the evolution and character of party finance in the Federal Republic of Germany and to analyze the effectiveness of some of the institutional arrangements that are to regulate, monitor and publicize party finance, including safeguards against corruption. In the next section, some fundamental constitutional and legal norms pertaining to party political funding will be discussed. In the following section, the role of the Federal Constitutional Court as an institutional check on the 'cartel' of the main parties will be outlined briefly. The fourth section will give a brief survey of the main political parties' income and spending, while the penultimate section will look in some more detail at the main sources of political funding in Germany: donations, state funding and membership dues. In the concluding section, the main results of this chapter will be summarized and the implications for the nature of 'party democracy' in Germany assessed.

## Fundamental legal norms

Article 21 of the Basic Law formally recognizes the crucial role of political parties in the 'formation of the political will of the people' and requires their internal life to be organized according to democratic principles. The provisions of the Basic Law are relatively general. The task of establishing more detailed norms was left to the Bundestag which passed a Political Parties Act in 1967 (see below). Unlike political parties, other political organizations such as interest groups or citizens' initiatives are not explicitly mentioned in, and recognized by, the Basic Law. The parties have therefore traditionally claimed a privileged status *vis-à-vis* other groups – a claim which, with some variations over time, has on the whole been supported by the rulings of the Federal Constitutional Court. This privileged position has had particular implications for public subsidies to political parties. Article 21 of the Basic Law also contains a number of general norms concerning the finance of political parties. In particular, the parties have to account publicly for their income sources, their expenditures and their assets.

The Political Parties Act 1967 is the statutory concretization of Article 21 of the Basic Law. The initiative for the Act came from the Federal Constitutional Court and not from the main parties themselves. In its landmark decision of 1966,[11] the Court outlawed generalized direct public subsidies to political parties (see below) and demanded the passage of a Political Parties Act as stipulated by the Basic Law. Not only did the 1967 Act require the parties to implement a number of basic principles of intra-party democracy which had hitherto remained unspecified. It also regulated the payment of public subsidies to political parties. Ever since, the financial part of the Political Parties Act 'has also been the most problematic. Whereas all other regulations remained intact without any major adjustment, the history of legislation on party finance has taken almost as many twists and turns as an average roller-coaster ride, with most of these turns being imposed upon law-makers by the Constitutional Court.'[12]

In its interpretations of Article 21, the Federal Constitutional Court has consistently emphasized that the state has to give all political parties *equal opportunities* to participate in the electoral process. It has left little doubt that 'equality of opportunity' must include the public funding of political parties and all other public services made available to them. The main exceptions to the principle of equality of opportunity are the powers of the Federal Constitutional Court to ban unconstitutional parties and the five-per-cent barrier of the Federal Elections Act, which mainly serves the purpose of maintaining a workable Bundestag. As far as the provision of public services or funds for political parties is concerned, clause 5(1) of the Political Parties Act allows discrimination between parties only according to their previous electoral performance. Some constitutional lawyers have argued that this may involve a problematic bias in favour of established parties at the expense of newly-founded or small parties,[13] although in cross-national comparison Germany's system of public subsidies to political parties is relatively open.[14]

In 1994 (taking effect on 1 January 1995), the Bundestag amended the Members of Parliament Act (*Abgeordnetengesetz*) to include legal

norms on the finance and financial accountability of the parliamentary parties, which receive considerable grants from the federal
budget.[15] It emphasizes that parliamentary parties assist the Bundestag in fulfilling its functions and are entitled to financial support and
other services in kind in pursuit of their duties. The distribution
formula is largely proportional, although opposition parties receive a
certain 'bonus'. The parliamentary parties administer these funds
themselves. They must only be used for purposes that are in agreement with the duties that parliamentary parties have according to
the Basic Law, the Members of Parliament Act and the Rules of Procedure of the Bundestag. They are expressly not allowed to use these
funds to finance extra-parliamentary party activities.[16] The parliamentary parties must account for the use of these funds annually.
The accounts have to be audited by a chartered accountant and published in the Bundestag's printed papers. The Federal Audit Office
(*Bundesrechnungshof*) has to scrutinize the accounts submitted by the
parliamentary parties regularly, consider the economic efficiency
and legal propriety of expenditure, to make recommendations for
improvements if necessary, and to publish a report on its findings.
There are certain restrictions, the most important of which is that
the Federal Audit Court is not allowed to pass judgement on the
political merits of the parliamentary parties' expenditure. It can,
however, establish whether a parliamentary party has used the funds
for purposes other than those connected with their parliamentary
work and whether the separation of parliamentary and extra-parliamentary party finance has been adhered to.[17]

## The Federal Constitutional Court as institutional check

There are three main institutional arrangements to control party
finance in Germany: first, certain constitutional and legal norms
defining and constraining lawful ways of revenue generation by the
political parties (see previous section); secondly, there are a number
of reporting requirements forcing the parties to report regularly and
publicly on their sources of income and expenditures; and thirdly,
the Federal Constitutional Court has consistently acted as an external
institutional check on the parties – that is, as an agent whose preferences differ from those of the political parties and who has the authority to veto or block their actions in parliament.[18] Court decisions

have usually been a response to constitutional complaints either by minority parties or individual citizens. Its role as an external 'veto player' has been crucial as the main parties control a legislative majority in the Federal Parliament, the Bundestag, and are therefore in a position to pass legislation on party finance. In matters of party finance, CDU/CSU, SPD and FDP, the three parties that have been represented in the Bundestag since 1949, have usually (if not always) sought a consensus. In the absence of an opposition, parliament has often not worked as a check on the main parties, who could be said to form a 'cartel'. Thus those whose finances are to be scrutinized have the power to define the rules of this scrutiny process. Without the Federal Constitutional Court as an external check, there would be no institution preventing the main parties from passing self-serving legislation.

Germany is not an isolated case in this respect, however Katz and Mair have identified a marked tendency towards the evolution of 'cartel parties' in many modern industrial democracies which, unlike their predecessors (the 'mass parties' and 'catch-all parties'), are no longer links or brokers between state and civil society, but agents of the state. While the catch-all parties of the 1950s and 1960s were highly competitive in the electoral arena, modern 'cartel parties' contain and manage inter-party conflict: 'Certainly, the parties still compete, but they do so in the knowledge that they share with their competitors a mutual interest in collective organizational survival.'[19] According to the authors, the electoral campaigns of modern 'cartel parties' are 'now almost exclusively capital-intensive, professional and centralized' and the parties 'rely increasingly for their resources on the subventions and other benefits and privileges afforded by the state'. To the extent that political parties have developed into 'cartel parties', the German case is an interesting example of the problems of party funding under such circumstances.

Nevertheless, it would be wrong to exaggerate the 'cartellisation' of the German parties and to 'credit' only the Federal Constitutional Court with the function of an institutional check. A significant degree of contention was re-introduced to German party politics when the Green Party arrived in the Bundestag in 1983. Being an 'outsider' the party had incentives to challenge the 'established' parties on a number of counts, including party finance. The outcome of the Flick affair and similar scandals also showed that the legal system and investigative journalists were eventually successful in exposing illegal practices in party financing.[20] Although a large number of grey areas remain,[21] these developments (combined with the rulings of the Federal Constitutional Court) have contributed to major improvements in the legal norms regulating the funding of political parties since 1983.

One characteristic feature of the development of party finance in Germany is almost a ping-pong game between the Federal Constitutional Court and the 'established' parties, that is, those parties that have been represented in the Bundestag uninterruptedly since 1949.

> Generally speaking, there were two main protagonists involved in the evolution of the German party financing system. . . . On the one hand, the *constitutional court*, invoking egalitarian–democratic principles of the Constitution, laid down in its 1958 and later decisions rather restrictive legal norms with regard to party financing. On the other hand, the *major political parties*, driven by ever-increasing financial desires, passed self-serving legislation. Since 1958 the history of party financing has been the history of a conflict over the division of powers and the role of political parties in a democratic state.[22]

The result of this is 'that in addition to unique constitutional requirements, much of the law dealing with German parties is judge-made law, with the Federal Constitutional Court forcing the Bundestag to act where it otherwise would have hesitated to rethink many of its decisions when it did resolve to act.'

## Party finance – a survey

As a result of reporting requirements that are far-reaching in international comparison, scholars have had a relatively (if not perfectly) accurate picture of party expenditure and assets since 1984. In the first half of the 1990s (1991–4), the total volume of expenditure of the (extra-parliamentary) German political parties is estimated to have amounted to approximately 750 million Deutsche Mark (DM) per annum, of which approximately 725 million DM were spent by the organizations of the parties represented in the Bundestag. The Social Democrats (SPD) spent almost 300 million DM per annum and the Christian Democrats (CDU) around 230 million per year. The smaller Bundestag parties such as the the CSU, the Christian Democrats' Bavarian regional 'sister party', the liberal Free Democrats (FDP), the Green Party (Bündnis 90/GRÜNE) and the post-socialist Party of Democratic Socialism (PDS) spent on average between 40 and 60 million DM per annum. The smaller parties not represented in the Bundestag spent around 25 million DM between them.[23]

These estimates do not include the considerable expenditures of the parliamentary party groups (*Fraktionen*) and, as a peculiarity of the German party system in international comparison, the 'political foundations' attached to the SPD, CDU, CSU, FDP and the Green Party. It has always been a point of contention in the German debate whether expenditures of the parliamentary party groups (more than 100 million DM in 1991) and the political foundations (they received bloc grants of approximately 545 million DM in 1990)[24] should be included in discussions of party finance. It is sometimes argued that the staff employed by the parliamentary party groups fulfil not only duties for their parties but contribute to the running of Parliament as a constitutional body. Similarly, it has been argued, the foundations cannot be treated as if they served predominantly as auxiliary organizations of their respective parties: they spend a considerable share of their funds on overseas development projects and actively attempt to promote democratization and civic education in democratizing countries.[25] Approximately two-thirds of their expenditure is earmarked for such purposes.[26] Nevertheless, part of their activities (e.g., policy analysis, research on voting behaviour, party archives, scholarships, domestic civic education) does benefit their parties domestically.[27] Therefore, Naßmacher includes a certain share of their expenditure in his estimate of approximately 1.3 billion DM as the total annual expenditure of all German political parties and their auxiliary organizations.[28]

Table 5.1 demonstrates that the parties' total expenditure increased considerably between 1970 and 1997. The interpretation of these increases is controversial. Given that a considerable share of their income comes out of the public purse (see below), vigorous criticism of a cost explosion accompanied by a 'subsidy explosion' has been mounted by scholars such as Hans Herbert von Arnim.[29] Naßmacher, by contrast, argues that most of the increases can be accounted for by inflation and the general growth of the German gross national

*Table 5.1:* Total annual income of the political parties in (West) Germany, 1970–1997 (in million DM)

| Year | SPD | CDU | CSU | FDP | Greens | PDS | Total |
|------|------|------|------|------|--------|------|--------|
| 1970 | 53.2 | 43.7 | 11.6 | 10.4 | | | 131.6 |
| 1975 | 118.8 | 111.6 | 19.8 | 22.7 | | | 289.2 |
| 1980 | 156.1 | 159.3 | 37.6 | 35.0 | | | 415.2 |
| 1985 | 193.7 | 176.7 | 39.5 | 30.3 | 26.8 | | 522.5 |
| 1990 | 353.9 | 330.4 | 89.8 | 83.8 | 48.5 | 191.9 | 1098.3 |
| 1991 | 339.6 | 212.8 | 51.7 | 52.2 | 32.5 | 60.7 | 749.5 |
| 1992 | 262.0 | 213.5 | 49.5 | 47.3 | 39.3 | 22.5 | 634.2 |
| 1993 | 280.8 | 225.9 | 56.1 | 49.5 | 37.7 | 27.3 | 677.3 |
| 1994 | 353.4 | 279.9 | 67.8 | 58.0 | 52.8 | 34.3 | 846.3 |
| 1995 | 285.2 | 218.3 | 52.9 | 45.9 | 48.4 | 40.8 | 691.6 |
| 1996 | 283.0 | 222.7 | 62.3 | 40.6 | 50.1 | 36.3 | 695.0 |
| 1997 | 281.0 | 218.2 | 56.0 | 41.6 | 51.3 | 36.8 | 684.9 |

*Note:* The data in the **Total** column refer to all political parties in the Federal Republic including those not represented in the Bundestag. Until 1983, the data do not include loans, from 1984 they do not include grants to lower levels of the party organizations. As a result of the significant public subsidies to the parties' election expenses (until 1994), their income has tended to peak in election years (e.g., 1980, 1990 and 1994).

*Sources:* 1970–85 Bundespräsidialamt (ed.), *Empfehlungen der Kommission unabhängiger Sachverständiger zur Parteienfinanzierung.* Baden-Baden: Nomos 1994, pp. 143–4; 1990–6 Deutscher Bundestag, 'DIP – Das Informationssystem für parlamentarische Vorgänge' (*http://www.bundestag.de/datbk/ pf gesei.htm*), 17 February 1999.

product.[30] In international comparison, Germany is amongst a group of nations where parties spend relatively large amounts of money. Austria, France, Italy and Sweden are also in this group of high-spending parties, whereas Canada, the Netherlands, the United Kingdom and the United States fall into the category of low spenders.[31]

What do German parties spend their money on? The two main expenditure items are the parties' organization and campaign expenditure. In years without a general election, approximately 60 per cent of the parties' total funds are spent on their organization. The main items in the parties' expenditure are costs for staff, office space, general administration, internal communication and party meetings. Most of the parties have expanded their central party and regional headquarters and their network of local offices considerably over the years. In election years, the overall expenditure increases. The parties then spend almost half of their funds on campaigning, whereas the share (not the level!) of their expenditures for organization is reduced to less than two-fifths. The main expenditure items are advertising and survey research. Naßmacher estimated that the campaign-related expenditure of the two major parties (SPD and CDU) increased by approximately 100 million DM in 1994 (compared to 1993). For the smaller parties, the campaign-related increases varied between 17 and 35 million DM. Apart from inflation, technological advances and the 'professionalization' of campaigns are the main causes for the fact that campaign expenditure has increased sharply over time.[32]

The German parties are, on the whole, relatively decentralized. On average, expenditure is almost evenly divided between the three main levels of party organization in the main parties: the national party, the organizations in the federal states (*Länder*) and the local and regional parties. There are, however, differences between the parties. In the Green Party, the local parties have traditionally enjoyed a particularly strong position. With the expansion of the party headquarters in the federal capital, the national level has increased its share of party expenditure in recent years. Similarly, the FDP is characterized by an expansion of the national parties' share of the expenditure, mainly at the expense of the party organizations at federal-state level. In the SPD, the weight of the national party increased as did the share of the local and regional parties – both at the expense of the party organizations at the *Länder* level. Finally, the CDU is the only party in which the share of funds spent by the federal-state organizations increased at the expense of the national and local level.[33]

## Sources of party funding

While the level of spending by political parties has been criticized, the main criticisms usually refer to the sources of party funding in Germany. The six parties represented in the Bundestag declared an aggregate income of almost 685 million DM in 1997. The SPD declared an income of approximately 281, the CDU of 218, the CSU of 56, the FDP of 42, the Green Party of 51 and the PDS of 37 million DM.[34] There are three principal sources of party income in Germany: donations, membership contributions and public subsidies. The (formally) voluntary contributions made by parliamentarians (sometimes referred to as 'party tax'), bank loans, revenues from party assets and income from sales are further important sources which cannot be dealt with here in detail (for some remarks on contributions by parliamentarians see sub-section below on public subsidies).

## Donations

Historically, large donations were the first major source of party funding in nineteenth-century Europe. This is also the case in Germany. Prior to 1871 (and after 1871 in the German states), the suffrage was restricted by property requirements and taxation. The consequent limited politicization of the electorate resulted in relatively low campaign costs. There was no need for the parties to maintain a large permanent organizational network. Campaigns were funded by relatively large but irregular donations from local notables (including the parliamentary candidates themselves), landowners, industrial magnates and bankers who derived benefits from easy access to important channels of communication in the political system. Extra-parliamentary party organizations of such 'cadre parties' remained weak and devoid of central direction.[35] With the expansion of the franchise and the related emergence first of mass and later of catch-all and cartel parties, the relative importance of large donations has declined in Germany.

Although there are important variations between the parties, donations have remained an important source of income for the German parties since 1945. In the calendar year of 1997, for example, the six parties represented in the Bundestag declared a total income of approximately 100 million DM coming from donations.[36] Thus in that year (a fairly typical one) almost one-sixth of the total income declared by these parties (685 million DM) originated from donations. The relative importance of donations varies across parties. The two organizations with a mass membership, SPD and CDU, depend on donations to a lesser extent than the smaller parties, especially those on the (socio-economic) right of the political centre. In 1997, the share of donations as percentages of the parties' declared total incomes was 8.2 per cent for the SPD, 15.5 per cent for the CDU, 15.9 per cent for the PDS, 17.7 per cent for the Green Party, 24.7 per cent for the CSU and 34.3 per cent for the FDP.[37]

The Basic Law does not limit the amount of money anyone can donate to a party, but Article 21, paragraph 1, sentence 4 requires the parties to account publicly for their income. This reporting requirement is to enable interested voters potentially to recognize who is financing the parties.[38] Details of public accountability are regulated by the Political Parties Act 1967, which contains two major provisions concerning the reporting of donations. First, large donors must be named in the published annual financial reports of the parties which have to be audited by chartered accountants. Until 1988, the names and addresses had to be reported of all those donors who contributed more than 20 000 DM per year. In 1989, the threshold was relaxed to limit reporting requirements to donations of more than 40 000 DM. Following the ruling of the Federal Constitutional Court on party finance in April 1992,[39] the threshold had to be reduced to 20 000 DM again. Second, the total income from donations has to be published annually as part of the parties' obligation to report their income by major categories (membership dues, donations and public subsidies).

Criticism has mainly referred to the generosity of and loopholes in the reporting requirements. In particular, the 40 000 DM threshold for naming individual donors between 1988 and 1992 was criticized as being too high, a criticism that the Federal Constitutional Court upheld in its 1992 ruling. Moreover, prior to the 1992 ruling, donations to individual Members of the Bundestag in excess of 10 000 DM had to be reported to the President of the Bundestag, yet the donors' names were not actually made available to the public. The 1992 ruling of the Federal Constitutional Court also put an end to this practice and required individual parliamentarians to report donations in excess of 20 000 DM publicly. It was also criticized that violation of the reporting requirements did not carry sufficiently severe penalties for the parties. Some critics, such as von Arnim, have questioned the effectiveness of the enforcement procedures which have mainly been based on tax incentives rather than punishments. Since 1983, the German party and tax laws have provided an incentive for parties and donors to make large donations public by granting tax benefits to donors (see below) dependent on their publication. Yet, as von Arnim claims, 'large donors appear to be more interested in anonymity than in tax deductions.'[40]

Yet by far the most problematic aspect of party funding, especially during the 1970s and 1980s, has been the issue of *Umwegfinanzierung*, the German expression for 'going around' the law in questions of party finance. Allegations of corruption arose mainly in this context. As a result of increasingly severe financial difficulties during the 1970s, the main parties began to intensify their attempts to attract large-scale donations. One traditional way of creating incentives for business corporations, interest groups and business associations to donate money had been to make donations to political parties tax deductible. For tax purposes donations to political parties have been treated as similar to donations to charitable organizations. During the 1970s, one of the main problems was that the Political Parties Act 1967, as amended in 1969 following the 1968 ruling of the Federal Constitutional Court,[41] limited tax deductions on donations to a maximum of 600 DM for individuals and legal persons. One way of circumventing the limit of 600 DM for individuals and 1200 DM for couples (1800 DM for individuals and 3600 DM for couples from 1980) and avoiding the publication of large donations from publicity-shy corporations was to engage in *Umwegfinanzierung*. Arthur Gunlicks describes one of the most important techniques, which was technically open to the parties until 1983, as follows:

> One [such technique] was to make donations to a professional association or nonpartisan organization concerned with citizenship education. Such groups, unlike the parties, were considered 'charitable' organizations for tax purposes. In contrast to the more restrictive American practice, such associations could make donations to political parties if these represented an insignificant proportion of dues and did not threaten in any way to influence unduly a recipient party. Accordingly, contributions up to 25 per cent of the dues income were allowable. Abuse began to occur when Association A gave 25 per cent of its dues to a party and the other 75 per cent to Association B. This group would give 18.75 per cent (25 per cent of 75) to the party and the remaining 56.25 per cent to Association C, etc.[42]

A further example provided by Gunlicks was the establishment by the CDU of a business consultancy (*Europäische Unternehmensberatungsanstalt*) in Liechtenstein. This firm sold research reports and briefings to companies for which the clients received the necessary receipts for their tax deductions for business expenses. The consultancy 'then contributed money to professional associations which, in turn, returned the money without receipts to the consulting firm.

Then the money was given to local CDU party organizations. . . . The FDP and SPD apparently engaged in similar practices.'[43]

During the 1970s, these practices came increasingly under the scrutiny of state prosecutors. The most spectacular scandal was the so-called Flick affair which broke in the early 1980s. For a number of years the management of Flick, a large holding company owned by Friedrich Karl Flick, gave large amounts of money to a charity operated by Augustine monks at a monastery near Bonn. According to one observer, Flick gave approximately ten million DM in total, of which eight million was returned to the company in cash. 'In the meantime Flick received a deduction for about half of the contribution. In the end, the charity got two million and Flick had about thirteen million, eight of which was untraceable.'[44]

The Flick company used part of the money generally to 'cultivate the political scene' ( that is, it made donations to all major parties and some of their leading representatives). It was also alleged that Flick – mainly via his general representative Eberhard von Brauchitsch – had donated considerable amounts of money to all major established German parties, allegedly in order to be granted a tax exemption for the sale of 1.8 billion DM worth of Daimler-Benz shares. In 1984, state prosecutors filed a law suit against Eberhard von Brauchitsch of the Flick group, Otto Count Lambsdorff, the Minister of Economic Affairs, and his ministerial predecessor, Hans Friderichs. Count Lambsdorff resigned from ministerial office. In 1986, a court decided that von Brauchitsch and another former agent of the Flick group were not guilty of bribery; Count Lambsdorff and Friderichs, who had to decide over the tax exemptions as Ministers of Economic Affairs, were found not guilty of accepting bribes. The court proceedings continued with regard to the question of tax evasion. In 1987, von Brauchitsch, Count Lambsdorff and Friderichs were found guilty of tax evasion and sentenced to fines.[45] Independent of the court proceedings the Bundestag's President, Rainer Barzel, had to resign in 1984 following allegations of his consultancy work for the Flick group.

The Flick affair developed into a more general scandal on party finance. The Bundestag appointed an Inquiry Committee to investigate the issue of Flick's donations to political parties. The Committee established that the Flick group made (1) 'official' payments to a number of fundraising bodies such as the *Staatsbürgerliche Vereinigung 1954*[46] for which it received receipts (according to Otto Schily, a member of the Committee, a total of approximately 18 million DM between 1969 and 1980); (2) 'unofficial' payments in cash to CDU, CSU, FDP and SPD as well as a number of individual politicians (between 1969 and 1980 approximately 8.5 million DM according to the same source), for which no receipts were given by the parties; and (3) payments from a so-called 'black bourse' (approximately 2.2 million DM between 1969 and 1980). Not only were the reporting requirements for large donations not complied with, the 'official' payments were partly channelled through organizations with charitable status in order to obtain tax reductions (see above). In 1983, another major scandal involved the anonymous donation of 6 million DM to the FDP (more than the party's aggregate membership dues in that year), for which the former owner of a department store chain, Helmut Horten, eventually accepted responsibility in 1984.[47] By 1984 there were hundreds of other cases of alleged illegal contributions pending, the majority involving the FDP.[48]

It was clear that the major parties' growing financial needs could no longer be met under the restrictive provisions of the Political Parties Act without resorting to practices such as *Umwegfinanzierung*. As noted above, these practices led to prosecutions and considerable public disaffection. At the initiative of the Bundestag parties, therefore, the Federal President appointed a commission of mostly academic experts in 1982. Its remit was to study the system of party finance in Germany systematically and make recommendations for reforms that would provide the parties with sufficient funding while simultaneously avoiding the problems associated with the practices of *Umwegfinanzierung*. The commission submitted its report in April 1983. In December 1983, the Bundestag amended the Political Parties Act 1967 and the tax laws in the light of the commission's recommendations, although the commission's recommendations were adopted only selectively. The reporting requirements were tightened up. Since 1983, the parties have been required not only to publish their sources of income (as previously), but also their expenditures and assets.

Arguably as a response to the Flick affair, the section on donations was completely rewritten. Parties have since been explicitly allowed to accept donations subject to a number of exclusions such as donations from the party foundations, from charitable and religious organizations, from foreigners exceeding 1000 DM and from any source that indicates expectations of political or economic favouritism. As before, contributors of 20 000 or more are to be listed separately by name and address. The income tax and corporation tax laws were changed to recognize the parties themselves (rather than certain fund-raising bodies) as 'charitable organizations' for tax purposes. This had the effect of making contributions up to 5 per cent of an individual's income and up to 2 millions of the total sum of wages, salaries and sales of a business tax deductible. The amended Act included a complicated formula according to which parties with less ability to attract donations and hence with a lower chance to benefit from tax deductions (that is, indirect public subsidies) are to be compensated by additional funds in order to avoid a violation of the constitutional principle of equality of opportunity. The penalties against parties that receive donations illegally, use funds not in conformity with the law, or do not report individual donations of 20 000 DM or more were increased. A party convicted of such violations must forfeit double the amount from its public subsidies and transfer the funds illegally obtained to the President of the Bundestag.[49]

### Membership contributions

Although all German parties except the Green Party lost members between 1991 and 1995, the two major parties, SPD and CDU, are still organizations with a large mass membership. In 1995, the SPD's membership was more than 817 000, while the CDU had more than 650 000 members. The two major parties, therefore, have considerable revenues from membership dues. In 1997 the SPD received more than 157 million DM in membership dues, the CDU over 100 million, the Green Party more than 21 million, the CSU over 19 million, the PDS nearly 17 million and the FDP almost 11 million DM. Membership dues account for approximately 56 per cent of the SPD's total income. The approximate share for the PDS was 46 per cent, for the CDU 46 per cent, for the Green Party 42 per cent, for the CSU 35 per cent, and 26 per cent for the FDP.[50]

Historically, the mass parties of the late nineteenth and early twentieth centuries were the first ones to rely primarily on a multitude of small subscriptions and donations. With the extension of the franchise in 1871, new forms of political organization and funding became necessary to canvass, mobilize and organize a much larger electorate. Party competition for the newly enfranchised voters intensified, requiring a permanent organization. In 1875, the German Social Democratic Party (SPD) emerged as a new type of party: a mass party with a large membership basis. The party was able to pay its full-time officials, support professional agitators and subsidize the publication and distribution of newspapers from the dues paid by more than 24 000 members (1875). Unlike the leaders of cadre parties, their leaders had no personal wealth to finance their campaign expenses.

> In such circumstances the irregular financial operations of cadre parties were insufficient to pay for the administrative costs of a mass organization and the caucus was eventually replaced with the branch, a permanent organization aimed at collecting funds. While the caucus was narrowly recruited, decentralized and semi-permanent, the branch was more widely based, tightly knit and permanent. The branch was financially reliant upon the subscriptions paid by party members.[51]

This new form of party organization also had implications for intra-party democracy. On the one hand, mass organizations offered an avenue for activists' input into the party by allowing them a say in the internal decision-making process; on the other, they were highly hierarchical and their operations were dominated by paid party workers (Michels).[52]

The mass party approach was emulated by the catholic Centre Party (*Zentrum*) during the Weimar Republic (1919–33). Until 1931, when the membership of the National Socialist Party began to rise dramatically,[53] the *Zentrum* was the only other party in the Weimar Republic able to make the transition to a mass party, thanks to the support of the mass memberships and associations of the catholic lay movement. After 1945, the SPD re-established itself as a mass party. The CDU also had a large membership, but it was not until the early 1970s that its membership rose to levels comparable to the SPD. Between 1969 and 1976 the CDU's membership more than doubled, from over 303 000 to more than 652 000[54] and, following the Political Parties Act 1967, the linkage between parliamentary leaders and extra-parliamentary organization and members was strengthened.

### Public subsidies

When the Parliamentary Council drafted the Basic Law in 1948–9, it was taken for granted that parties would be funded exclusively from membership dues and donations: 'the idea of public political financing did not even occur to anyone.' Yet with technological change and the further metamorphosis of political parties in Germany – especially their development into 'catch-all parties'– membership contributions and donations were no longer sufficient to finance the main parties' needs. Electronic media helped party leaders to reach large audiences more efficiently than previously. Although political parties were entitled to free radio and TV broadcasting, the cost of campaigning in this new and rapidly developing media environment increased dramatically. Political parties were less and less reliant on a fee-paying membership and more dependent on other funding sources such as state funding and interest groups. The gap between the material resources needed for political persuasion and the resources available in terms of voluntary work and institutionalized support widened. 'When the party organization became increasingly independent from membership dues the ties between leaders and rank-and-file loosened. Party survival did not depend on the grass-roots fees. Freed from the straitjacket of the *classe gardée*, the catch-all party enjoyed greater strategic flexibility to design policies aimed at achieving immediate electoral success.'[55]

State funding of political parties presents a fundamental dilemma. On the one hand, inequality of opportunity in the competition between parties can be reduced as their ability to extract resources from members and donors varies and distorts electoral competition. It can also reduce the dependence of parties on powerful economic interests in society and help curb corruption. On the other hand, it may create a problematic dependence on public funds. Not only may such a dependence contribute to a loosening of the links between party elites and rank-and-file (whose contributions become less important for the leadership),[56] but also it is sometimes argued that it may lead to a fundamental problem of accountability: the fact that the parties in parliament award themselves funds may cast doubt on the legitimacy of this process and contribute to a disaffection with parties in general.[57]

The amount of public subsidies to German political parties is difficult to estimate. In 1997, for example, direct public grants to the six parties represented in the Bundestag amounted to more than 225 million DM. The SPD received approximately 90.0 million DM, the CDU 73.2, the CSU 19.4, the Green Party 17.3, the FDP 13.1 and the PDS 12.3 million DM. These amounts constitute approximately one-third of each party's total declared income (from a minimum of 31.6 for the FDP to a maximum of 34.7 per cent for the CSU).[58] Yet, these figures do not include indirect forms of public support such as tax deductions for donors or free radio and television advertising. Nor do they include the grants paid out to the parliamentary parties and the main parties' political foundations. Finally, they do not include the considerable contributions Members of Parliament are paying to their parties. Formally, these contributions are voluntary. In practice, they seem to be virtually compulsory and are considered to be 'problematic' in terms of their constitutionality.[59] They account for a substantial part of the major parties' incomes. Since 1984, the parties have not reported such contributions from parliamentarians at the national, federal-state and local level in their annual financial reports. Naßmacher estimates for the late 1980s that such contributions are likely to have increased the SPD's income from membership contributions by at least one-fifth and accounted for approximately one-tenth of the total income of FDP, CDU and CSU.[60]

Indirect public subsidies in the form of tax deductions for donations started with a tax law in December 1954. Against the votes of the Social Democrats, the Christian Democratic Adenauer government passed legislation according to which up to 10 per cent of an individual's income or 2 millions of a company's total sales, wages and salaries could be deducted from the taxable income for contributions to political parties represented in the Bundestag or in a *Land* parliament. In 1957 and 1958 the Federal Constitutional Court quashed some of these provisions, mainly on the grounds that they violated equality of opportunity (*Chancengleichheit*) between the parties. In its 1957 ruling it established that the requirement that parties must have at least one representative in the national or a *Land* parliament to qualify for indirect subsidies favoured parties that were already represented in parliaments and discriminated against those who were not represented. In 1958 the Court ruled that tax deductions for all political parties were unconstitutional violations of the principle of equality of opportunity or equality of treatment (*Chancengleichheit*) because some parties were more likely to attract large donations from individuals and corporate donors than others were. Indirect public subsidies via tax benefits compounded this bias therefore.[61]

In its ruling, however, the Court stated that it was constitutional to pay direct public subsidies to those political parties which participated in elections, because participation in elections was a public duty.[62] This opened the way for direct public funding. The Bundestag passed a law that authorized the payment of public funds from the federal budget to the political parties represented in the Bundestag. This arrangement was in place until 1966. Between 1959 and 1961 SPD, CDU, CSU and FDP received an annual grant of 5 million DM to support their contribution to 'civic education'. In 1962 a new item was added to the Federal Budget. In addition to the 5 million DM for purposes of civic education the parties were given 15 million DM in general support of their tasks according to Article 21 of the Basic Law. In 1963 the definition of a specific purpose (civic education) was dropped. The government grant was increased to 38 million in 1965. Although there were certain changes in detail, the monies were distributed roughly in proportion to the parties' share of seats in the Bundestag, but only parties in parliament qualified for such grants.[63] Federal-state parliaments soon followed in giving qualifying parties financial support at the sub-national level.

Following a constitutional complaint from several smaller parties and the SPD-controlled state of Hesse, the Federal Constitutional Court ruled in 1966 that funds from the federal budget could not be used to subsidize political parties for purposes other than waging election campaigns. The ruling also effectively compelled the parties in the Bundestag to pass the Political Parties Act stipulated in the Basic Law. Section 4 of the Political Parties Act 1967 granted parties a direct subsidy of DM 2.50 for each eligible voter in Bundestag elections in compensation for election-campaign costs. The funds were to be allocated in proportion to the percentage of votes gained by the parties. Yet, only parties with 2.5 per cent of the vote in a federal state or, under certain circumstances, 10 per cent of the vote in a constituency, were to be eligible for compensation. Payments were to be made over a four-year period, with no more than 10 per cent of the reimbursement to be paid in the second year following the election, 15 per cent in the third year, and 35 per cent during the election year.[64]

In its 1968 ruling the Federal Constitutional Court decided with regard to public funding that the requirement that a party receive 2.5

per cent of the total vote in a federal state in order to qualify for reimbursement of campaign expenditure was excessively high. It suggested a threshold of 0.5 per cent, which was followed by the Bundestag. In 1974 the Bundestag revised the party law to raise the reimbursement per voter to DM 3.50. In 1979, the same reimbursement was authorized for the elections to the European Parliament. Following a decision of the Federal Constitutional Court in 1976, the Bundestag legislated in 1979 to make independent candidates eligible for reimbursement of campaign expenditure if they reached at least 10 per cent of the vote in a constituency.[65]

In 1983, the reimbursement per voter was raised from DM 3.50 to DM 5.00, and it was increased retroactively to DM 4.50 for the 1983 election. However, direct public subsidies were not allowed to be a party's predominant source of income. The sum of the public election campaign reimbursement for any one year was not to exceed the total income from other sources.

In 1988, an overwhelming majority of the Bundestag passed further amendments to the Political Parties Act 1967. The reimbursement for campaign expenditure was to be supplemented by a 'base payment' (*Sockelbetrag*) for all parties with more than 2 per cent of the vote. In its 1992 ruling, the Federal Constitutional Court revised its earlier view and eliminated the previous limitations on the public financing of election campaign costs. However, the Court held to its insistence that no more than 50 per cent of the revenue of the parties may come from public funds. Also, the Court established an absolute maximum aggregate figure. In the future public funds may not exceed a total amount larger than the average for the years 1989–92. The distribution of the funds has to be based on three criteria: the number of voters, the amount of membership contributions and the volume of donations. The details of the law were left to the Bundestag.[66]

In 1994, therefore, the Political Parties Act 1967 had to be amended again. Since 1994, the parties have received DM 1.00 per annum for each voter and DM 0.50 for each DM the respective party received in membership contributions and donations, as long as the donations come from 'natural persons' (a German legal term referring to individuals rather than 'juridical persons' such as associations or corporations) and are not higher than DM 6000 per annum. For its first five million voters, each party receives DM 1.30. Public subsidies are reduced, should they amount to more than 50 per cent of a party's total income ('relative limit') or if it is higher than DM 230 million for all parties together ('absolute limit'). The absolute limit can be revised in proportion to the inflation rate. In order to be eligible for public subsidies, a party must have gained at least 0.5 per cent of the vote at the previous Bundestag or European parliament elections, or 1.0 per cent at a federal-state election.[67] The main difference between the situation between 1966 and 1993 on the one hand, and since 1994 on the other, is the fact that the limitation of public subsidies to compensation payments for election expenses was dropped. Parties are no longer encouraged to 'dress up' their expenditure as election-related.

In addition to these direct public subsidies, party-related foundations have received considerable public subsidies since 1967. The main parties created these foundations partly in response to the Federal Constitutional Court's 1966 decision that parties as such could not be subsidized for purposes of 'civic education'. These foundations are the Friedrich-Ebert-Stiftung (SPD), Konrad-Adenauer-Stiftung (CDU), Hanns-Seidel-Stiftung (CSU), Friedrich-Naumann-Stiftung (FDP) and (since 1989) Stiftungsverband Regenbogen (Green Party). 'These foundations were and are not part of the individual party organizations, and they do enjoy considerable autonomy – both legal and practical – from the parties; nevertheless, their activities have been an undisputed aid to the parties.'[68] They receive an annual block grant from public funds for general purposes of civic education, plus support for specific projects (support of European integration, support of the reforms in Central and Eastern Europe, development projects in the less developed countries, scholarships for students) largely provided by the Ministry of Education and Research as well as the Foreign Office. According to data provided by Gunlicks, the party-related foundations employed more than 3200 staff. At least half of the staff was based in foreign countries. More than 90 per cent of the foundations' income came from public sources.[69] In 1992, the Friedrich-Ebert-Stiftung received 220 million DM in public subsidies; the Konrad-Adenauer-Stiftung received 217.5 million, the Friedrich-Naumann-Stiftung 103.3 million, the Hanns-Seidel-Stiftung 102.8 million, and the Stiftungsverband Regenbogen 25.8 million DM.[70]

A further public subsidy, which was not a part of the public reimbursements for election campaigns and not reported as public funding in the parties' annual reports, is the payment received by all parliamentary parties or party groups (*Fraktionen* and *Gruppen*) at national and federal-state (*Länder*) level. These funds are mainly used for secretarial assistance, office equipment and supplies, and research staff. In the fiscal year of 1998, for example, the parliamentary parties in the Bundestag received a total amount of over 112 million DM on top of the funds received by individual Members of the Bundestag.[71] In 1993 a Commission of Experts appointed by the Federal President criticized the lack of transparency of the finances of parliamentary parties and – given the fact that they decide themselves in the Bundestag about their own subsidies – the absence of a statutory upper limit to public funds paid to parliamentary parties.[72] In response to the criticism, the Members of Parliament Act (*Abgeordnetengesetz*) was amended in 1994 (with effect from 1995). A new section was inserted, tightening up the parliamentary parties' accountability for their use of any public funds they receive (see above).

## Conclusions

The German political discourse knows the term 'established parties'. For much of (West) Germany's history this term covered those parties that have been represented in the Bundestag without interruption since 1949. They had a monopoly of parliamentary representation at the national level between 1961 and 1983. In 1983, this monopoly was broken as the Green Party, whose leaders initially defined themselves as an 'anti-party party' (Petra Kelly), managed to overcome the 5 per cent threshold in Germany's electoral law and have had continuous parliamentary representation since.[73] Since 1983, the Green Party (now called Bündnis '90/Die Grünen) has achieved representation in government coalitions not only in local government and at the federal-state level, but (since October 1998) also at the national level. It has become an 'established party', too. The German 'established parties' resemble, at least to some extent, the ideal type of a 'cartel party' (Katz and Mair) 'in which colluding parties become agents of the state and employ the resources of the state (the party state) to ensure their own collective survival.'[74]

The fundamental problem of political finance in Germany is this: the 'established parties', driven by ever-increasing financial needs, dominate parliament. They do not always agree on every detail of party finance but, fundamentally, share an interest in securing funds for their organizational survival and development. Party competition, which ideally serves as a check on a parliamentary majority, has often been suspended in the area of political finance – that is, the 'established parties' have generally attempted to agree on compromises which were then presented to the chamber and self-serving legislation was passed by a vast majority. Only when the Green Party entered the Bundestag in 1983 did parliamentary debates on issues of party finance become more controversial – and public.

Given the very encompassing parliamentary coalition on questions of party finance, the Federal Constitutional Court's role as an independent institutional check has been crucial. Much of the law dealing with German parties has been prompted by the Federal Constitutional Court. Moreover, the Court intervened on numerous occasions to prevent the 'established parties' from passing self-serving legislation and violating the fundamental principle of equality of opportunity for all parties. This has arguably contributed to the fact that the German party system has not developed strong indications of 'ossification' or 'petrification', despite the considerable public funds distributed to the political parties in general and the 'established parties' in particular. In other words, the 'established parties' in the Bundestag have not managed to use their privileged access to public funds as a device to close the political market completely. Although funds have generally been distributed in proportion to past electoral performance, the threshold for small or new parties was, at the insistence of the Federal Constitutional Court, lowered to an extent that less-established parties have also had access to public funds. The rise of the Green Party and recent electoral successes of the extreme right-wing Republikaner party 'came about not least because of public party financing'.[75]

Allegations of political corruption in the context of party donations have repeatedly surfaced since the early 1980s. Cases such as the Flick affair or the Amigo affair in Bavaria have occupied the newspaper headlines and seem to suggest that high-level corruption has become more widespread. Alternatively, one could argue, perceptions of the 'acceptable' and 'corrupt' have changed as German democracy has matured. This hypothesis is consistent with data provided by Transparency Watch. This organization provides data on perceptions of political corruption based on surveys of businesspersons.

Over the last years, Germany has consistently occupied a middle position amongst the member states of the European Union. The Nordic countries (Denmark, Finland and Sweden) are perceived to be least affected by corrupt public services, the southern European states (Spain, Greece and Italy) are deemed to be most affected. In 1995, for example, Germany occupied rank 7 amongst 14 members of the European Union (Luxembourg was not included). The reputation for corrupt public services is measured on a scale from 0 to 10, where 10 indicates the complete absence of corruption. With a 'lack of corruption value' of 8.14 Germany was much closer to Denmark (9.32), Finland (9.12) or Sweden (8.76) than to Spain (4.35), Greece (4.10) or Italy (2.99).[76]

The issue of political corruption has mainly arisen in the context of large-scale donations to political parties. Yet, how much influence can large donors really 'buy'? Lösche maintains that it depends very much on the respective party's size: 'even very large contributions cannot "buy" one of the two large parties in Germany. Their funding is much too diversified. . . . However, if a small party cannot operate on membership dues and public funding, it will depend on large private contributions (e.g., the Free Democrats in the 1960s, 1970s and early 1980s) and an impact can be observed.'[77]

It is important to stress the significant implications that the system of party funding in Germany has for intra-party democracy. Lösche argues (as do others) that 'party executive committees on the *Land* and federal levels have become independent of the party membership, that is, independent of membership dues and small donations'[78] as campaigns and party organizations are mainly financed from public funds, large donations and loans. As a result, party leaderships on the regional and national levels are 'almost autonomous, rather like independent monarchs not accountable to the membership'.[79] Lösche emphasizes, however, that the model of party presented in Robert Michels's 'iron law of oligarchy' is not an adequate description of the reality of the German party system. Rather, he uses the metaphor of a 'loosely coupled anarchy' of different national and regional organizations that coexist and often compete. Nevertheless, even in Lösche's view the lack of dependence of the party leaderships at national and regional levels on their grass roots compounds problems of intra-party democracy and participation.

## Notes

1 Compare, *inter alia*, Christiane Landfried, *Parteifinanzen und politische Macht: Eine vergleichende Studie zur Bundesrepublik Deutschland, zu Italien und den USA*, Baden-Baden: Nomos, 1990; Karl-Heinz Naßmacher, 'Parteienfinanzierung in Deutschland', in Oscar W. Gabriel, Oskar Niedermayer and Richard Stöss (eds), *Parteiendemokratie in Deutschland*, Opladen: Westdeutscher Verlag, 1997, pp. 157–76; Karl-Heinz Naßmacher, 'Structure and impact of public subsidies to political parties in Europe: the examples of Austria, Italy, Sweden and West Germany', in Herbert E. Alexander (ed.), *Comparative Political Finance in the 1980s*, Cambridge: Cambridge University Press, 1989, pp. 236–67; Andrea Römmele, *Unternehmensspenden in der Parteien- und Wahlkampffinanzierung: Die USA, Kanada, die Bundesrepublik Deutschland und Großbritannien im internationalen Vergleich*, Baden-Baden: Nomos, 1995; Rolf Schwartmann, *Verfassungsfragen der Allgemeinfinanzierung politischer Parteien*, Berlin: Duncker und Humblot, 1996; Göttrik Wewer, *Parteienfinanzierung und politischer Wettbewerb*, Opladen: Westdeutscher Verlag, 1990.
2 Peter Lösche, 'Problems of party and campaign financing in Germany and the United States – some comparative reflections', in Arthur B. Gunlicks (ed.), *Campaign and Party Finance in North America and Western Europe*, Boulder, CO: Westview, 1993, p. 219.
3 Compare Susan Rose-Ackerman, 'Democracy and "grand" corruption,' *International Social Science Journal*, 48, 1996, pp. 365–80.
4 Erhard Blankenburg, Rainer Staudhammer and Heinz Steinert, 'Political Scandals and Corruption Issues in West Germany', in Arnold J. Heidenheimer, Michael Johnston and Victor T. le Vine (eds), *Political Corruption: A Handbook*, New Brunswick: Transaction, 1989, p. 913.
5 Ibid.
6 Max Kaase, 'Political Alianation and Protest' in Mattei Dogan (ed.), *Comparing Pluralist Democracies: Strains on Legitimacy*, Boulder, CO: Westview, 1988, p. 125.
7 The definition of corruption used in this article draws on the principal-agent-client ('PAC') framework. This approach interprets the workings of public agencies as the relationships between a principal, who is charged with carrying out a public function – an agent, who actually performs the operational functions of the agency – and a client, with whom the agent also interacts. Following from this constellation, Rose-Ackermann defines corruption as follows:

While superiors would like agents always to fulfil the superior's objectives, monitoring is costly, and agents will generally have some freedom to put their own interests ahead of their principals'. Here is where money enters. Some third person, who can benefit by the agent's action, seeks to influence the agent's decision by offering him a monetary payment which is not passed on to the principal. The existence of such a payment does not necessarily imply that the principal's goals have been subverted – indeed the payment may even increase the principal's satisfaction with the agent's performance. Both tips to waiters and bribes to low-level officials may often improve service beyond the level attained by employees paid only a regular salary. Thus my focus is not limited to payments that conflict with the principal's goals. Nor is it limited to payments that have been formally declared illegal. Rather it embraces all payments to agents that are not passed on to superiors. Nevertheless, many third-party payments *are* illegal, and it is only these which I shall call 'corrupt'. (Susan Rose-Ackerman, *Corruption: A Study in Political Economy*, New York: Academic Press, 1978, pp. 6–7.

8  Compare *The Economist*, 8 January 2000, p. 39.
9  Compare Karl-Heinz Naßmacher, 'Comparing Party and Campaign Finance in Western Democracies', in Arthur B. Gunlicks (ed.), *Campaign and Party Finance in North America and Western Europe*, Boulder, CO: Westview, 1993, pp. 244–7; Karl-Heinz Naßmacher, 'Structure and impact of public subsidies to political parties in Europe: the examples of Austria, Italy, Sweden and West Germany', in Herbert E. Alexander (ed.), *Comparative Political Finance in the 1980s*, Cambridge: Cambridge University Press, 1989, pp. 259–61.
10  A summary of the findings and recommendations of the 1983 commission is provided by one of its members, Hans-Peter Schneider, in 'The new German system of party funding: the Presidential committee report of 1983 and its realization', in Herbert E. Alexander (ed.), *Comparative Political Finance in the 1980s*, Cambridge: Cambridge University Press, 1989, pp. 220–35; the findings and recommendations of the 1992–4 commission were published as Bundespräsidialamt (ed.), *Empfehlungen der Kommission unabhängiger Sachverständiger zur Parteienfinanzierung*, Baden-Baden: Nomos, 1994.
11  *Entscheidungen des Bundesverfassungsgerichts*, Vol. 20, 19 July 1966, pp. 56 ff.
12  Thomas Poguntke, 'Parties in a Legalistic Culture: The Case of Germany.' in Richard S. Katz and Peter Mair (eds), *How Parties Organize: Change and Adaptation in Party Organizations in Western Democracies*, London: SAGE, 1994, p. 191.
13  See the references in Dimitris Th. Tsatsos, 'Die politischen Parteien in der Grundgesetzordnung', in Oscar W. Gabriel, Oskar Niedermayer and Richard Stöss (eds), *Parteiendemokratie in Deutschland*, Opladen: Westdeutscher Verlag, 1997, pp. 145–6.
14  Naßmacher (1989), *op. cit.*, p. 248.
15  The amendment also includes provisions on the role of parliamentary parties as an employer and their legal status in the courts.
16  It remains to be seen how this distinction can be upheld in political practice.
17  Sven Hölscheidt, 'Keine Kontrolle des "Erforderlichen": Das Finanzgebaren der Bundestagsfraktionen ist gesetzlich geregelt', *Das Parlament* No. 38, 12 September 1997, p. 10; Florian Becker, 'Defizite im Fraktionsgesetz des Bundes: §50 AbgG', *Zeitschrift für Parlamentsfragen*, 27:2, 1996, pp. 189–99.

18   D. Roderick Kiewiet and Mathew D. McCubbins, *The Logic of Delegation: Congressional Parties and the Appropriations Process*, Chicago: University of Chicago Press, 1991, p. 34.

19   Richard S. Katz and Peter Mair, 'Changing Models of Party Organization and Party Democracy: The Emergence of the Cartel Party', *Party Politics*, 1:1, 1995, pp. 19–20.

20   Compare Blankenburg *et al.*, *op. cit.*, pp 924–6. It has to be added that Blankenburg and his co-authors interpret the same facts in a less sanguine way.

21   Compare the critical comments of Hans-Herbert von Arnim, 'Campaign and party finance in Germany', (translated by A. Gunlicks) in Arthur B. Gunlicks (ed.), *Campaign and Party Finance in North America and Western Europe*, Boulder: Westview, 1993, pp. 201–18.

22   Blankenburg *et al.*, *op. cit.*, p. 919.

23   All data were taken from Karl-Heinz Naßmacher, 'Parteienfinanzierung in Deutschland', in Oscar W. Gabriel, Oskar Niedermayer and Richard Stöss (eds), *Parteiendemokratie in Deutschland*, Opladen: Westdeutscher Verlag, 1997, p. 158.

24   Both the figures for the parliamentary party groups and the party foundations were taken from von Arnim, 1993, *op. cit.*, p. 211.

25   Naßmacher (1997), *op. cit.*, p. 158; more generally on the foundations see Michael Pinto-Duschinsky, 'Foreign Political Aid: German Political Foundations and their US Counterparts', *International Affairs*, 67:1, 1991, pp. 33–63; Michael Pinto-Duschinsky, 'International Political Finance: The Konrad Adenauer Foundation and Latin America', in Laurence Whitehead (ed.), *International Dimensions of Democratization*, Oxford: Oxford University Press, 1996, chapter 9.

26   Landfried, *op. cit.*, p. 110.

27   See Poguntke, *op. cit.*, p. 196.

28   Naßmacher (1997), *op. cit.*, p. 158.

29   von Arnim (1993), *op. cit.*, p. 211.

30   Naßmacher (1997), *op. cit.*, pp. 160–1.

31   Naßmacher (1997), *op. cit.*, p. 160.

32   Naßmacher (1997), *op. cit.*, pp. 172–3.

33   Naßmacher (1997), *op. cit.*, p. 174.

34   Deutscher Bundestag, *DIP – Das Informationssystem für Parlamentarische Vorgänge* (*http://www.bundestag.de/datbk/ pf_gesei.htm*, 17 February 1999). The figures exclude 'intra-party money transfers' (presumably the substantial income from the 'party tax').

35   Compare Rosa Mulé, 'Financial uncertainties of party formation and consolidation in Britain, Germany and Italy: the early years in theoretical perspective', in Peter Burnell and Alan Ware (eds), *Funding democratization*, Manchester: Manchester University Press, 1998, pp. 49–53.

36   Deutscher Bundestag, DIP (*http://www.bundestag.de/datbk/pf spend.htm*, 17 February 1999).

37   Calculated from Deutscher Bundestag, DIP (*http://www.bundestag.de/datbk/pf_ gesei.htm and http://www.bundestag.de/datbk/pf_spend.htm*).

38   von Arnim (1993), *op. cit.*, p. 203.

39 *Entscheidungen des Bundesverfassungsgerichts*, Vol. 85, 9 April 1992, pp. 264 ff.

40 von Arnim (1993), *op. cit.*, p. 204.

41 *Entscheidungen des Bundesverfassungsgerichts*, vol. 24, 3 December 1968, pp. 300 ff.

42 Arthur B. Gunlicks, 'Campaign and Party Finance in the German "Party State"', *Review of Politics*, 50:1, 1988, p. 37.

43 Gunlicks, ibid. p. 37.

44 Gunlicks, *op. cit.*, p. 39.

45 Data on the Flick affair were largely taken from Otto Schily, *Politik in bar: Flick und die Verfassung unserer Republik*, München: Beck, 1986, pp. 50–5; for brief discussions of the Flick affair see also Arthur B. Gunlicks, 'Campaign and Party Finance in the German "Party State"', *Review of Politics*, 50:1, 1988, pp. 31–4; Landfried (1990), *op. cit.*, pp. 143 ff.; Göttrik Wewer, *Parteienfinanzierung und politischer Wettbewerb*, Opladen: Westdeutscher Verlag, 1990, pp. 420 and 443 ff.

46 Most large donations have traditionally been given by corporate donors or the interest associations of business and employers. In cooperation with the parties, business and employers, associations have set up special fund-raising organizations and 'civic associations' (*staatsbürgerliche Vereinigungen*) which collect donations from the business community and distribute funds among those parties that seem best suited to safeguard business interests (including the Social Democrats if and when they are in power at the federal or federal-state level). These bodies function as 'financial intermediaries between business and political parties'. See Blankenburg *et al.*, op. cit., p. 917. Compare also Andrea Römmele, *Unternehmensspenden in der Parteien-und Wahlkampffinanzierung: Die USA, Kanada, die Bundesrepublik Deutschland und Großbritannien im internationalen Vergleich*, Baden-Baden: Nomos, 1995, pp. 139–57.

47 Naßmacher (1997), *op. cit.*, p. 166.

48 Gunlicks, *op. cit.*, p. 39.

49 Gunlicks, *op. cit.*, pp. 36–43.

50 Deutscher Bundestag, DIP (*http://www.bundestag.de/pf_gesei.htm* and *http://www.bundestag.de/pf_mitg.htm*, 17 February 1999).

51 Mulé, *op. cit.*, p. 53.

52 Mulé, *op. cit.*, pp. 53–4.

53 Michael Kater, *The Nazi Party: A Social Profile of Members and Leaders, 1919–1945*, Oxford: Blackwell, 1983, Figure 1 (after p. 261).

54 Wulf Schönbohm, *Die CDU wird moderne Volkspartei: Selbstverständnis, Mitglieder, Organisation und Apparat 1950–1980*, Stuttgart: Klett-Cotta, 1985, p. 166.

55 Mulé, *op. cit.*, p. 62.

56 Compare, for example, Lösche (1993), *op. cit.*, pp. 226–7.

57 This argument has been put forward by von Arnim, for example, in his 'Campaign and party finance in Germany', *op. cit.*, pp. 201–18.

58 Deutscher Bundestag, DIP (*http://www.bundestag.de/datbk/pf_staat.htm*, 17 February 1999).

59  Naßmacher (1997), *op. cit.*, p. 168 with further references.
60  Ibid., including footnote 44.
61  Gunlicks, *op. cit.*, p. 32.
62  *Entscheidungen des Bundesverfassungsgerichts*, Vol. 8, 24 June 1958, pp. 51 ff.
63  Peter Schindler, *Datenhandbuch zur Geschichte des Deutschen Bundestages 1949 bis 1982*, 2nd (ed), Bonn: Presse- und Informationszentrum des Deutschen Bundestages, 1983, pp. 90–1.
64  Gunlicks, *op. cit.*, p. 33.
65  Schindler (1983), *op. cit.*, p. 90.
66  For an English summary of the ruling see von Arnim (1993), *op. cit.*, pp. 215–17.
67  Naßmacher (1997), *op. cit.*, p. 170.
68  Gunlicks, *op. cit.*, p. 34.
69  Gunlicks, *op. cit.*, pp. 34–5.
70  Bundespräsidialamt (ed.), *Empfehlungen der Kommission unabhängiger Sae hverständiger zur Parteienfinanzierung*, Baden-Baden: Nomos, 1994, p. 161.
71  *Bundestag Drucksache*, 13/11458 and *Blickpunkt Bundestag*, 4/98, p. 21.
72  *Bundespräsidialamt*, *op. cit.*, pp. 85–6.
73  In the 1990–4 Bundestag, the Greens were only represented in the form of the East German Alliance '90. The two parties merged in 1993.
74  Richard S. Katz and Peter Mair, 'Changing Models of Party Organization and Party Democracy: The Emergence of the Cartel Party.' *Party Politics*, 1.1, 1995, p. 5.
75  Lösche, *op. cit.*, p. 227.
76  Compare Arnold J. Heidenheimer, 'The topography of corruption: explorations in a comparative perspective', *International Social Science Journal*, 48, 1996, p. 338.
77  Peter Lösche, 'Problems of party and campaign financing in Germany and the United States – some comparative reflections', in Arthur B. Gunlicks (ed.), *Campaign and Party Finance in North America and Western Europe*, Boulder: Westview, 1993, pp. 223–3.
78  Ibid., p. 226.
79  Peter Lösche, '"Lose verkoppeite Anarchie." Zur aktuellen Situation der Volksparteien am Beispiel der SPD.' *Aus Politik und Zeitgeschichte*, No. 43, 1993, pp. 34–45, Elmar Wiesendahl, 'Changing Party Organizations in Germany: How to Deal with Uncertainty and Organised Anarchy.', In Stephen Padgett and Thomas Saalfeld (eds) *Bundestagswahl '98: End of an Era?*, London: Frank Cass, 1999, pp. 108–125.

## Bibliography

Alexander, Herbert E. (1989), 'Money and politics: rethinking a conceptual framework', in Herbert E. Alexander (ed.), *Comparative Political Finance in the 1980s*, Cambridge: Cambridge University Press, pp. 9–23.
Alexander, Herbert E. and R. Shiratori (eds) (1994), *Comparative Political Finance Among the Democracies*, Boulder: Westview.

Arnim, Hans Herbert von (1988), *Macht macht erfinderisch. Der Diätenfall: ein politisches Lehrstück*, Zürich: Interfrom.

Arnim, Hans Herbert von (1993), 'Campaign and party finance in Germany' (translated by A. Gunlicks), in Arthur B. Gunlicks (ed.), *Campaign and Party Finance in North America and Western Europe*, Boulder: Westview, pp. 201–18.

Arnim, Hans Herbert von (1995), *'Der Staat sind wir!' Politische Klasse ohne Kontrolle? Das neue Diätengesetz*, München: Droemer Knaur.

Arnim, Hans Herbert von (1997), 'Misleading the German Public: The New Bundestag Law on Parliamentarians', *German Politics*, 6:2, pp. 58–75.

Blankenburg, Erhard, Rainer Staudhammer and Heinz Steinert (1989), 'Political Scandals and Corruption Issues in West Germany', in Arnold J. Heidenheimer, Michael Johnston and Victor T. le Vine (eds), *Political Corruption: A Handbook*, New Brunswick: Transaction, pp. 913–32.

Bundespräsidialamt (ed.) (1994), *Empfehlungen der Kommission unabhängiger Sachverständiger zur Parteienfinanzierung*, Baden-Baden: Nomos.

Burnell, Peter (1998), 'Introduction: money and politics in emerging democracies', in Peter Burnell and Alan Ware (eds), *Funding democratization*, Manchester: Manchester University Press, pp. 1–21.

Geis, Norbert (1997), 'Korruption in Staat und Wirtschaft', in Heinz Reichmann, Winfried Schlaffke and Werner Then (eds), *Korruption in Staat und Wirtschaft*, Köln: Deutscher Instituts-Verlag, pp. 47–60.

Gunlicks, Arthur B. (1988), 'Campaign and Party Finance in the German "Party State"', *Review of Politics* 50:1, pp. 30–48.

Hafner, Georg M. and Edmund Jacoby (eds) (1994a), *Die Neuen Skandale der Republik*, Reinbek bei Hamburg: Rowohlt.

Hafner, Georg M. and Edmund Jacoby (eds) (1994b), *Die Skandale der Republik, 1949–1989: Von der Gründung der Bundesrepublik bis zum Fall der Mauer*, Reinbek bei Hamburg: Rowohlt.

Heidenheimer, Arnold J. (1963), 'Comparative Party Finance – Notes on Practices and Towards a Theory', *Journal of Politics*, 25:4, pp. 790–811.

Heidenheimer, Arnold J. (1996), 'The topography of corruption: explorations in a comparative perspective', *International Social Science Journal*, 48, pp. 337–47.

Homann, Karl (1997), 'Korruptionsbekämpfung – Begründung und Ansatzpunkte', in Heinz Reichmann, Winfried Schlaffke and Werner Then (eds), *Korruption in Staat und Wirtschaft*, Köln: Deutscher Instituts-Verlag, pp. 32–46.

Johnston, Michael (1996), 'The search for definitions: the vitality of politics and the issue of corruption', *International Social Science Journal*, 48, pp. 321–35.

Kaase, Max (1988), 'Political Alianation and Protest', in Mattei Dogan (ed.), *Comparing Pluralist Democracies: Strains on Legitimacy*, Boulder: Westview.

Käsler, Dirk, Hans Peter Albers *et al.* (1991), *Der politische Skandal: Zur symbolischen und dramaturgischen Qualität von Politik* , Opladen: Westdeutscher Verlag.

Katz, Richard S. and Peter Mair (1995), 'Changing Models of Party Organization and Party Democracy: The Emergence of the Cartel Party', *Party Politics*, 1:1, pp. 5–28.

King, Anthony (1976), 'Modes of Executive-Legislative Relations: Great Britain, France, and West Germany', *Legislative Studies Quarterly*, 1:1, pp. 11–36.

Koch, Peter-Ferdinand (1992), *Das Schalck-Imperium: Deutschland wird gekauft*, München: Piper.

Kulitz, Peter (1983), *Unternehmerspenden an die politischen Parteien*, Berlin: Duncker & Humblot.

Landfried, Christiane (1994), *Parteifinanzen und politische Macht: Eine vergleichende Studie zur Bundesrepublik Deutschland, zu Italien und den USA*, second edition, Baden-Baden: Nomos.

Lösche, Peter (1984), *Wovon leben die Parteien? – Über das Geld in der Politik*, Frankfurt: Fischer Taschenbuch Verlag.

Lösche, Peter (1993), 'Problems of party and campaign financing in Germany and the United States – some comparative reflections', in Arthur B. Gunlicks (ed.), *Campaign and Party Finance in North America and Western Europe*, Boulder: Westview, pp. 219–30.

Mair, Peter (1994), 'Party Organizations: From Civil Society to the State', in Richard S. Katz and Peter Mair (eds), *How Parties Organize: Change and Adaptation in Party Organizations in Western Democracies*, London: Sage, pp. 1–22.

Mair, Peter (1997), *Party System Change: Approaches and Interpretations*, Oxford: Clarendon Press.

Meny, Yves (1996), 'Politics, corruption and democracy. The 1995 Stein Rokkan lecture', *European Journal of Political Research*, 30:2 pp. 111–23.

Mintzel, Alf and Heinrich Oberreuter (eds) (1992), *Parteien in der Bundesrepublik Deutschland*, second edition, Bonn: Bundeszentrale für politische Bildung.

Mulé Rosa (1998), 'Financial uncertainties of party formation and consolidation in Britain, Germany and Italy: the early years in theoretical perspective', in Peter Burnell and Alan Ware (eds), *Funding democratization*, Manchester: Manchester University Press, pp. 47–72.

Naßmacher, Karl-Heinz (1982), Öffentliche Rechenschaft und Parteienfinanzierung', *Aus Politik und Zeitgeschichte*, B14–15.

Naßmacher, Karl-Heinz (1989), 'Structure and impact of public subsidies to political parties in Europe: the examples of Austria, Italy, Sweden and West Germany', in Herbert E. Alexander (ed.), *Comparative Political Finance in the 1980s*, Cambridge: Cambridge University Press, pp. 236–67.

Naßmacher, Karl-Heinz (1993), 'Comparing Party and Campaign Finance in Western Democracies', in Arthur B. Gunlicks (ed.), *Campaign and Party Finance in North America and Western Europe*, Boulder: Westview, pp. 233–66.

Naßmacher, Karl-Heinz (1997), 'Parteienfinanzierung in Deutschland', in Oscar W. Gabriel, Oskar Niedermayer and Richard Stöss (eds), *Parteiendemokratie in Deutschland*, Opladen: Westdeutscher Verlag, pp. 157–76.

Pinto-Duschinsky, Michael (1991), 'Foreign Political Aid: German Political Foundations and their US Counterparts', *International Affairs*, 67:1, pp. 33–63.

Pinto-Duschinsky, Michael (1996), 'International Political Finance: The Konrad Adenauer Foundation and Latin America', in Laurence Whitehead (ed.), *International Dimensions of Democratization*, Oxford: Oxford University Press, chapter 9.

Poguntke, Thomas (1994), 'Parties in a Legalistic Culture: The Case of Germany', in Richard S. Katz and Peter Mair (eds), *How Parties Organize: Change and Adaptation in Party Organizations in Western Democracies*, London: Sage, pp. 185–215.

Reichmann, Heinz (1997), 'Korruption – Einführung in die Problematik', in Heinz Reichmann, Winfried Schlaffke and Werner Then (eds), *Korruption in Staat und Wirtschaft*, Köln: Deutscher Instituts-Verlag, pp. 8–11.

Römmele, Andrea (1995), *Unternehmensspenden in der Parteien- und Wahlkampffinanzierung: Die USA, Kanada, die Bundesrepublik Deutschland und Großbritannien im internationalen Vergleich*, Baden-Baden: Nomos.

Rose-Ackerman, Susan (1996), 'Democracy and "grand corruption"', *International Social Science Journal*, 48, pp. 365–80.

Scheuch, Erwin K. (1997), 'Korruption in einer freiheitlichen Gesellschaft', in Heinz Reichmann, Winfried Schlaffke and Werner Then (eds), *Korruption in Staat und Wirtschaft*, Köln: Deutscher Instituts-Verlag, pp. 12–31.

Scheuch Erwin K. and Ute Scheuch (1992), *Cliquen, Klüngel und Karrieren: Über den Verfall der politischen Parteien – eine Studie*, Reinbek: Rowohlt.

Schily, Otto (1986), *Politik in bar: Flick und die Verfassung unserer Republik*, München: Beck.

Schindler, Peter (1994), *Datenhandbuch zur Geschichte des Deutschen Bundestages 1983 bis 1991*, Baden-Baden: Nomos.

Schneider, Hans-Peter (1989), 'The new German system of party funding: the Presidential committee report of 1983 and its realization', in Herbert E. Alexander (ed.), *Comparative Political Finance in the 1980s*, Cambridge: Cambridge University Press, pp. 220–35.

Schwartmann, Rolf (1996), *Verfassungsfragen der Allgemeinfinanzierung politischer Parteien*, Berlin: Duncker und Humblot.

Tsatsos, Dimitris Th. (1997), 'Die politischen Parteien in der Grundgesetzordnung', in Oscar W. Gabriel, Oskar Niedermayer and Richard Stöss (eds), *Parteiendemokratie in Deutschland*, Opladen: Westdeutscher Verlag, pp. 133–56.

Wagner, Joachim (1986), *Tatort Finanzministerium: Die staatlichen Helfer beim Spendenbetrug*, Reinbek bei Hamburg: Rowohlt, Spiegel Buch, Vol. 70.

*Werkzeuge des SED-Regimes: Der Bereich Kommerzielle Koordinierung und Alexander Schalck-Golodkowski* (1994), Bericht des 1. Untersuchungsausschusses des 12. Deutschen Bundestages, Bonn: Deutscher Bundestag.

Wewer, Göttrik (1990), *Parteienfinanzierung und politischer Wettbewerb*, Opladen: Westdeutscher Verlag.

# 6
# Russia: from a Corrupt System to a System with Corruption?

*Richard Sakwa*

Russia is moving from metacorruption, that is a system which is corrupt in its very essence, to 'normal' corruption; from a corrupt system to a system with corruption. The communist system was metacorrupt in that it never subordinated itself to the rule of law (although of course it ruled by and through the law), because of its lack of accountability, and because of the systematic enjoyment of privileges granted its leadership from the common ownership of the means of production.[1] A new form of metacorruption, however, has emerged, rooted in the transition from a state-owned economy to a market-based system. The enormity of the attempt to disentangle the political process from its deep embedment in the economy, while at the same time structuring political life as an autonomous activity governed by the impartial rule of law and accountable to the electorate, can hardly be exaggerated. The extrication of the Russian state from, on the one hand, deep involvement in the economy and, on the other, from its dominance by a single party that governed for some seventy years in an arbitrary and voluntarist manner, represents an act of political reconstitution unprecedented in its scope and complexity. What has emerged, though, is a dual system where new forms of systemic metacorruption coexist with what we shall call venal corruption, the pursuit of individual gain out of the pursuit or attainment of public office.

## The historical context

Although communist systems presented themselves as dedicated to the popular good and fought a constant struggle against political degeneration, by the end almost all had succumbed to a social degeneration. Political processes were subverted by the emergence of social patronage systems, venal corruption on a grand scale, and the etiolation of the whole socialist labour process. Fraud and deception became integral to the system's survival. The Stalinist system itself destroyed public values and ensured that the only bonds of trust were highly personalized and informal. The Gulag system itself, formally established in 1929 although founded by Lenin, was based on an alliance of criminal and state power to control the millions of 'politicals' flowing through the labour camp archipelago. Communist rule was characterized by arbitrariness, 'telephone law' [the practice of party officials determining judicial outcomes informally], and the subordination of constitutional principle to political expediency.

The last days of the Soviet Union were inextricably linked with the battle against corruption.[2] How one part of the system tried to root out systemic corruption is one of the more fascinating stories of the final period of actually existing socialism. The campaign became part of the succession struggle to Leonid Brezhnev and then with attempts by the reformers around Mikhail Gorbachev to consolidate their rule. Eduard Shevardnadze epitomizes both the communist and the postcommunist ends of the cycle. Appointed party leader in Georgia in 1972 specifically to combat the widespread corruption, he returned to Georgia in 1992, after having helped destroy the Soviet 'empire' in Eastern Europe and elsewhere, only to rule in alliance with deeply corrupt paramilitary forces until his election as president in 1995 allowed him once again to launch another anti-corruption campaign.[3] Shevardnadze's career, indeed, was made by his anti-corruption crusade. Having brought down Otari Lolashvili, the extravagantly flamboyant First Secretary of the Tbilisi party organization, he was appointed Minister of the Interior in 1965:

> As interior minister, Shevardnadze arrested more than 25 000 people, including 17 000 members of the Communist Party, numerous government ministers, and 70 KGB officials. He was responsible for the torture and execution of many innocent people, including dissidents. This campaign and the purges he initiated as first secretary earned him the undying enmity of many Georgians. They also won him greater notice in Moscow.[4]

His campaign against the notoriously corrupt Vasilii Mzhavanadze, the First Secretary of the Georgian Communist Party, allowed him to take this post in 1972 until called to Moscow as Foreign Minister by Gorbachev in July 1985.

Yurii Andropov, head of the KGB from 1967 to 1982, was uniquely placed to understand the depth and scale of corruption gnawing away at the very basis of Soviet society. It appears he sponsored Shevardnadze's appointment as republican party leader, and on his election as General Secretary following Brezhnev's death in November 1982 he launched a vigorous anti-corruption and discipline campaign that in many respects drew on Shevardnadze's experience in Georgia. It appears that he was 'enchanted by the effectiveness and inventiveness displayed in the Georgian version of the police state'.[5] Andropov sought to use police methods to combat corruption and as Party leader launched a programme of authoritarian reform designed to counter the social degeneration of the regime. His untimely death in February 1984 allowed his successor, the *apparatchik* Konstantin Chernenko, temporararily to halt the assault against corrupt practices. The campaign, however, was renewed by Gorbachev on his accession in March 1985, although it was soon drowned out by other pressing concerns.

Initially, the idea of authoritarian reform was once again pursued by Gorbachev. According to Yegor Ligachev, an advocate of moderate reform of the Andropov type and thus an ally of Gorbachev until he became alarmed by the increasingly radical turn that perestroika took after 1987:

> The real drama of perestroika was that the process of self-cleansing of our society begun in the depths of the Communist Party, not only slowed down, but was, I would say, distorted. In place of the old corrupt elements that for decades had been festering in the body of the Communist Party and the society at large, suddenly, in the space of a year or two, came even more horrible and more absolutely corrupt forces that stifled the healthy start made in the Party and the country after April 1985.[6]

The legalization of limited forms of capitalism from 1987, epitomized above all by the emergence of co-operatives, allowed the criminal structures deeply embedded in Soviet life to take advantage of the new opportunities. As the only agencies with capital and organizational resources, Gorbachev's half-hearted economic reforms could not have been better designed to ensure the criminalization of the nascent market economy. Buying goods cheaply at state prices and selling them with a large mark-up in the burgeoning market sector largely defined the type of rent-seeking entrepreneurialism that would become prevalent in Russia. The lifting of most restrictions on foreign trade in 1990, combined with the liberalization of the banking sector, allowed huge fortunes to be made in the export of Soviet natural resources and encouraged the establishment of financial-trading empires that survive to this day as one of the enduring legacies of perestroika.

It was Boris Yeltsin who as leader of the Moscow party organization from late 1985 until 1987 took up the campaign with Shevardnadzeite zeal. In one year he charged some 800 people with corruption, often using anonymous denunciations.[7] According to the Ministry of Internal Affairs (MVD) at least three-quarters were found to be unsubstantiated and the practice of informing was abolished in February 1988. The anti-corruption theme was one of Yeltsin's most potent weapons in his struggle for power, but once secure in office as the first popularly elected president of Russia his own regime succumbed to new forms of venality and corruption.

The social bases and political nature of Soviet and postcommunist metacorruption differed radically, yet similar mechanisms were at work. In the Soviet system the lack of distinction between a public and a private sphere in economic life was a matter of principle, and the emergence of what Milovan Djilas called the 'New Class' allowed a privileged ruling elite to enjoy the fruits of socialized property. Communist Party rule was sustained by its colonization of the state, including its use of state resources to fund its political predominance. Towards the end this took increasingly criminal forms. As Galeotti puts it, 'The 1970s saw a further blossoming of organised crime within and alongside the CPSU, and corruption, embezzlement and black-marketeering became endemic.'[8] The details remain unclear, but there is little doubt that the CPSU's funds were augmented by transfers from the state treasury.[9] The CPSU earned considerable profits from its newspapers and membership dues, but this was probably not enough to cover the costs of its central apparatus and regional organizations. In particular, there is much evidence that in the final period the Central Committee of the CPSU was preparing for the fall of its political power by converting its resources into liquid assets, some of which were banked abroad.[10]

While grandiose in scale and pervasive in essence, postcommunist political corruption can be distinguished from Soviet metacorruption in that the new system seeks to differentiate the political level from the social and the economic. The task of state reconstitution in post-communist Russia has been arduous and incomplete, but the basic outlines of a democratic constitutional state have emerged, however flawed. The duality of postcommunist corruption is derived from the transitional process, above all in the deeply corrupt privatization process, but may become a systemic feature of the new order. Such an outcome is challenged by the other side of the duality, the norm-ative recognition that certain practices are corrupt and the emer-gence of a state and administration founded on principles of law, accountability and impartiality. It was this second side of the dual-ity, the politics of anti-corruption, that was weakly legitimated and difficult to ground in an autonomous political practice (distinct from personal power struggles) in the Soviet era. This is not to suggest that the successful establishment of a democratic polity is inevitable but to argue that, theoretically, Soviet metacorruption was systemic whereas in postcommunist Russia it is incidental and can be chal-lenged at the level of politics and society.

## Contemporary (meta) corruption and political finance

The legacy of the late Soviet period hangs like a dark shadow over the postcommunist era.[11] Not only the CPSU but the criminal under-world prepared for the new era.[12] According to Stephen Handelman, 'A post-Soviet mafiya incorporating the most obdurate elements of the former system – from the old *nomenklatura* and KGB bureaucracy – and the frontier capitalism of the new, eclipsed all other political forces in Russia. And it went on to penetrate the loose coalition of reformers which had accomplished Russia's second revolution.'[13] At a congress in Tbilisi in 1982 the 'thieves in law' (*vory v zakone*, the fraternity of thieves whose strict code of criminal ethics forbade col-laboration with the authorities – as opposed to the 'renegades', *suki*) allegedly 'discussed the question of taking political control in the country in the future. Already by that time the authorities in many regions had effectively become mafia-like structures'.[14] According to the MVD, in June 1997 there were some 9000 organized criminal groups with some 100 000 members,[15] controlling banks, money exchanges and systematically subverting the state administration and new entrepreneurial activity. At least a quarter of Russia's businesspeople were linked to the criminal world.[16] According to Boris Fedorov, 'Corruption has permeated our entire society. . . . Corruption, that is a demand for remuneration, is encountered at every step.'[17] Whereas in Eastern Europe a civic counter-culture had developed in the framework of the decaying communist system, in Russia the main counter-culture appeared to be a criminal one.

The 'democratic' reformers themselves were soon overwhelmed by this culture. Moscow mayor Gavriil Popov resigned in June 1992, facing serious corruption allegations. In the event, it was only his deputy, Sergei Stankevich, who was pursued concerning an alleged $10 000 bribe for his services in organizing a concert in Red Square in 1992. The former mayor of St Petersburg, Anatolii Sobchak, also faced questions concerning his financial dealings. Instances of post-communist venality abound. The former Vologda governor Nikolai Podgornov in January 1998 was accused by the Prosecutor General of taking bribes, stealing state property and distributing credits from the oblast budget for his personal benefit, and he was removed from office by Yeltsin in March 1998. The former governor of Tula, Nikolai Sevryugin, also faced corruption charges, accused of taking a $100 000 bribe.[18] The most detailed exposure of the pervasive criminalization of the state concerned the case of the mayor of Leninsk-Kuznetsk (Kemerovo oblast), Gennadii Konyakhin, a rich local businessman with criminal connections arrested on embezzlement charges in October 1997. Despite having spent a year in gaol for fraud, he won the election in April of that year with the slogan that he was so rich that he didn't have to steal, although that did not stop him later siphoning off public funds and merging his state office with his private business concerns, including – possibly – contract murders of rivals.[19] It was this incident that appears to have prompted Yeltsin's radio talk of 26 September 1997 in which he stated that crime and corruption were 'Russia's most serious problem', warning that criminals were concentrating on gaining access to public office so as to get 'closer to federal and municipal coffers'. He revealed that over 2500 representatives of the authorities were suspected of corruption and were being investigated.[20]

No clear line can be drawn between venality and metacorruption. The whole privatization programme, for example, masterminded by Anatolii Chubais, was a huge exercise in transferring public goods into private assets. All sides of the Russian political spectrum, however, charge that privatization favoured a small group of 'oligarchs', immiserated large sections of society and enriched Chubais' friends in the elite. From a structural perspective, however, privatization was considered a necessary component in establishing a market economy. Chubais, moreover, perhaps unconsciously following Barrington Moore's well-known dictum 'no bourgeois, no democracy', insisted that the creation of a new middle class would create the social basis for democracy. Privatization, however, hardly changed the behaviour of many of the new 'owners', and they continued to form alliances with state bureaucrats to gain resources and to shield them from hostile alliances of competing interests.

The 'loans-for-shares' scandal of November 1995 took the process one step further when the state itself favoured certain 'insider' interests in the privatization process in return for funds that would ensure that the machinery of government could continue to turn. Insider banks were granted shares in the country's top companies as collateral for loans to a desperate government, but it was understood by all sides that the government would default on the loans and the oligarchs would get the companies for a song. In this way Vladimir Potanin's Oneksimbank 'purchased' the giant Norilsk Nickel works (the world's largest), the Sidanko oil company, and the Northwest River Shipping Company, while the Menatep Bank got hold of Yukos, Russia's second largest oil company. The growing budget deficit was exacerbated by various tax exemptions granted to bodies like the Russian Orthodox Church for the import of alcohol and cigarettes, and above all to the National Sports Fund (NFS) established by presidential decree on 1 June 1992. Having been granted generous export quotas on a range of valuable raw materials, out of the billions of roubles that passed through its hands only a tiny proportion contributed to the development of sport, and not a single audit was conducted on the fund throughout its existence until its privileges were revoked in 1995.[21] In the absence of a state able to enforce rules and to adjudicate between interests, organized crime stepped in to enforce contracts, regulate economic struggles and protect property rights. Metacorruption, in other words, worked from the top down and from the bottom up, squeezing honest business and endeavour almost entirely out of existence. The chaotic, arbitrary and punitive tax system, moreover, not only undermined the revenue-raising powers of the state but also drove small entrepreneurs as well as larger enterprises into the technically illegal activities of the black, grey and other-coloured sections of the economy. While the proportion of economic activity conducted outside the law tended to decrease after some three years in most postcommunist societies, the inability of the state to deal with organized crime and official corruption prevented a similar pattern occurring in Russia (as well as Bulgaria and Ukraine).

The criminalization of Russian politics is a theme of much alarmist writing, and the role of organized crime and the *mafiya* is obviously crucial in examining political corruption. A recent volume edited by Phil Williams argues that the development of the market and democracy in Russia had become fatefully entwined with organized crime. Criminal networks had entered the banking system, were in control of many companies, and distorted the evolution of market relations by extortion and protection rackets, thus forcing costly security operations.[22] Gangs were involved not only in typically gangsterish behaviour but also penetrated the 'legal' open economy; indeed, in postcommunist Russian conditions it was very difficult to tell where the black economy (estimated to be roughly the same size as the official economy) ended and various shades of the grey economy began. In a report delivered to the Academy of Social Sciences in July 1997, Anatolii Kulikov, then Minister for Internal Affairs and also a Deputy Prime Minister, argued that 'Organised crime is dictating to individual Russian industries how to behave on the market and controls whole areas of the country.' According to Kulikov, 'underworld godfathers are setting up closed syndicates and having them infiltrate the state's economic institutions.'[23]

The funding of political parties and electoral campaigns is at the sharp edge of political corruption. The best-known example where venality intersected with metacorruption was the 1996 presidential campaign. There is no doubt that the Yeltsin team (from March 1996 led by the ubiquitous Chubais) spent several dozen (if not thousands) times more money than the law allowed (each candidate could spend 14.5 billion old roubles, or $3.2 million). In February 1996 Russia's leading moguls, inspired by Boris Berezovskii, met at the Davos Forum in Switzerland and created a war chest to bankroll Yeltsin's re-election. The gulf between what the Yeltsin campaign actually spent on the campaign, whose upper estimates reach over $500 million,[24] and the modest sum that he declared is impressive.[25] There was no serious attempt to implement election and campaign laws – except against his opponents. Not only did Yeltsin clearly exceed the legal maximum financial outlay on the campaign itself, but he debased the whole process by promising generous social programmes. In his 24 campaign trips he lavished generous 'gifts' on schools, enterprises and whole regions (formalized in bilateral treaties between the federal authorities and the region in question, many of which to this day have not been published). While Yeltsin promised an enormous amount, it is unlikely that many voters believed that he would be able to deliver on his promises of the rapid payment of wage arrears, higher salaries, public works and improved social benefits. He knew, and the voters probably knew too, that there were simply not enough resources.[26] In the event, by a single decree in August 1996 Yeltsin consigned some seventy separate promises of 'pork' to oblivion.[27] Yeltsin's victory, however, was due to far more than electoral bribery: a recognition of the positive benefits his re-election would bring; and fear of what a victory for the communists would entail. Yet the shameless and extravagent promises, and their equally brutal repudiation, indicates a profound corruption of the political process that exceeds even the illegal over-spending on the campaign.

The symbol of the campaign was not the ballot box but a cardboard box containing $538 000 in campaign cash that two of Chubais' aides were caught carrying out of the White House on 19 June, just three days after the first round of voting.[28] One of the two caught with the box was Sergei Lisovskii, one of the masterminds behind the campaign and head of the 'Premier SV' advertising agency, one of Russia's largest advertising companies. There have been allegations that he was somehow involved in the murder in 1995 of Vladislav List'ev, a television journalist and executive at ORT (Russia's main TV channel) who had temporarily frozen all advertising contracts, including that with Premier SV. Lisovskii stood (unsuccessfully) in the by-election on 27 September 1998 for a seat in the Duma in a constituency in Nizhnii Novgorod region, a region that had already become notorious on 29 March of that year for electing a criminal mayor of its capital. Andrei Kliment'ev won the mayoral election despite having two petty criminal convictions in the 1980s and at the time of his election was awaiting the result of an appeal on charges of embezzling $3 million from a $30 million federal government loan. The result was subsequently annulled by the local electoral commission, provoking outrage among voters and removing immunity from further prosecution. The Russian Supreme Court's decision on 10 August to extend his prison sentence to six years suggested a political and judicial conspiracy to keep him out of the running in the new elections – convicted criminals serving sentences are barred from office. For Stankevich – someone who was in a position to know – the episode was symbolic of the late Yeltsin era, above all revealing the 'pathological dependence of the whole Russian judicial system, including judges, on the whims of the political authorities'. For him Kliment'ev's election in the first place was 'a symbolic form of the contemporary Russian uprising (*bunt*)', revealing the alienation felt by the humiliated masses and having nothing to do with municipal administration.[29]

A year after the presidential elections the charges of corruption focused on Chubais' own personal enrichment, with *Izvestiya* alleging that in February 1996, a month after he first left office, the Stolichnyi Savings Bank granted a five-year interest-free $2.9 million loan to his new Centre to Defend Private Property. The funds were allegedly used for his personal speculation in the treasury bills (GKO) market, allowing him to reap lucrative profits which he then pocketed.[30] In a letter to the paper Chubais did not dispute the facts but claimed (quite logically within the framework of what we call metacorruption) that what he had done was 'absolutely normal' in any democratic country.[31] His action was perhaps not strictly speaking illegal, but using funds donated for charitable purposes for personal speculation is irregular, to say the least. The whole story of Western 'aid' to Russia is similarly beset by a mixture of venality and systemic metacorruption.[32] There is a similar confusion over the legal status of the use of authors' 'advances' in the case of a number of officials in 1997. The story was linked to the intra-elite struggles over the Svyazinvest sale in July 1997, and led to the exposure of a $100 000 advance payment from Servina, a Swiss financial group with links to Potanin's Oneksimbank (the winner of the auction), to Alfred Kokh, head of the state property committee (GKI) responsible for the disbursement of state property; as a consequence Kokh was sacked in August 1997.[33] A similar case was exposed in November 1997 when five high officials, including Chubais, were together found to have received a \$450 000 advance. Maksim Boiko, Kokh's successor at GKI, was forced to resign, but Chubais once again weathered the storm. Criminal charges were not filed against the officials on the grounds that there was no evidence that they had embezzled money from the state, although presumably Oneksimbank, in making the excessive payments, expected to receive something in return for its 'investment'.

At the heart of the metacorruption view of the Yeltsin regime is the notion of a 'party of power' closely entwined with financial–commercial interests. The concept of the 'party of power' is misleading in that it implies a coherence and unanimity among ruling groups that in actuality was never there, but the notion does at least indicate the prevalence of informal relations behind the allegedly democratic facade of elections and constitutional government.[34] Although the 1996 presidential election encouraged a temporary coalescence in the face of the perceived communist threat, later events demonstrated just how fragmented it was. The 'Our Home is Russia' (NDR) party, headed by Viktor Chernomyrdin, the former head of the huge utilities company Gazprom and Prime Minister from December 1992 until March 1998, suffered numerous splits, while economic elites engaged in bitter internecine warfare in which each side sought to mobilize the media and sections of the administration. The Svyazinvest auction revealed a complex pattern of alliances, with Potanin's Oneksimbank ranged alongside Chubais and First Deputy Prime Minister Boris Nemtsov (formerly governor of Nizhnii Novgorod oblast) against Boris Berezovsky of Logovaz and Vladimir Gusinsky of Mostbank. Gazprom is one of the most politically experienced companies in Russia, with its former head, Chernomyrdin, retaining close links with the company even as he served as Prime Minister. It is alleged that in the 1996 presidential elections Gazprom invested \$450 million in Yeltsin's re-election campaign.[35] It was plans drawn up by Nemtsov to challenge the privileges of the oligarchs, and in particular of natural resource monopolies like Gazprom, that by some accounts provoked the dismissal of Sergei Kirienko's government on 23 August 1998 and the attempt to restore Chernomyrdin as Prime Minister, thus gratuitously adding a political crisis to an already severe economic one.

Postcommunist Russian party financing must be seen in the context of a country that has moved from a one-party system to a no-party system. Although there are a myriad small groups, only four were formally represented in the Sixth Duma elected in December 1995, and only one of these (the communists) had a mass base whose membership dues could support party activity. We have already suggested the way that the NDR was entwined with business interests as an element of the 'party of power'. The NDR above all was a party of regional interests and, lacking a mass party membership, relied on funds gained through political office. The funding of Vladimir Zhirinovskii's Liberal Democratic Party of Russia (LDPR) must remain a matter of conjecture, although its links with at least some semi-criminal business networks is well-known, together with the marketing of its own brand of vodka. In her last interview before her murder Galina Starovoitova revealed that the LDPR received funds from Iraq, North Korea and Libya.[36] According to one report, the LDPR had assets of $80–100 million.[37] The Yabloko party, headed by Grigorii Yavlinskii, relied on more orthodox methods of party financing: membership dues, voluntary donations and state contributions, although he did not lack supporters in the United States who presumably provided some financial support. Most politicians did not enquire too closely into the source of funds donated by private sponsors. It has even been argued that the fundamental reason why Russia's democrats were unable to unite was that 'they all have different and competing sponsors'.[38]

For the Communist Party of the Russian Federation (CPRF), the fourth and largest party in the Sixth Duma and the main successor organization to the CPSU, there was no 'Moscow gold' even in Moscow. Having failed to regain some of the CPSU's assets sequestered after August 1991, the CPRF supplemented its income derived from membership dues by fostering contacts in the world of business. Surprising patterns sometimes emerged. According to Jeremy Lester, the CPRF 'has fairly good financial resources at its disposal thanks to a number of close links with lucrative business organizations and business people such as the "Mosbusiness Bank" and Vladimir Semago – a casino owner. And, in general, it has good connections with a whole range of powerful social and economic elites.'[39] Parts of the regional bureaucracy affiliated themselves with the CPRF but were careful not to alienate the government, the source of much of their funds. The

CPRF itself from 1996 changed from a party struggling for power to one hoping to share the spoils of power in a system that was not so much a polis but a spolis!

The above discussion clearly reveals the limited role played by mass membership in party financing. The majority of the CPRF's half million members, for example, are from low-income categories or pensioners, and thus the percentage due to the party is small. The NDR has no serious individual membership at all, relying instead on regional governors, while Yabloko endures endless discussions about how best to launch itself as a mass membership political party. For those parties and groups fortunate enough to find themselves represented in parliament, the Duma itself became the great incubator of party development. Each deputy is allowed up to five full-time assistants at the expense of the state. The murder of at least a dozen of these accredited assistants suggests a link between the mafia and the political elite.[40] Some deputies employed family members as assistants, but the CPRF exploited the privilege to the full. Typically each communist deputy would have two assistants based in the Duma while the rest would be out in the regions, often running local communist organizations, all at the expense of the state. The Duma building, moreover, is where the parties were based (although formally they were registered elsewhere) and conducted most of their affairs. It costs the taxpayer some $20 000 a month for every deputy in salaries and perks, including a chauffeur-driven car and much else. While formally barred from running a business or receiving a second salary, many registered their activities in the name of a family member. As Vyacheslav Nikonov put it, 'For many the Duma is the perfect place to do business. A seat opens many doors and it provides a good life.'[41] Semago, chair of the Duma's commission on fighting corruption, declared that lobbying 'in its dirtiest forms' existed there.[42] According to Konstantin Borovoi all Duma deputies took bribes, and indeed all major bills were decided by paying deputies off.[43] In these circumstances it is not surprising that they sought to avoid the risk of new elections, where they stood to lose not only their seats but also an extensive network of privileges, including apartments in Moscow, free telephones and faxes, and access to the exclusive Duma supply network which included food, clothes, furniture and much else besides. Not surprisingly, the parliamentary aspect of party development tended to be privileged over the hard work of developing party organization in the localities.

The role of private research and educational foundations in sustaining party life and in shaping the terms of public debate has been significant; indeed, in some cases they have acted as substitutes for more narrowly defined political parties. On his forced retirement in December 1991 Gorbachev established the Gorbachev Foundation to pursue research work, and it became the base for several attempts to create a functioning social democratic party, efforts that have so far borne little fruit. On the patriotic–communist wing, Aleksei Podberezkin was one of the most effective and financially successful political operators. He established his RAU-Corporation in June 1990 as a closed joint-stock company to conduct scientic research and educational work. The use of CPSU funds and far more generous bank support for his activities, despite his disclaimers, is probably the only way to explain how in 1990–1 RAU was able to maintain on generous salaries 2500 staff, mostly former employees of the Defense Ministry, the KGB, the Central Committee apparatus, the Foreign Ministry, and the Komsomol Central Committee.[44] Podberezkin helped the CPRF to establish itself organizationally in 1994, and he remained an important intermediary between the CPRF and the bankers. The 'Spiritual Heritage' movement was created based on RAU, with its constituent congress being held in May 1995, and by 1997 the movement allegedly had over 10 000 members. Podberezkin entered parliament in December 1995 on the CPRF slate, and he was a member of the communist faction in the Sixth Duma although not formally a member of the party. He was above all a close adviser to Zyuganov, having supported the latter after the 1991 coup and providing intellectual support for his nationalist rhetoric. The source of the RAU-Corporation's lavish funds has always been a mystery, with much talk of CPSU money, links with the new banks and Western investments. Podberezkin himself denied ever gaining Party or state money or money from abroad, but admitted private funds from patriotic 'new Russians'. The top ten banks had all helped him, usually for specific projects.

One traditional source of support for left parties has remained unexploited, namely financial donations from the trade unions. In the 1995 elections the legatee of the old Soviet-style trade union umbrella organization, the Federation of Independent Trade Unions

(FNPR), ultimately stood as an electoral organization itself. Earlier it had given limited support to various attempts to create a Social Democratic Party, but none had borne fruit. Unlike South Korea, it is not illegal for trade unions to engage in organized political activity, but the FNPR leadership under Mikhail Shmakov was careful not to become identified too closely with any one tendency. In particular, the FNPR resolutely sought to distance itself from the communist successor parties, no doubt fearing (correctly) reprisals by the presidential administration if it allied itself too closely with the political opposition to the regime.

Although there is no direct state funding of political parties, there are subsidies for electoral associations contesting parliamentary elections, a factor which encouraged the proliferation of small groups standing for election. The main form of support is guaranteed free airtime on television, amounting to half an hour each in the December 1995 elections. Support for party development also comes from a variety of indirect measures, above all reduced rents for the several dozen associations and parties that are based in what had formerly been the headquarters of the Komsomol organization. The Russian Social Political Centre (ROPTs) housed there was established in 1991 by presidential decree to foster the development of civil society, in particular by supporting political parties and socio-political organizations. Since 1995 its work has diversified, including a regional programme and research work.

Parties outside parliament devised a variety of orthodox and unorthodox ways of raising funds. The extreme right-wing organization Russian National Unity (RNE) led by Alexander Barkashov appeared well-endowed with funds. Barkashov hinted at the source: 'We help some people resolve their problems, within the framework of the law, of course. They pay for the service. Purely business.' The party, in other words, had gone into the debt collection business and 'contract enforcement'. Barkashov offered another example: 'Say someone threatens a businessman, and we settle that situation. The grateful businessman finds a way to express his gratitude.'[45]

Vladimir Gel'man titles his discussion of the issue 'the iceberg of Russian political finance',[46] and the image is an accurate one – far more is taking place under the water than is visible on the surface. A discussion of political corruption, moreover, deals by definition with something hidden from sight. It is the role of the scandal to throw the spotlight on to some hidden corner, but the very absence of major political corruption scandals in postcommunist Russia (so far they have tended to be confined to the regions, as with the case in Leninsk-Kuznetsk) is itself indicative of a system that has not yet matured enough, where the line between acceptable and unacceptable behaviour is not clear enough, and where the media and the judiciary is not yet brave enough, to allow the country the enjoyment of a fully-fledged scandal with judicial follow-up. The closest Russia has come to it is the incident with the half million dollars in June 1996, but even here the case was mired in intra-elite power struggles, and no judicial case followed. The case was scandalous, but not a scandal. The parallels with postwar Japan and Italy are notable, where effective one-party rule institutionalized factional politics for decades, and only when the Cold War stasis began to break up did scandals emerge that prompted a realignment of the systems.[47] As in Italy, the internal fragmentation of Russia's alleged 'party of power' inhibited the development of coherent policies and encouraged the fusion of public and private roles.

## The political economy of political corruption

Any discussion of political corruption in Russia must examine its roots in the political economy of the transition. Yves Mény has defined corruption as 'a clandestine exchange between two markets – the political and/or administrative market and the economic and social market.'[48] This definition is at the core of John Girling's recent analysis of the issue:

> Corruption is the illegitimate reminder of the values of the market place (everything can be bought and sold) that in the age of capitalism increasingly, even legitimately, permeate formerly autonomous political and social spheres.[49]

For Girling corruption was more than a 'criminal' problem but a social one, derived in part from the incommensurability of the economic and political spheres that in practice eroded the distinction between public and private matters. Seen in this light, the spread of capitalism to Russia could not but subvert the realization of the proclaimed democratic ideals together with good governance in its entirety.

We have noted above the close relationship, and in many cases the indistinguishability, between economic and political elites. A professional political class has yet to emerge in Russia, one which could adapt to the norms most developed countries expect from their rulers. The whole postcommunist regime, moreover, can be dubbed one of redistribution, in which state assets were privatized with minimal legal controls and with no public oversight. In these circumstances it is not only not surprising that political corruption thrived, but that its very definition is difficult to pin down. What if Chubais was right and that it did not matter how state property was disbursed as long as it was done quickly and created a substantial class (however narrow its composition) with a vital stake in the preservation of the postcommunist order? In those circumstances corruption, ranging from the venal to the political, could be considered a progressive phenomenon. The common good could, it is argued, be achieved by metacorrupt means, something that is tautologically incoherent but is typical of the paradoxes of postcommunism. Mayor Yurii Luzhkov's style of managing affairs in Moscow, where the city government took its cut of all deals and reinvested the proceeds in the city itself (like mayor Richard Daley in Chicago in an earlier epoch), suggested that metacorruption might be the price of efficiency.

Even more venal forms of corruption, moreover, can be considered functional. While the emergence of Yeltsinite metacorruption has been defended, by Chubais and his allies, as systemically progressive, allowing the rudiments of a capitalist system to be transferred to Russia and a middle class to emerge, a similar argument has been advanced by economists concerning venal corruption. Do its costs always out weigh its benefits? Might it not encourage economic growth by subverting a stifling bureaucracy and allowing the accumulation of capital?[50] This may be the case in individual cases, but the evidence suggests that corruption deters foreign investment, and in Russia encouraged capital flight totalling at least $100 billion between 1991 and 1998, dwarfing the $6 billion in foreign direct investment and the various painful International Monetary Fund (IMF) loans. If allowed to proliferate corruption ultimately undermines government itself as bureaucrats become more concerned with private profit than public duties. This has certainly been the case in Russia, where the very existence of the state was threatened by corruption, both meta and venal. For Leslie Holmes, indeed, corruption represented a distinctive type of crisis of the state.[51] The British consultancy Control Risks Group ranked Russia the most corrupt country in the world,[52] while in Transparency International's Corruption Perception Index for 1997 Russia came in 49th place,[53] not a healthy position for a country aspiring to great power status.

The 'political economy' approach to corruption is already well-established.[54] It stresses that political actors will act rationally to advance their (typically material) interests, usually at the expense of the public interest.[55] The approach focuses on the behaviour of agents, which in a situation where property rights were fluid and negative rights unenforced allowed enormous scope for rent-seeking and corruption. Up to August 1998 Russia had some 1800 banks, but the 20 largest banks alone controlled 57.8 per cent of the total assets in the banking system.[56] Until 1998 the very management of state assets had been 'privatized', with some 50 authorized banks dealing with transfers from the state budget at the central and local levels, allowing unimaginable profits to be made at the state's expense – and above all at the expense of those whose wages were delayed as the banks speculated with funds designated for social purposes. Some ten so-called 'court' banks were at the heart of this system of financial manipulation. A system of tax benefits granted to so-called charitable foundations siphoned billions of roubles away from the state budget, as with NFS. In short, the Yeltsin regime allowed the state budget itself to become the object of private speculative manipulation, contributing to the bankruptcy of the state in mid-1998 and the effective default on foreign loans and the moratorium on servicing the domestic debt.

It is clear that the monopolies and financial groups exerted a disproportionate and direct influence on politics. Bureaucratic, political and economic corruption became entwined as the semi-feudal court politics around Yeltsin allowed a financial–industrial oligarchy to replace formal politics by a system of informal deals. The 'corridors of power' were no longer to be found in government ministries but in the softly-carpeted executive suites of the new oligarchs. The very notion of 'lobbying' became pathetically inadequate to describe the way that whole areas of the state were colonized by external interests. We have noted allegations that Duma deputies were routinely bribed – in the words of one paper, 'everything can be bought and sold.'[57] The focus of political corruption, however, was the presidency – in a presidential system lobbying will inevitability focus more narrowly on the presidential apparatus than in the more complex multi-layered game typical of parliamentary systems. In Russia the relationship between special interest groups and the presidency was exceptionally close. The presidency was not only the source of 'reform' but was also at the apex of the metacorruption with which it was accompanied.

The key issue increasingly became not the open contest between political parties but the struggles between the financial–industrial groups (FIGS). To succeed in the battle to gain the spoils of privatization the FIGS and other conglomerates needed their own lobbyists within the political system and the ability to whip up media campaigns against their opponents. The major television and newspapers are owned in whole or in part by the economic moguls, like Vladimir Potanin, Boris Berezovsky and Vladimir Gusinsky, while the remaining electronic media is certainly dominated by the executive authorities, precluding investigative reporting on their activities. The classic case of this was the struggle to control Svyazinvest in summer 1997. The political process became less and less focused on the traditional instruments of politics like parliament, parties and the presidency, and was reduced to the law of the jungle of primitive economic empire-building. In an attempt to restore the presidency to its customary role under Yeltsin as balance-holder, in September 1997 he called in six of the top barons and ordered a ceasefire, but to little effect.

## Political corruption and political outcomes

Neal Ascherson has noted the emergence of 'post-Communist one-party police states, where semi-free economies nourish seething corruption'.[58] Russia is neither a one-party nor a police state, but the latter part of the statement certainly holds true. Yergin and Gustafson point out that 'Money and property are emerging as independent political resources in their own right' . . . they are the "currency" with which all other resources, including political position, are bought.'[59] They go on to argue that 'Regular mass to voting would lead quickly to the development of mass political parties, which would change the political landscape dramatically.'[60] This, however, has not yet come to pass and the political landscape in party terms remains remarkably featureless. The mountain of the CPRF remains to the left, accompanied by various other leftist foothills, while to the right the volcano that was once the LDPR looks increasingly extinct. In the centre the frenetic activity of party formation resembles nothing more than a series of molehills in an increasingly pockmarked field.

Yergin and Gustafson were right, however, in arguing that 'The importance of votes is bound to keep growing. In today's Russia no politician can expect to build or win power without using votes as a resource – unless he is willing to take the authoritarian path.'[61] Votes are a central resource commodity in a liberal democratic system, but the rules surrounding the degree to which they can be 'bought' or 'sold' are a matter of convention that evolves with the changing technologies of electoral campaigns and shifts in a society's normative perception of what is acceptable behaviour.

Mounting an election campaign becomes increasingly expensive in an age of television advertisements and billboard campaigns. The main expense in Russian electoral campaigns is indeed television advertising, allowing a political party to get its message to a large number of voters directly. All studies have demonstrated, however, that there is little correlation between the money spent on television advertising and electoral outcome. In the 1995 Duma elections by far the biggest spender in this respect was Chernomyrdin's NDR, pouring some $2 million into the campaign and winning 10.13 per cent of the party list vote. The Bloc of Ivan Rybkin, set up apparently on Yeltsin's initative in an artificial attempt to establish a classic two-party system (in this case as the leftist counterweight to the conservative NDR), spent just under half ($900 000) that of its rival, yet won only 1.1 per cent of the vote. Yegor Gaidar's Democratic Choice of Russia (DVR) spent $600 000 on television advertising yet came out with only 3.9 per cent, a performance that was worse than the four main non-liberal parties, even though their combined expenditure was less than half that of the DVR. Above all, the election's clear winner, the CPRF, devoted almost no resources to television advertising (coming 26th out of 43 in this respect), and spent a total of only some quarter of a million dollars (1.2 billion roubles) on the entire campaign, yet won 22.3 per cent of the party list vote. Thus the CPRF spent only some 80 old roubles (about one-and-a-half cents) for every vote, while for all other significant parties the figure was markedly higher. Thus there was little correlation between the amount of television advertising and electoral outcome.[62] This is a finding that holds equally true for the December 1993 Duma elections, when it cost nearly 50 million old roubles to elect one deputy from Russia's Choice but only some 2 million for an LDPR deputy.[63]

In the light of this it is clear that in Russia, as elsewhere, money alone is not a sufficient resource to influence the results of electoral competition. Money, official position and an ability to influence media coverage certainly help but – as many governors found to their cost in regional elections – by no means guarantee victory, and indeed can be counter-productive. Against heavy odds Alexander Lebed won the 17 May 1998 gubernatorial election in Krasnoyarsk krai against the incumbent, Valerii Zubov.[64] With typical bluntness he was open about the financing of his campaign. When asked by a heckler where his funds came from, he stated:

> From people who work and earn money, and who – like you – tend to be on the fiddle. I won't name them. Isn't that clear enough? I repeat: it is so-called 'gray' money – money honestly earned, but on which you pay no tax because the tax system in this country is crazy. It is a sin that everyone in this country is guilty of. Everyone.[65]

Following his election it was claimed that money started flowing in to prepare for his presidential campaign, but nevertheless his ratings began to slip. Money alone would not buy him the presidency. In the by-election for a Duma seat in the Altai Republic on 31 May 1998 Andrei Vavilov, with close links to Gazprom, failed to win against Mikhail Lapshin, head of the Agrarian Party of Russia, despite having spent far more and enjoying the support of the republican authorities. Despite its financial resources, it is likely that the LDPR will suffer a significant electoral decline in the Duma elections due in 1999. The CPRF in both 1993 and 1995 relied on low-tech and increasingly obsolete campaigning methods, using leaflets, public meetings and door-step exchanges. Able to draw on a large pool of campaign workers, often pensioners with time on their hands, the approach was effective. It was notable, however, that the CPRF did not seek to build up its working-class membership (the *class gardée* of traditional socialist parties), confirming once again arguments of Kirchheimer and Panebianco on the decline of the 'mass party' model.[66]

The premium in Russian politics became 'professionalism' and a technocratic ethos of efficient managerialism, but the absence of the mediating role of parties meant that individuals were forced to seek support and financing directly. The personalization of postcommunist Russian politics stemmed in part from the failure of a stable multi-party system to emerge. Russia, like Japan in the first postwar election in 1946 when 260 parties fielded candidates, suffered from over-partification, in the sense of numerous groupuscules, most of whom withered at the first frost-like touch of a genuine electoral contest. A model of party development that stresses leadership involvement largely in terms of personal advantage, and where the party as an institution becomes little more than an instrument of the leader's advancement to be jettisoned when it no longer serves that purpose, is required. By entering a party in the proportional elections the leader was entitled to free access to the media and campaign funding that could be of advantage in the single-member races where they could simultaneously stand. Attempts by rich business people to fund their own entrance into politics either through a party or individually, however, has not been a success. Borovoi's Party of Economic Freedom in 1993 sank without trace, as did Irina Khakamada's small business party in 1995. In the presidential elections Vladimir Bryntsalov, the proprietor of Russia's largest pharmaceuticals company, did even worse than Gorbachev to come last, despite frequent television advertisements showing him and his comely wife as a model 'new Russian' family. In this context it might be noted that the psychology of television political advertisements is often dreadfully misjudged, appealing to a middle class that does not yet exist (as in Gaider's counter-productive campaign in 1993), and ignoring the real concerns of millions of people eking out their existence on minuscule wages or pensions, which themselves are often delayed.

Despite the veneer of democracy Russian politics remained focused on elite intrigues involving the leaders of corporate groups affiliated to the state and various government organizations, with only a residual role for the representatives of public associations, including political parties. While the idea of the 'cartel party', largely detached from civil society and focused on the state for financial and organizational support, has some resonance in the Russian context,[67] the more important feature is the marginalization of formal political representation in its entirety. The distinction between public and private roles was almost entirely erased, most spectacularly in the case of the extraordinary career of Berezovskii. The head of one of the most dubious business organizations, Logovaz, that held the concession for the distribution of Lada cars, and exploiting many other business interests, he entered government in 1997 as deputy secretary of the Security Council, and in 1998 became Secretary General of the Commonwealth of Independent States. He was one of the main 'oligarchs' funding Yeltsin's re-election in 1996, and was a key player trying to ensure a smooth succession to Yeltsin in the run-up to the 2000 elections. Potanin was also central to President Yeltsin's re-election in 1996, and his reward was a spell as a government minister while continuing to head his powerful Oneksimbank financial–industrial empire.

One of the effective tools in Yeltsin's armoury was his ability, quite simply, to buy-off the opposition. The under-development of a dense network of public organizations meant that politics was overwhelmingly focused on the state, above all the struggle to gain access to it, favours from it, or to work in it. In his struggle to ensure Kirienko's confirmation as Prime Minister in April 1998, Yeltsin openly sought to bribe Duma deputies, offering rewards to those who 'show a constructive approach'.[68] Time and again Yeltsin masterfully divided his opponents by offering them jobs in the government, a tactic that finally seems to have exhausted itself with Lebed's refusal of the offer in August 1998 to become a Deputy Prime Minister in what Yeltsin hoped would be Chernomyrdin's new cabinet. One of the advantages of incumbency is the array of patronage posts to be allocated, but by the end it was clear that even the value of this commodity was declining and Chernomyrdin failed in his bid to return as Prime Minister. Nevertheless, patronage systems and extended patron–client relations remain central to the operation of Russian politics, reinforcing traditional networks of *blat* (fixing and influence peddling). Clientelistic networks are challenged by the nascent principles of meritocracy, and indeed by open electoral competition, but there remains a long way to go.

The lure of office in postcommunist Russia may well have involved a degree of personal fulfilment, but perhaps equally important were the enormous personal 'fringe benefits' derived from office-holding. The Stalinist system of extravagent rewards for top state and administrative officials remained largely intact. The weakness of market mechanisms gave officials enormous powers, while the old 'special' distributive system rewarded them irrespective of the quality of their work. Indeed, the premium was on loyalty to the system rather than merit, and while many honest people entered government service after 1991, most in intangible ways were corrupted. Officialdom once again faced the main enemy – the great mass of the people.[69] A stark example was the Central Bank that spent 15 billion new roubles on wages, administration and operational expenses, a sum that was 1.5 times greater than federal expenses on the presidential administration, the government, the Duma, the Federation Council, and some other state organizations taken together; calculated differently, the sum exceeded by 1.5 times the total amount spent on the health service.[70] The extravagant emoluments paid to the Central Bank chairman, Sergei Dubinin, and some of his staff was confirmed in an investigation by the Audit Chamber, an independent government agency mandated by Article 101.5 of the Russian Constitution to monitor federal expenditures and appointed jointly by the two houses of the Federal Assembly, after his sacking in the wake of the 17 August 1998 financial collapse. The Audit Chamber discovered that the Bank under Dubinin had been engaged in profiteering from its transactions with precious metals, whose profits went not into government coffers but into the personal remuneration of Bank officials.[71] The Central Bank was also investigated about the whereabouts of the $4.8 billion first instalment of an IMF loan granted in late July 1998.[72]

There is an important regional and republican dimension to political corruption, to which we can only allude. The presidents of some of the ethno-federal republics, and indeed the governors of some regions, have emerged with virtually the powers of medieval princes, channeling finances through 'court' banks with little or no accountability to the federal authorities or local legislatures. In Kalmykia this 'postcommunism feudalism' was taken to the limit, with the president, Kirsan Ilyumzhinov, in June 1998 announcing the dissolution of the government as an institution and concentrating executive powers in his person. Fulfilling due procedures, he revealed that in 1997 he had earned 5.8 million new roubles ($1 million), stressing that he had paid taxes on the full amount but did not reveal the sources of such a huge income.[73] President Aslan Maskhadov stands accused of having been bankrolled in the 1997 elections by the Chechen-controlled Ivanovo crime syndicate, and he retains close links with a leading Moscow gang leader.[74] Even criminals can be patriots! There is a different story to tell about political financing in every Russian region and republic, and indeed in every city and local administration, with endless variations on the theme of corruption, both venal and systemic. The weakness of local legislatures and the concentration of power in executives has allowed many local leaders to emerge with the powers of medieval potentates, confirming the emergence of a distinctive type of postcommunist feudalism in Russia.

Although the fall of communism allowed much of the media to escape from state ownership, the difficult economic situation has meant that few remained genuinely independent: most survived by becoming dependent on state subsidies or sponsorship from other organizations (often banking–industrial conglomerates) to survive. A case in point is *Nezavisimaya gazeta* (*The Independent*), whose very name proclaims its independence, yet following a financial crisis in August 1996 it was taken under the wings of one of the most predatory of Russia's postcommunist tycoons, Berezovskii. The under-developed condition of the advertising industry and its concentration in just a few hands means that this form of support is limited. Only *Moskovskie novosti* (*Moscow News*) was able to maintain its independence by a mix of income from sponsorship and advertising. While some moguls bought up existing media outlets, others established new ones, while bodies like Gazprom set up its own voice in the form of Gazprom-Media. The aim of the latter, according to Sergei Karaganov (a member of its board), was to 'build up Gazprom's political muscles in accordance with its economic might' and to provide it with 'the proper means for influencing politics'.[75] With the presidential ambitions of its former head, Chernomyrdin, destroyed by his failure to return as Prime Minister in September 1998, in the run-up to the presidential elections scheduled for 9 July 2000 Gazprom shifted its support to the new Prime Minister, Yevgenii Primakov. Berezovskii, as usual, was frank about the role of big business in those elections, noting in early 1998 that Russia's businessmen were already preparing for the next parliamentary and presidential elections and hoped to avoid the panic of 1996 when financial and industrial groups only agreed to back Yeltsin five months before the election.[76] It remained unclear whether these interests could agree on a common candidate.

Given the enormous concentration of wealth in Moscow, with the capital's budget making up 40 per cent of the federal budget and with 75 per cent of the country's financial capital located in the city, whoever controlled Moscow could influence events in the country. In the run-up to the first post-Yeltsin presidential election Luzhkov built up an impressive war-chest. Even before openly declaring his candidature he created an agitprop empire formally managed by a holding company called Metropolis, spanning the print and electronic media. He controlled Centre Television and the newspapers *Rossiya* and *Literaturnaya gazeta*, the latter one of the most respected cultural fora in the country. By late 1998 he had succeeded in taking over the *Moskovskaya pravda* printworks, that printed not only Moscow's most popular daily newspaper *Moskovskii komsomolets* but a range of other titles (40 journals and 128 newspapers) as well. In subtle but effective ways Luzhkov ensured favourable coverage in his media empire, and was not averse to ensuring a rent rise or some other unpleasantness (including frequent threats to sue) for concerns that criticized him. Luzhkov's press officials, as *The Moscow Times* noted, 'openly divide media into two camps: those friendly to the mayor and those hostile to him'.[77] Clearly, a Luzhkov presidency would challenge, if not threaten, freedom of speech, although it is not clear how the media empires of the other oligarchs would react to his leadership. From a period of anarchic profusion in the very late Soviet period, the bulk of the Russian media is now owned by five financial or industrial groups. As Anne Nivat puts it, 'The problem is not the lack of plurality but of independence.'[78]

In discussing issues of freedom and fairness in the Russian context, it is important not to try to impose absolute standards in a political process that by definition will be a tough competitive struggle for power. It might be argued that elections are seldom absolutely free and fair in the sense that all competitors enjoy equal access to resources. The media bias and financial imbalance in British elections are notorious (at least, until recently). What is crucial is that the judicial and regulatory terrain remain impartial for all competitors, and here the Russian case is deeply flawed. The detailed results of the December 1993 Duma elections have never been published, and much of the evidence has been destroyed, while controversy rages over the real turnout figures in the plebiscite held at the same time over the new constitution. In the 1995 elections attempts to bar two opposition parties (Yabloko and Derzhava) from participation by the Central Electoral Commission (CEC) were reversed by the Supreme

Court, even though technically both had infringed electoral regulations. Above all, the advantages of incumbency have been exaggerated to a point that threatens the very legitimacy of the electoral process. The notorious examples are the 1996 presidential campaign and in the Moscow mayoral elections held at the same time, when Luzhkov won a second term with 90 per cent of the vote, and numerous provincial and republican elections, notably in Tatarstan. But the electoral system has, despite all the advantages enjoyed by the incumbents, showed that it has bite. In the gubernatorial elections held from Autumn 1996 some two dozen incumbents were voted out of office; most left with ill grace, but they left.

## Attempts at reform

In keeping with our dual model, anti-corruption drives and attempts at political reform are enlisted in political struggles but they are not totally cosmetic. Attempts at reform can be listed as follows.

### The legal definition of corruption

In contrast to Russia's old Criminal Code, adopted in 1960, that made no mention of corruption, the new Code adopted by the Duma on 24 May 1996, that came into force on 1 January 1997, at least recognizes the problem.[79] Article 291.1 criminalizes the payment of bribes either directly or indirectly to an official whether in a state or private office, while 291.2 outlawed payments to an official to undertake wittingly illegal actions (or inaction). Article 292 defines 'administrative forgery' as an official inserting into official documents known falsehoods or distorting their contents out of mercenary or personal interest. Punishments ranged from a stiff fine to imprisonment. The very definition of the crime represented an important step in combating it, but few prosecutions have yet been brought against officials. In 1995, 3504 charges were brought against corrupt civil servants, the great majority accused of bribery, while according to MVD statistics 700 cases had been found between 1995 and 1998 linking bureaucrats to organized crime, although few prosecutions resulted.[80] A new law on government service came into effect on 1 January 1998 which defined the rights and obligations of civil servants and marked a small step towards overcoming the functional corruption that had defined the Russian state bureaucracy since at least the time of Peter the Great.[81] At the same time, although it is illegal for public servants to work in business, this is only irregularly policed. The enforcement of existing laws would mark a significant step towards combating corruption.

### Anti-corruption campaigns and income declarations

The Yeltsin presidency launched a number of anti-corruption campaigns, but they tended to be a substitute for the kind of changes that would have genuinely tackled the problem.[82] Their primary purpose was symbolic and political. As Valerii Streletskii, the head of the anti-corruption section of the Presidential Security Service in 1995–7, put it: 'We existed on two planes. On the one hand we carried out the war against corruption. On the other, we proceeded out of political interests.'[83] By 1998 Yeltsin had vetoed three Duma anti-corruption laws that might have threatened the interests of his newly enriched allies. A presidential decree of 4 April 1992 was the first official anti-corruption measure, focusing on petty crime in the civil service, and was followed by numerous equally ineffective campaigns. In his annual address to the Federal Assembly on 6 March 1997 Yeltsin acknowledged that corruption had undermined all levels of public service, noting that 'the criminal world has openly challenged the state and launched into open competition with it.'[84] The new anti-corruption campaign encompassed a number of measures, including a decree (drafted by Nemtsov) of 20 May 1997 that forced all government officials, members of parliament, public officials and political appointees to declare their incomes and assets (above all property holdings) in writing on special forms, and one of the sanctions for the first time against officials was the confiscation of personal property. From 1 January 1999 all government officials whose lifestyle exceeded their official incomes had to declare the source of their excess wealth. The actual declarations by leading officials at times verged on the farcical. Chernomyrdin, whose personal wealth in foreign bank accounts was reputed to be in the region of $5 billion, filed earnings of 1.4 million new roubles ($233 000) for 1997, a figure 31 times higher than what he had declared the previous year.[85] Yeltsin himself declared his 1997 income at 1.95 million new roubles ($320 000), derived mainly from his salary, royalties from his memoirs published in 1994, and interest on Russian bank accounts.[86]

As elsewhere, anti-corruption drives are used to punish opponents and to strengthen those politicians who can claim to have 'clean hands'. No campaign is complete without a few sacrificial lambs. The victims in this case were once again Stankevich, who had already been arrested in April 1997 in Warsaw on an international arrest warrant in connection with the ill-fated Red Square concert, and General Konstantin Kobets, the hero of August 1991 but who in May 1997 was charged with abuse of office, bribery and the illegal possession of firearms. Both had long ago left the top rank of government, and thus their prosecution did not taint the existing authorities. A notable element in any anti-corruption campaign was the use of *kompromat* (evidence of malfeasance) in power struggles among the elite to blacken (compromise) one's opponents. The battle of *kompromat* was waged from the highest to the lowest levels, and not only in Russia.[87] It was a typical response of challengers to incumbent governors and deputies to regional assemblies. It was particularly evident in the Nizhnii Novgorod mayoral elections in early 1998, and in the elections to the Krasnodar krai legislative elections in November 1998.

### Public supervision and transparency

From the above it is clear that effective anti-corruption campaigns have to be distanced from executive authorities. In keeping with the dual nature of Russian politics, there were moves in this direction. A General Control Inspectorate was established in 1992 to combat corruption, and its first head from March 1992, Yurii Boldyrev, proceeded to do so with gusto, exposing malfeasance in the Moscow mayor's office, GKI and, most notoriously, in the Western Army Group in the former East Germany. For his pains, Boldyrev was forced to resign as Comptroller General in March 1993.[88] Yeltsin had intended the anti-corruption campaign to be directed against his enemies, not his political allies.[89] And thus this case, as we suggested above with other anti-corruption campaigns, was politicized. In 1995 Boldyrev continued his lonely struggle against corruption as the deputy head of the Federal Audit Chamber. His exposure of the 'loans-for-shares' scam helped put an end to the practice, but the fact that the exposure of these cases hardly caused a ripple let alone a scandal indicates that we are dealing here with metacorruption, not 'simple' corruption.

In this context public oversight and media campaigns can have only a marginal role. It is not so much that the executive branch is too powerful, but that accountability for its actions is too weak. This is not a counsel for despair, and while what we described above is part of systemic metacorruption, we also argue that Russia is a dual system where venal forms of corruption can be challenged, and by doing so the legitimacy of metacorruption is also undermined. Already Yeltsin's March 1997 address to the Federal Assembly recognized the danger that metacorruption posed to his own power, and promised to abolish the system of authorized banks and replace them with a national treasury, and insisted that future privatization auctions should be more transparent. Independent watchdog institutions play an important part in reversing the culture of corruption and ensuring that anti-corruption struggles are perceived as more than part of political gamesmanship. The struggle at least sustains an alternative normative system that refuses to accept corruption as 'normal' and upholds a concept of the public good. The abuse of the concept of civil society has led to it being abandoned by some analysts, yet Girling is absolutely right to argue that 'the emergence of "civil society" provides the potential for normative counter-claims.'[90] These claims, moreover, as Rutland and Kogan stress, must be rooted in the realities of the country itself. Only Russians, they insist, 'can come up with a formula for a "capitalism with a Russian face" that stands a chance of working in that country', and here legal abstractions should come to terms with the realities of political power: 'Unless one specifies the political conditions conducive to the emergence of a coalition in favor of battling corruption, reforms promoting the rule of law will remain mere castles in the air.'[91] The roots of political corruption lie not in the social psychology of Russians but in specific institutions, structures and practices, and well-formulated and implemented reforms can deal with it at that level.

### Parliamentary and other forms of immunity

Many criminals had run for, and some were elected to, parliament to take advantage of the immunity from criminal prosecution that this conferred on them.[92] In many cases investigations have had to be dropped when the suspect successfully ran for office. Vitalii Savitskii, head of the Christian Democratic Union – Christians of Russia (CDU/CR) bloc, had repeatedly advocated limiting parliamentary immunity for deputies from criminal prosecution.[93] His death just before the December 1995 elections in a car accident was considered suspicious by some. His cause continued to be fought, and by late 1998 there were concrete plans to lift the immunity from deputies indicted on criminal offences. Already the Constitutional Court ruled against attempts to grant deputies in regional legislatures immunity, ruling that only a federal law could decide the issue.[94] Managers of partially state-owned enterprises also enjoyed *de facto* immunity, since their prosecution faced numerous legal obstacles, allowing the luxuriant growth of corruption. The business ethics of Russia's new semi-market economy in fact became part of the larger process of metacorruption.

## Controlling campaign expenses

Another element is the strengthening of supervision over campaign expenses. All candidates have to file financial declarations to the CEC or its equivalents at the local level, stating the amount and source of campaign funds. Attempts to smear rivals with the charge that they received support from abroad (which is illegal) or foreign NGOs based in Russia have led to the publication of some of these declarational.[95] Both parliamentary elections held in postcommunist Russia to date have been accompanied by accusations that the CEC had failed to establish clear rules for the financing of electoral campaigns. In the December 1993 campaign there had been confusion over how much a candidate could spend on themselves, allowing (it is claimed) corruption on a grand scale.[96] There is no doubt that 'lobbying' interests have 'invested' in candidates, hoping for a substantial return on their election. The failure of deputies to perform to expectations in this respect prompted business interests and other groups to participate directly in the December 1995 elections. The CEC has gradually refined the financial rules concerning elections, but the problem, as before, remains implementation.

## The structure of elections

The electoral system devised in 1993 sought to encourage the development of a stable party system. Half the 450 deputies to the State Duma are elected in single-member districts, and the other half proportionately on party lists. From early 1998 Yeltsin sought to abolish the party list section, a proposal that would not only undermine the development of Russian political parties but would, in Zyuganov's words, 'turn the Duma into a corporation of mafia clans'.[97] Although some dubious characters might have entered on the party lists, especially that of the LDPR, purely constituency elections would indeed open the door to the criminalization of parliament. As far as corruption is concerned, the proposed electoral reform would be counterproductive.

### More market or authoritarianism?

One of the leading analysts of the Russian 'transition', Anders Aslund, has argued that a rapid move to free markets would eliminate corruption.[98] The reduction of state intervention and bureaucratic interference would, in his view, remove some of the sources of distortion that allowed corruption to flourish. The analysis is undoubtedly correct in part, but failed to understand that an effective (from the classical perspective) market required also an effective state, and this Russia spectacularly lacked. A strong market required a strong state. It is at this point that more authoritarian solutions to the problem of corruption became increasingly popular. Already Lebed, advancing a distinctive mix of authoritarian populism to resolve the economic crisis and the criminalization of politics, was preparing his bid for power. Having won the governorship of Krasnoyarsk krai his problems with financing his presidential campaign appeared to be resolved. Luzhkov, too, advanced a *dirigiste* model to tackle Russia's problems, and with his power base in Moscow at his disposal he certainly did not lack funds for his presidential bid.

## Conclusion

The Russian system of political finance combines a small measure of legal regulation with a very large dose of quasi-legal informal relationships. While it is easy to understand the historical and social roots of corruption among state officials in postcommunist countries, it is no less clear that the phenomenon threatens the whole democratization process, undermining the rule of law, democracy, human rights and the very foundations of the emerging civil societies. Mény has argued that the prevalence of corruption undermines the democratic process itself, above all by fuelling a withdrawal from political participation and cynicism.[99] In Russia these features were apparent, with a widespread lack of trust in the new political elite and a grudging participation in the political process. A common attitude to the new leaders was that they were all thieves, but the very definition of what constituted theft was blurred in context where the whole transitional regime was built on an *enrichessez-vous* programme. Despite the systemic corruption, at the individual level the communist system had been imbued by an ethic of public service, but this was now thrown out with the bathwater of communism. The problem was exacerbated by the postcommunist bias against idealism of whatever hue and by the dominance of a neo-liberal paradigm that elevated market forces into a new utopia.

Corruption extended not only into many areas of public administration but also into the law-enforcement and other security agencies, including in Russia the army. When combined with the increasingly transnational character of organized crime and the vast resources it was able to control, the very bases of state autonomy came under threat. With its roots in the communist period, contrary to expectations the fall of the regimes did not lead to the decline of corruption and organized crime, but to their luxurient growth in the new market conditions.[100] At a meeting in Prague of justice ministers from the Council of Europe's member states on 11 June 1997 Ukraine's Justice Minister Serhiy Holovaty stressed the roots of the problem in the legacy of the past and the adaptation of old communist elites to new conditions. Former Soviet elites in those countries, he argued,

> continue to cling to power. Having wielded tremendous administrative control over the lives and activities of their citizens [under Communism], the members of the 'nomenklatura' are now the virtually uncontrolled arbiters of the distribution and use of state property . . . Today, because of the absence of accountability within hierarchical power structures, the scope for fraud, corruption, and self-aggrandizement is broad, to put it mildly. The nomenklatura is not interested in serious economic and administrative reform because its members profit handsomely from the existing unregulated environment.

He stressed in addition the link between organized crime and corruption, noting that 'The distinction between organized crime and certain aspects of government activity is often indistinguishable,' giving rise to the 'increasing institutionalization of corruption, enormous losses of revenue to state budgets, retardation of the development of the private sector, the monopolization of certain aspects of economic activity, and pervasive unjust enrichment.[101] Criminal and bureaucratic forces in Russia have combined to form a new and ruthless power.

Corruption undermined the rudimentary systems of financial market regulation, discouraged foreign direct investment and contributed to the currency crises that unrolled out of East Asia from late 1997. It was also clearly an element in Russia's failure to move out of the long recession from 1990 and which from August 1998 took on catastrophic proportions. Metacorruption distorted the whole economic system, and indeed a semi-reformed economy trapped between bureaucratic regulation and the market was clearly to the advantage of those who could take advantage of the opportunities for rent-seeking behaviour. While the struggle against corruption could to a degree become a public project, with the mobilization of the media and social and international organizations (for example, Transparency International) to expose wrong doing and to act as a watchdog to deter malfeasance by public officials, metacorruption could only be combated by systematic political action. Corrupt behaviour by public officials could be countered by judicial measures, whereas metacorruption required political reform.

## Notes

1  The classic statement of this is Milovan Djilas, *The New Class*, New York: Praeger, 1957; with the profound political corruption described later by Mikhail Voslenskii, *Nomenklatura: Anatomy of the Soviet Ruling Class*, London: Bodley Head, 1984; and the social corruption by Konstantin Simis, *USSR: Secrets of a Corrupt Society*, London: Dent, 1982.
2  William A. Clark, *Crime and Punishment in Soviet Officialdom: Combatting Corruption in the Political Elite, 1965–1990*, Armonk, New York: M.E. Sharpe, 1993; Leslie Holmes, *The End of Communist Power: Anti-Corruption Campaigns and Legitimation Crisis*, Oxford, Polity Press, 1993.
3  For details, see Carolyn McGiffert Ekedahl and Melvin A. Goodman, *The Wars of Eduard Shevardnadze*, University Park: Pennsylvania State University Press, 1997, especially chapters 1 and 11.
4  Ekedahl and Goodman, *The Wars of Eduard Shevardnadze*, p. 12.
5  Vladimir Solovyov and Elena Klepikova, *Yury Andropov: A Secret Passage into the Kremlin*, New York: Macmillan, 1983, pp. 90–1.

6 Yegor Ligachev, *Inside Gorbachev's Kremlin*, Boulder: Westview Press, 1996, p. 44.

7 For details, see John Keep, *Last of the Empires: A History of the Soviet Union, 1945–1991*, Oxford University Press, 1996, p. 351.

8 Mark Galeotti, 'The *Mafiya* and the New Russia', *Australian Journal of Politics and History*, Vol. 44, No. 3, 1998, p. 419. For more details see John Millar, 'The Little Deal: Brezhnev's Contribution to Acquisitive Socialism', *Slavic Review*, Vol. 44, No. 4, 1985, pp. 694–706, and Arkady Vaksberg, *The Soviet Mafia*, London: Weidenfeld & Nicolson, 1991.

9 Keep, *Last of the Empires*, p. 73.

10 For example, the one-time prime minister of Kazakhstan, Akezhan Kazhegeldin, later admitted working for the KGB and conducting speculative financial deals on behalf of the party, *RFE/RL Newsline*, 11 September 1997. A week after the August 1991 putsch the business manager of the CPSU's Central Committee, Nikolai Kruchina, the man with all the secrets about the party's appropriation of state assets and foreign speculations, jumped to his death from his seventh-floor apartment.

11 For Victor M. Sergeyev, *The Wild East: Crime and Lawlessness in Post-Communist Russia*, Armonk, NY: M.E. Sharpe, 1997, the problem is more profound: the very definition of deviant behaviour was destroyed in the overthrow of the old regime and no replacement has emerged, especially when sections of the old elite in alliance with the criminal world can exploit the uncertainties of the new period. For detailed studies of the contemporary situation, see S. Lovell, A. Ledeneva and A. Rogatchevskii (eds), *Blat and Corruption in Russia*, Basingstoke and London, Macmillan, forthcoming.

12 According to Stephen Handelman, the KGB was involved in illegal business and extortion in the final days. Aslambek Aslakhanov argued that, 'The nomenklatura knew years ago that the system would come tumbling down, and prepared themselves', *Comrade Criminal: The Theft of the Second Russian Revolution*, London: Michael Joseph, 1994, p. 349, fn 3.

13 Stephen Handelman, *Comrade Criminal: The Theft of the Second Russian Revolution*, London: Michael Joseph, 1994, p. 311.

14 Georgii Podlesskikh and Andrei Tereshok, *Vory v zakone: brosok k vlasti*, Moscow: Khudozhestvennaya literatura, 1994, p. 27.

15 Tanya Frisby, 'The Rise of Organised Crime in Russia: Its Roots and Social Significance', *Europe-Asia Studies*, Vol. 50, No. 1, 1998, p. 40.

16 According to Moscow region police chief Alexander Kulikov, Interfax, 13 June 1997.

17 *Rossiiskie vesti*, 23 July 1997.

18 IEWS, *Russian Regional Report*, Vol. 3, No. 2, 15 January 1998.

19 *Izvestiya*, 17–19 September 1997.

20 *Rossiiskaya gazeta*, 27 September 1997.

21 *Novaya gazeta*, No. 35, 1–7 September 1997.

22 Phil Williams (ed.), *Russian Organized Crime: The New Threat*, London: Frank Cass, 1997.

23 RIA-Novosti, 2 July 1997.

24  Rustam Narzikulov, *Nezavisimaya gazeta*, 11 March 1997.
25  Yeltsin declared an expenditure of 14.4 billion roubles (3.1 million dollars). See 'El'tsyn deneg ne zhalel', in *Ot El'tsina k... El'tsinu: prezidentskaya gonka-96*, Moscow: Terra, 1997), pp. 547–9. For the full income reports of Yeltsin and the other 16 candidates, see *Deklaratsii o dokhodakh kandidatov v prezidenty na vyborakh 16 iyunya 1996*, compiled by G. Belonuchkin, Moscow: Panorama, 1996. Zyuganov officially spent 11.3 billion roubles (2.1 million dollars).
26  M. Steven Fish, 'The Predicament of Russian Liberalism: Evidence from the December 1995 Parliamentary Elections', *Europe-Asia Studies*, Vol. 49, No. 2, 1997, pp. 214–15, advances this argument. For the view that Yeltsin successfully bribed the electorate, see Daniel Treisman, 'Why Yeltsin Won', *Foreign Affairs*, Vol. 75, No. 5, September–October 1996, pp. 64–77.
27  *Rossiiskaya gazeta*, 19 August 1996.
28  Peter Reddaway, 'The West's Spoilt Russian Son', *New Statesman*, 22 August 1997, p. 26.
29  Sergei Stankevich, 'Simvolicheskaya forma russkogo bunta', *Vremya MN*, No. 37, 28 July 1998.
30  *Izvestiya*, 1 July 1997.
31  *Izvestiya*, 5 July 1997.
32  See Janine R. Wedel, *Collision and Collusion: The Strange Case of Western Aid to Eastern Europe 1989–1998*, Basingstoke and London: Macmillan, 1998, in particular chapter 4.
33  In the event, perhaps taking advantage of his enforced leisure, Kokh did actually write a book, called appropriately *The Selling of the Soviet Empire*.
34  For a discussion of this, see my 'The Regime System in Russia', *Contemporary Politics*, Vol. 3, No. 1, 1997, pp. 7–25.
35  *Russia Briefing*, Vol. 5, No. 3, 30 May 1997, p. 2.
36  *Moskovskii komsomolets*, 25 November 1998.
37  *Rossiiskaya gazeta*, 31 July 1998.
38  Yurii Rodygin, 'After Starovoitova Murder, Competing Funding Sources Prevent Democrats From Uniting', EWI *Russian Regional Report*, Vol. 3, No. 49, 8 December 1998.
39  Jeremy Lester, 'Overdosing on Nationalism: Gennadii Zyuganov and the Communist Party of the Russian Federation', *New Left Review*, No. 221, January–February 1997, pp. 34–5.
40  Frisby, 'The Rise of Organised Crime in Russia', p. 35.
41  *The Sunday Times*, 12 October 1997.
42  *RFE/RL Newsline*, 4 August 1997.
43  *Nevskoe vremya*, 20 October 1997.
44  *Moskovskie novosti*, No. 30, 27 July–3 August 1997.
45  *Time* Magazine, 9 June 1997.
46  Vladimir Gel'man, 'The Iceberg of Russian Political Finance', in Peter Burnell and Alan Ware (eds), *Funding Democratization*, Manchester: Manchester University Press, 1998, chapter 8, pp. 158–79.

47 The role of scandals in forcing party realignment in Japan is discussed by Steven R. Reed, 'Political Corruption in Japan', *International Social Science Journal*, No. 149, September 1996, pp. 395–405.

48 Yves Mény, 'Fin de Siècle Corruption', *International Social Science Journal*, No. 149, September 1996, p. 313.

49 John Girling, *Corruption, Capitalism and Democracy*, London: Routledge, 1997, p. vii.

50 For a discussion of the issue, see Natasha Kogan, 'Thinking About Corruption', *Transitions*, March 1998, pp. 46–9.

51 Leslie Holmes, 'Corruption and the Crisis of the Post-Communist State', *Crime, Law & Social Change*, Vol. 27, No. 3/4, 1997, pp. 1–23.

52 *Moscow Times*, 10 January 1998, p. 11.

53 *Transitions*, March 1998, p. 61.

54 Above all by Susan Rose-Ackerman, *Corruption: A Study in Political Economy*, New York: Academic Press, 1978.

55 In his analysis Federico Varese stresses precisely this, making reference to the 'tragedy of the commons' where the pursuit of individually rational goals leads to a less-than-optimal outcome, 'The Transition to the Market and Corruption in Post-socialist Russia', *Political Studies*, Vol. 45, No. 3, 1997, pp. 579–96.

56 These were figures given by Sergei Dubinin, then head of the Central Bank, in July 1997. For details, see 'Krupneiskie banki Rossii', *Finansovye izvestiya*, No. 58 (508), 11 August 1998.

57 *Novye izvestiya*, 6 November 1997.

58 Neil Ascherson, 'Post-Communism Triumphs by Default', *Independent on Sunday*, 26 November 1995, p. 14.

59 Daniel Yergin and Thane Gustafson, *Russia 2010 and What it Means for the World*, New York: Random House, 1993, p. 52.

60 Ibid., p. 53.

61 Ibid., p. 53.

62 Fish, 'The Predicament of Russian Liberalism', pp. 197, 199.

63 For the official figures, see *Byulleten' TsIK*, No. 12, 1994, pp. 82–105. For an analysis, see Richard Sakwa, 'The Russian Elections of December 1993', *Europe-Asia Studies*, Vol. 47, No. 2, 1995, pp. 209–10.

64 The funding of his campaign has aroused considerable speculation and there is no doubt that both candidates exceeded spending limits. It appears that Lebed's main backer was Boris Berezovskii and Rossiiskii Kredit bank, while Zubov was supported by Oneksimbank (the owner of a controlling stake in Norilsk Nickel, one of the krai's main employers) and Inkombank.

65 Martin Walker, 'After Yeltsin: Russia Faces Free-fall', *Transitions*, June 1998, p. 21.

66 O. Kirchheimer, 'The Transformation of Western European Party Systems', in J. LaPalombara and M. Weiner (eds), *Political Parties and Political Development*, Princeton: Princeton University Press, 1966, pp. 177–200; A. Panebianco, *Political Parties: Organisation and Power*, Cambridge: Cambridge University Press, 1988.

67    Richard Katz and Peter Mair, 'Changing Models of Party Organization and Party Democracy: The Emergence of the Cartel Party', *Party Politics*, Vol. 1, No. 1, January 1995, pp. 5–28.

68    *RFE/RL Newsline*, 15 April 1998.

69    On this see, for example, Sergei Khaitun, 'Chtoby ostavat'sya chestnym, nado byt' glupym', *Izvestiya*, 28 August 1998, p. 5.

70    Andrei Illarionov, *Argumenty i fakty*, No. 34, 1998, p. 4.

71    *The Moscow Tribune*, 27 November 1998.

72    *Financial Times*, 11 January 1999.

73    IEWS, *Russian Regional Report*, Vol. 3, No. 1, 8 January 1998.

74    Aslan Dukayev, 'Grozny's Pyrrhic Victory', *Transitions*, May 1998, p. 84.

75    *Kommersant-daily*, 5 March 1998.

76    ITAR-TASS, 1 February 1998; *RFE/RL Newsline*, 2 February 1998.

77    *The Moscow Times*, 14 August 1998, p. 9. The newspaper, incidentally, was classified as 'unfriendly', as were, notably, *Kommersant* and *Segodnya*.

78    Anne Nivat, 'His Mater's Voice', *Transitions*, June 1988, p. 47.

79    *Ugolovnyi kodeks Rossiiskoi Federatsii*, Moscow, 1997.

80    Svetlana P. Glinkina, 'The Ominous Landscape of Russian Corruption', *Transitions*, March 1998, pp. 16–17.

81    Tsarist experience is discussed by Clark, *Crime and Punishment in Soviet Officialdom*, pp. 30–8.

82    This is a point made by Paul Goble in relation to anti-corruption campaigns in Kazakhstan, 'The Corruption of Power', *RFE/RL Newsline*, 14 July 1998.

83    *Moskovskii komsomolets*, 8 October 1997.

84    *OMRI Daily Digest*, 6 March 1997.

85    *RFE/RL Newsline*, 3 April 1998.

86    *RFE/RL Newsline*, 30 March 1998.

87    In the Czech Republic the ruling Civic Democratic Party (ODS) stood accused of corrupt financial deals whereby secret business donations were rewarded with political influence. It was even suggested that the prime minister himself, Vaclav Klaus, had built himself a villa in Switzerland out of party funds. An ironic twist in the story was that Klaus's arrogance had provoked some ODS leaders to expose the scandal (using *kompromat* that they had long known about) in order to unseat him and to take revenge on his dictatorial style of government that had humiliated them all.

88    For an analysis of Boldfyrev's career, see 'Kontroler-ispytatel', *Figury i litsa: Nezavisimaya gazeta*, No. 11 (12), June 1998, pp. 9, 11.

89    See Brian Whitmore, 'Russia's Top Crime Fighter', *Transitions*, March 1998, pp. 35–9.

90    Girling, *Corruption, Capitalism and Democracy*, p. xi.

91    Peter Rutland and Natasha Kogan, 'The Russian Mafia: Between Hype and Reality', *Transitions*, March 1998, p. 32.

92    It remains a moot point whether criminal ties subvert democracy. It has been alleged, for example, that up to a third of sitting MPs in India are criminals.

93  Vladimir Wozniuk, 'In Search of Ideology: The Politics of Religion and Nationalism in the New Russia (1991–1996)', *Nationalities Papers*, Vol. 25, No. 2, 1997, p. 203.

94  *RFE/RL Newsline*, 4 February 1998.

95  For example, in the mid-1997 gubernatorial campaign in Nizhnii Novgorod State Duma deputy and Communist-backed candidate Gennadii Khodyrev charged that the Carnegie Endowment's Moscow centre was financing the campaign of Ivan Sklyarov, then mayor of Nizhnii Novgorod city and ultimate victor in the campaign, *RFE/RL NEWSLINE*, Vol 1, No. 57, Part I, 20 June 1997.

96  *Moscow News*, No. 47, 19 November 1993, p. 2.

97  *RFE/RL Newsline*, 16 January 1998.

98  Anders Aslund, 'Economic Causes of Crime in Russia', in Jeffrey D. Sachs and Katharina Pistor (eds), *The Rule of Law and Economic Reform in Russia*, Boulder: Westview Press, 1997.

99  Yves Mény, 'Politics, Corruption and Democracy: The 1995 Stein Rokkan Lecture', *European Journal of Political Research*, Vol. 30, No. 2, 1996, pp. 111–23. On the covert funding of parties and the like, see his *La corruption de la République*, Paris: Fayard, 1992.

100  Pal Vastagh, the Hungarian justice minister, noted that some corrupt practices that had developed under communist rule continued to flourish in postcommunist Hungary. He admitted that 'at the time of the change of regime, it was believed corruption would no longer pose a big problem in an emerging market economy, since the reasons for it would have ceased to exist. This expectation, unfortunately, proved to be wrong', *RFE/RL Newsline*, Part II, 13 June 1997.

101  *RFE/RL Newsline*, Part II, 13 June 1997.

# 7
# Political Corruption in Southeast Asia

*William A. Callahan*

> 'Our crisis is not only economic but also political and psychological. People are fed up with the same government that is corrupt, nepotistic and full of cronies.'[1]
>
> Amien Rais, Indonesian opposition leader

Enormous changes have been taking place in Southeast Asia in the 1990s, particularly towards the end of the decade. First there was a pattern of equitable economic growth that was striking enough to be characterized by the World Bank as a 'miracle', and hailed by professional and pop economists alike as a new capitalist utopia. On 2 July 1997 all of this started to unravel in a financial crisis which in less than one year had radically devalued currencies in Thailand (by 32 per cent), Indonesia (71 per cent), Malaysia (31 per cent), the Philippines (29 per cent) and South Korea (35 per cent).[2] Suddenly what had seemed to be a miracle actually turned out to be a curse that the region will have to bear for the remainder of the 1990s, and probably into the next millennium.

As Amien Rais tells us above, the crisis has not just been financial. It has also been political and cultural. Since July 1997 there have been changes of government in Thailand, Indonesia and South Korea. What used to be called 'Asian Values' is now called 'crony capitalism' – often by the same analysts and critics.[3] In Asia, there has been a backlash which has traced the origin of the financial crisis to the door of racist and envious political-economic elites in the West – Malaysian Prime Minister Mahathir Mohamad's charge in August

1997 that George Soros was leading a 'Jewish conspiracy' is just one case in point.[4]

Corruption has been an important political and cultural issue in both the miracle and its unravelling. Luminaries such as Chalmers Johnson and Lucian W. Pye have argued that corruption in East Asia is not a problem, but the secret of the region's success. Similar to the problems of defining 'corruption' in general, many Asian Studies scholars ask whether 'corruption' is merely a Western concept with dubious utility in Asia. Indeed, in Thai the word for 'corruption' is the phonetic loan-word *kawrupchun*, leading us to believe that it is not an indigenous concept or concern.[5] Like 'democracy' and 'human rights', using 'corruption' is not necessarily helpful in understanding the grammar of Asian society.

What some called 'structural corruption' in Japan, Johnson argued in 1986, was certainly 'structural', but not necessarily 'corruption'. It actually was a key part of the democratization of the bureaucratic state. (Pye made an argument linking corruption with democratization in East Asia as late as 1997.[6]) Since the sale of access in such large state structures is 'unavoidable', Johnson reasons that we should change our analytic questions to ask 'what is the overall performance record of any given strong bureaucratic state? How is the purchased access actually used? And does the citizenry tolerate the sale of access?' He answers these new questions for us by rehearsing the story of Japan's broadbased economic success where patterns of what we might call 'corruption' have actually redistributed income from rich to poor, and opened up the secretive ministries to parliamentary scrutiny. The only hesitation Johnson had in 1986 was to state that the Japanese public felt that corruption had gone too far.[7]

When Johnson republished this article in 1995, he added a paragraph at the end which completely undermined his argument: corruption was no longer helpful, but had become a disease rampant not only in politics, but in the bureaucracy and business.[8] Corruption had gone too far: citizens were disillusioned with parliamentary democracy, and the Japanese economy had been in the doldrums since the early 1990s. Likewise, in most countries in Southeast and East Asia corruption has become a major public issue, with criticisms of corruption widespread both via public opinion mobilizers in the press, and popular political reform movements.

Johnson's 1995 reassessment seemed to foreshadow the flip-flop of 'Asia' from being a utopia to a distopia, from a positive example to a negative one. But rather than see corruption as a clear and unproblematic concept which can yield reliable judgements of societies as either 'clean' or 'dirty', it is best to jettison this 'either/or' framework to consider corruption in terms of the more 'Asian' concept of harmony. When we hear that Japanese and Thai citizens[9] feel that there is 'too much' corruption, they are implicitly saying that they judge their governments in terms of 'degree' (harmony), rather than 'kind' (either/or). In this chapter, first I will sketch the practices of political corruption in Thailand, the Philippines, Indonesia, Singapore and Malaysia. Though I will limit my brief examination of these countries to a consideration of electoral corruption, this analysis can also tell us more about wider issues of political and social change in these societies. In the second section, I will examine the different routes to reform for these various patterns of corruption using a critical schema proposed by Michael Johnston which looks to the value of 'balance'.

## Elections and political corruption

It is common to portray Thailand and the Philippines as quite backward in relation to their neighbours Singapore and Malaysia. The corruption of widespread vote-buying and frequent coups in Thailand and the Philippines does not compare well with the apparently regular, clean and fair elections in Singapore and Malaysia.[10] But I would argue that the electoral systems of Thailand and the Philippines are actually more developed – albeit in odd ways – than those in Malaysia and Singapore. More to the point, it is useful to note that election irregularities in Malaysia and Singapore have more in common with those of the authoritarian government of Indonesia than with Thailand or the Philippines. Since the dramatic changes in Indonesia, which saw President Soeharto resign in May 1998, now promise to lead to widespread political reform, Indonesia could surpass Malaysia and Singapore as well.

Unlike Western countries where 'campaign finance' is a guiding issue in the analysis of political corruption, it has yet to become a major issue in Southeast Asia. As the other chapters in this book show, the main issues in Western countries and Japan concern economic elites using money to buy political power, access and influence: scandals involve interest groups bribing politicians. Since the politicians largely use these funds not for personal gain, but to cover the high costs of campaigning in the television age, scholars often argue that the way to correct this political corruption is through reform of campaign finance laws.

But in much of Southeast Asia, it is the politicians who bribe, threaten or manipulate the electorate for votes. The politicians and political parties do not need to go hat in hand to private sources for funds, for they themselves are typically wealthy. The Nationalist Party in Taiwan is the richest party in the world, and the ruling United Malays National Organization (UMNO) in Malaysia owns a wide portfolio of assets, at times raising campaign funds from manipulating the stock market in Kuala Lumphur.[11] It is only recently that large corporations and small businesses have been approached for campaign donations in Thailand. As we will see below, business and politics are often complementary activities in the region: but in the opposite way to that in most Western democracies. Political power allows politico-business people to firm up and expand their business activities, while income generated from business gives them access to political power in what Gomez calls 'state capitalism and political business' (Gomez, 84ff.). Certainly, campaign finance is becoming more of an issue as calls for more 'transparency' are increasingly heard. But I would argue that studying problems of party finance – in particular the institutional arrangements that regulate, monitor and publicize party finance – is not the best route towards an understanding of political corruption in Southeast and East Asia. For example, to gain and maintain this political power, corrupt politicians need the co-operation of government officials, both locally and nationally.

Thus, rather than focusing on campaign finance as the root of political corruption, it is useful to divide electoral corruption in Southeast Asia into two broad categories: vote-buying by candidates and official manipulation by bureaucrats. My argument is that while Thailand and the Philippines are well known for the economic-based electoral corruption of vote-buying and bribing officials, the well-entrenched ruling parties of Indonesia, Malaysia and Singapore rely on their firm control of state power to guarantee their re-election. Thus informal corruption like vote-buying is not necessary in Singapore and Malaysia because the ruling parties can manipulate the election through official channels, and thus reproduce their power on a regular basis. Examples of such activities help to explain the similarities and differences of Singapore and Malaysia with Thailand and the Philippines.

## Thailand

Thailand's Eighteenth Constitution was promulgated in September 1997 in an effort to curb the exploding problem of political corruption. This controversial constitution, which was opposed by most politicians since it restricted their powers, was finally pushed through as a reaction to the economic crisis of 1997. Although elites in Malaysia often pointed to a 'Western conspiracy' for their woes, people in Thailand largely felt that their economic crisis was in large part due to the rampant corruption in parliament and in the bureaucracy. Hence the new constitution was organized around a grand plan of 'political reform' to set in place checks and balances on state and parliamentary power. This included the formation of six independent institutions: the Constitutional Court, the Administrative Court, the Court of Justice, the National Counter Corruption Commission, the Office of the Ombudsman, and lastly the organization which most concerns this chapter, the Election Commission. The Election Commission of Thailand (ECT) was founded in 1997 to deal with electoral fraud. The ECT's duties include scheduling elections, designating constituencies, urging voters to exercise their voting rights, monitoring campaign spending and receiving complaints about poll fraud. It was stated in the constitution that the agency's structure must allow for public participation and be free from partisan politics. Only time will tell if the ECT will be part of a new era of co-operation between public and private groups, or if it will once more demonstrate that the more things change, the more they stay the same.

To understand the problem of political corruption in Thailand it thus is necessary to understand how elections work. One of the Bangkok newspaper columnists stirred up controversy in 1995 by calling politicians 'electorocrats-*nakluektang*' rather than candidates or representatives.[12] The idea was that the election was a prime example of professional politicians and rural machine politics in action, where money is everything and 'issues' are so much rhetoric.[13] Indeed, a report on democracy in Thailand also characterized the political system as more 'electoralism' than democracy.[14] By the 1990s electoral fraud had become a national issue. An editorial from *Thai Rat*, the largest newspaper in Thailand, declared:

> The practice of using money to buy votes, without regard for the nation's laws, has spread epidemic-like down to local elections. It has spread throughout the country like fire spreads through a field. . . . The power of the country will fall into the hands of capitalists whose supporters are local 'dark powers'. The democratic platform will become dominated by economic power and vested interests.[15]

As Thai political scientist Sombat Chantornvong argues, such election fraud cannot be viewed in isolation, but must be situated firmly in the context of the Thai political order.[16] The nature of the Thai party system is particularly relevant to an understanding of vote-buying and electoral malpractices by government officials. Most parties are loosely structured groups of factions, based around a number of senior patrons who compete with one another to gain lucrative Cabinet posts.[17] Thai parties typically use their control of ministries to recoup election expenses, to establish war-chests for future elections, and to distribute favours to supporters. Beginning in the 1970s, national politicians and faction leaders have formed increasingly close ties with local 'influential figures' in provincial areas (Sombat, 1993:111–20).[18] These 'influential figures' have achieved significant wealth and influence in provincial areas, largely through semi-legal or illegal business practices: sub-standard construction contracting, underground lotteries, smuggling, and illegal logging. In many cases, successful parliamentary candidates are either influential figures themselves, or are relatives or close associates of such figures.

For politicians of this ilk, business and politics are two complementary activities: political power allows them to firm up and expand their business activities, while income generated from business gives them access to political power. To gain and maintain this political power, such politicians need the co-operation of local government officials, creating a 'political–bureaucratic–business iron triangle' which makes the electoral process increasingly exclusionary.[19] The participation of influential figures in the campaign process has led to a commercialization of parliamentary elections, which are typically viewed by them as an investment opportunity. Beyond the quasi-legal activities of influential figures, Sombat also charts the general rise of business in politics. The result is not simply the increasing monetarization of campaigns, but a new marketing strategy approach to electioneering which Sombat argues has institutionalized common forms of election fraud (Sombat 1993:169–74, 180).

Cultural factors which contribute to the prevalence of vote-buying include the idea of *bunkhun*, indebtedness to the benevolence of others. In Thailand's hierarchical society, some rural voters will readily agree to support candidates who are known to have the backing of leaders such as the district or village headman, the school teacher, or the abbot of the local temple. Rural voters with limited education often feel obligated to candidates who have made payments to them, and are inclined to support them at the ballot box. Many devout Buddhists, especially older people, believe that failing to vote for a candidate who had paid them would be a *bap*, an act of demerit.[20] During the 1995 general election campaign, a famous Buddhist abbot declared that not voting for a vote-buyer did not constitute a *bap*, but his statement – widely covered by the media – had little impact on the outcome of the election.

Though such 'political culture' arguments are useful in explaining electoral fraud, both politicians and academics also attribute the rise of vote-buying to changes in electoral legislation enacted in 1979.[21] This legislation banned candidates from showing films and using traditional entertainers at election rallies, eliminating a very low-cost form of campaigning. Unable to offer free entertainment to attract villagers to political rallies and so gain their interest, candidates were obliged to pay voters directly for their support.

By the time of the General Election of July 1995, electioneering involved huge amounts of money. One campaign worker described the election as '21 days of big spending', while the Thai Farmers' Bank Research Centre estimated that 17 billion baht would be circulated over the course of the 45-day campaign.[22] Even though there was a rush to hi-tech methods of electioneering through the electronic media, the bulk of the campaign in 1995 took place at the village level where all the main political parties bought votes.[23] Ten or twenty years previously, candidates would distribute small gifts such as cigarettes or betel nut, gifts which showed their interest in the people and were more symbolic than material. Gradually, however, rural people began to expect cash payments, though payment in kind did persist in some areas: gifts of food, fish sauce, and sacks of rice.

But the bulk of vote-buying involved a simple cash transaction, with votes selling for anywhere between 50 and 1000 baht, depending on the local conditions. Though this might sound like a small amount of money, it amounted to a huge flow of cash. One informed estimate suggested that to ensure successful election in a competitive constituency, a candidate would need to spend in the region of 20 to 25 million baht (the official legal limit for campaign spending is one million baht per candidate). By no means all of this money would be passed on to the voters: perhaps only 5 or 6 million baht. Some of the remaining money would be used for legitimate expenses such as campaign vehicles, remunerating *huakhanaen* (canvassers), making donations to temples and community groups, and bribing local officials.

In a provincial centre like Khon Kaen, votes cost around 300 baht, dramatically up from 50–100 baht at the time of the September 1992 election, due to heavy spending by parties with wealthy and ambitious leaders. Some political commentators predicted that the inflationary trend of election expenses would exhaust the coffers of political parties, and thus vote-buying would exhaust itself. But these predictions were not borne out by the campaign of 1995. In any case, few parties were spending their own money: at the national level, parties were funded by banks and major corporations, which often made multi-million baht under-the-table donations to a range of different parties. A parallel process was at work at the local level, where hoteliers and other business people would give donations in the order of 100 000 or 200 000 baht to promising candidates.

To avoid being tricked out of money by voters, some *huakhanaen* bought votes by 'renting' the identity cards of voters on election day; the actual votes would be cast by agents of the *huakhanaen* who impersonated the voters, rather than by the voters themselves. This is just one of the many strategies that *huakhanaen* used on election day which necessitated the co-operation of government officials. Others included padding the voter's registration lists to create 'ghost voters'. For example, during the March 1992 election one house registered 2673 eligible voters.[24]

Buying individual votes was not the only way of dispensing cash. Some candidates made multiple 'donations' of several thousand baht to organizations such as housewives' groups and youth clubs; others gave donations of hundreds of thousands of baht to temples in order to win endorsement from well-respected monks. Local officials such as police officers, district officers, and even provincial governors sometimes receive generous 'gifts' from parliamentary candidates at election times.

The election campaigns also included violent attacks on candidates and *huakhanaen*: one way to get elected is to intimidate and threaten rivals. The police were very public about keeping an eye on known assassins during the 1995 election campaign, and reported sobering statistics. There were 12 000 arrests in an 11-day national crackdown before the elections; the bulk of the arrests were for gambling, but also included a significant number of arrests for drugs, explosives, handguns, war weapons and assault.[25] Candidates often make well-known canvassers offers that they cannot refuse: numerous *huakhanaen* were shot because they turned down offers from rival candidates.[26] After the election, failed candidates typically go after the *huakhanaen* who do not get their quota of votes.[27]

The PollWatch Organization in Thailand was formed in 1992 as a quasi-official neutral body to curb election fraud by monitoring elections for irregularities, as well as organizing civic education programmes to promote meaningful democracy through elections. PollWatch is an independent state organization, formed through an alliance of NGO leaders and Prime Minister Anand Panyarachun. Though it was an *ad hoc* committee with no legal jurisdiction to enforce the election law, under Anand's patronage in 1992 Poll-Watch received the co-operation of the police and the bureaucracy. Indeed, PollWatch took advantage of state infrastructure to organize its activities. It received a budget from the Prime Minister's Office. It used office space in government buildings throughout the country. Civil servants and state enterprise workers took paid leave to work as PollWatch volunteers.

One of PollWatch's mandates was to increase popular participation in the election. This was accomplished, in part, by turning Poll-Watch into a social movement which recruited between 50 000 and 60 000 volunteers for each general election. Its 'civic education' campaign section made grants to NGOs for independent projects for grassroots civic education. Thus PollWatch used state resources to mobilize the people, and strengthen the network of civil society throughout Thailand.

PollWatch fought for years to transform itself from an *ad hoc* body which was only active during election campaigns into a permanent organization. As noted above, this was finally accomplished with the formation of the Election Commission of Thailand (ECT) in 1997. The ECT combines the mission of the Interior Ministry with that of PollWatch through its activities: scheduling elections, designating constituencies, civic education campaigns, monitoring campaign spending and receiving complaints about poll fraud. Since the ECT is quite similar to the Commission on Elections in the Philippines, the next sub-section suggests both the problems and the possibilities that lay ahead for Thai electoral politics.

### The Philippines

Philippine elections are characterized by the three Gs: Guns, Goons and Gold. Much like Thai elections, votes are illegally obtained through a mixture of persuasion, coercion, and official manipulation. Similar patterns of vote-buying and the bribery of government officials are commonplace. Violence and intimidation are more widespread in the Philippines where warlord candidates carry private armies in tow: 953 violence-related incidents which resulted in 447 casualties were reported in the four elections between 1986 and 1992.[28] Volunteers of the election watchdog organizations are also targeted: four volunteers were killed and 160 injured in the 1986 campaign alone.[29] Villaneuva argues that much of this violence comes from the nature of Philippine politics; for common people 'candidates are not just persons to be chosen but heroes to be revered, and if need be, defended by any means' (Villaneuva, 182). There are not enough police to enforce the election law and keep order.

To address these enduring problems an independent body called the Commission on Elections (Comelec) was formed in 1940 to organize the elections for the American colonial regime.[30] Though Comelec is independent of the government, it is given the full support of the bureaucracy. For example, though Comelec has only 5000 full-time regular employees, for the 1992 Presidential elections Comelec used its extraordinary powers to deputize 1.3 million people. This included over 800 000 government officials from the Philippine National Police, the Armed Forces of the Philippines, the

Department of Education, Culture and Sports, and 30 other government agencies.[31] With these resources, Comelec engages in voter education, registration, enforcing election law, running the polls on election day, and counting the election returns.[32] It is given the power to act quickly to settle disputes and adjudicate issues to facilitate campaigning and the elections. Its authority is subject to review only by the Supreme Court.

Even with all these powers – or just because of them – Comelec still has major problems. Even though it is technically independent, the seven Commissioners who run Comelec are appointed by the President, and approved by the Senate. Even though this process is set up so that Commissioners outlast their appointing President's term in office, it is up to the President to determine the strength and character of the Commission. For example, during the Marcos years the Commission was very much a tool of the ruling government, running what came to be known as 'sham elections' which were characterized by widespread fraud. Thus Comelec was among the least trusted government agencies at this time.[33] (This is a potential problem for the Election Commission of Thailand, which is packed with commissioners who come out of corrupt state bureaucracies.) The Commissioners appointed by Corazon Aquino after the 1986 People Power Revolution received more trust, and built up the credibility of Comelec. There were real fears that the 1992 election, the first free Presidential election since 1969, would have huge problems with the 3 Gs. So Comelec put certain measures in place to meet this challenge: a gun ban and a ban on paid political advertising, while free 'Comelec Space' was provided in newspapers and 'Comelec Time' was given on radio and television (Comelec 1992 Report). Such measures restored confidence in the election process and led to a legitimate poll in 1992.[34]

But the common feeling in Manila after the wholesale fraud of the May 1995 election is that the 1992 election was the peak of Comelec's credibility. President Ramos' appointees are seen as, if not partisan, then very inept: 'Since the Comelec waffles and changes its mind from day to day, its decisions are not respected.'[35] For example, even though this was the second election which had a Gun Ban to discourage the use of warlord intimidation, Comelec did not enforce its own rules: one candidate marched into the Comelec office itself with a private army in tow, but he still was not disqualified.[36]

Furthermore, Comelec is notorious for taking a month to tabulate national election results. In this way, it actually encourages fraud because candidates can determine where they are losing in the polls and go to pay off the officials in those selected provinces. Thus this new genre of the fraud was called 'wholesale' rather than 'retail' because it had shifted from buying individual votes in local polling places to purchasing the election at the provincial level. Provincial Comelec committees engaged in a form of corruption that has come to be known as 'Operation Add-Subtract' where the local numbers were 'massaged' in the provincial tallies to favour certain government candidates over others. For example, by Comelec's own count, 80 731 votes were added and subtracted out of 279 751 voters in the province of Ilocos Norte: 29 per cent of the votes are suspect.[37] Maambong's argument is that even though there were problems in the tabulation, they did not affect the outcome of the election. This begs the question because candidates who Add-Subtract are breaking the law, and thus should be disqualified.

The charges of wholesale fraud became even more meaningful when a former Senator who was running under the ruling party banner complained of widespread fraud which benefited other government candidates in lots of 20 000 and 30 000 votes.[38] This was seen as a failure of Comelec because it was Comelec officials who sold the tabulations. Hence one of the reasons that this former Senator made an 'electoral protest' was so Comelec officials would be made responsible for their actions. But Comelec itself is more concerned with the carrot of 'Values Formation' training of its officials, than with the stick of disciplinary action, for such problems were not described as fraud, but as a 'management problem'. Only 2 per cent of the Comelec staff were sanctioned for this wholesale fraud (Maambong, Interview). As of 1995, no Comelec official had ever been imprisoned for corruption.

Comelec has become just another bureaucracy – including both the full-time employees and special election workers – with the same problems of influence peddling that plague any bureaucracy. Much like in Thailand, everyone knows what is happening, but because it is difficult to find hard evidence, it is difficult to prove these charges in court. So in 1983 the National Movement for Free Elections (NAMFREL) was founded as a nationwide non-partisan umbrella organization of civic, religious, professional, business, labour, educational and youth organizations. It gathered together the 'informed and concerned' citizenry to promote an honest and meaningful election as a citizen's arm of Comelec. NAMFREL was formed to challenge the Marcos dictatorship through the election process. While PollWatch relied on the infrastructure of the Thai state, NAMFREL was formed with the co-operation of the Catholic church and Manila's economic elite in the Makati Business Club. These two organizations provided NAMFREL with both influence and infrastructure to place 500 000 volunteers at polling stations all over the Philippine archipelago for the 1986 presidential election. The reasoning was that Marcos could only win by cheating: buying votes and manipulating the vote count. Again, like PollWatch, NAMFREL organizes two sets of activities. First, during the election campaign NAMFREL engaged in civic education programmes in order to change the election from the patronage of personality politics to a more democratic issue-based politics. Second, on election day it sought to place a volunteer 'poll watcher' at each polling station in the country to guard against blatant electoral fraud.

Hence, while Thailand is becoming more like the Philippines by formalizing neutral election watchdogs through the transformation of PollWatch into the ECT, the Philippines has gone in the opposite direction by forming independent private organizations like NAMFREL to watch over official bodies like Comelec. What the Philippine and Thai electoral systems tell us is that there is no silver bullet to eliminate election fraud; they both are trying to strike a balance between public and private, formal and informal, political and economic.

**Indonesia**

Like Nero fiddling as Rome burned, Soeharto was sworn in for his seventh term as the President of Indonesia in March 1998 in the midst of the financial crisis which soon became a political revolution which consumed him in May. This surreal event highlighted the deep-seated corruption in a regime that put Indonesia at the top of the list of the most corrupt nations of the world.[39] Indonesians themselves describe the system as KKN: corruption, collusion, nepotism. In addition to the economic corruption which enriched Soeharto's family and friends, the regime also engaged in electoral fraud.

The government's manipulation of the election process was most graphically shown in the summer of 1996 when Megawati Soekarnoputri was ousted from the leadership of the opposition Indonesian Democratic Party (PDI). This action was taken by an unconstitutional party conference which her rival Suryadi organized with the help of the Indonesian military. The military was uncomfortable with the potential challenge that Megawati posed to President Soeharto in the March 1998 presidential election, for she is the daughter of Soeharto's predecessor, Soekarno, who represents the 'chief rival in the national myth'.[40] Thus this illegal conference replaced her with the more pliant Suryadi.

Then in July when Megawati and her supporters refused to recognize the change and surrender the PDI's Jakarta headquarters, the police and Suryadi's supporters attacked. This triggered what was – up until May 1998 – Jakarta's worst riot since the founding of the New Order regime in 1965–6.[41] In addition to such direct violence, government propaganda also used anti-communist rhetoric to de-legitimize Megawati and her supporters, recalling the terrifying memory of the political blood-bath of 1965–6 against 'communists' and 'sympathizers'.[42] This blatant government interference in internal party affairs appalled Indonesians. The heavy-handed official overreaction alienated moderates and made radical solutions more popular.[43]

Such state intervention into the internal workings of the three official political parties is nothing new. Indeed, the government used 'unashamedly gross' measures to try to block Megawati's election to the leadership of the PDI in 1993. But she received popular support from thousands of people who came to the party convention despite serious intimidation. Hence it came as a 'great embarrassment' when all of the government's efforts to block Megawati's election as the PDI leader failed in the end.[44]

Elections in New Order Indonesia are not quite as straightforward as in the parliamentary systems of Thailand, Singapore and Malaysia, or the presidential system of the Philippines. The Indonesian president is elected indirectly by the People's Consultative Assembly (MPR) every 5 years. They have always elected the same man, Soeharto, and actually Soeharto has been the only person nominated for the seven successive terms since the election of 1971 (thus Megawati posed a threat to his legitimacy just by contemplating running as an opposition candidate). Soeharto's regular election success is not surprising since the president himself appoints 600 of the 1000 MPR members. The other 400 are elected as members of parliament, the People's Representative Assembly (DPR). The DPR is dominated by the ruling government party Golong Karya (Golkar, 'Functional Group')[45] which has always had the majority of votes in parliament.[46]

In addition to giving Golkar the use of the 'resources both political and financial of the military, presidency, and state bureaucracy' (Robison, 1993, 44), the state has engineered the political party system. In 1973 the ten existing political parties were forcibly fused into three convenient groupings, while the formation of new political parties was prohibited. In addition to Golkar, there is the Islamic-based United Development Party (PPP) and the Indonesian Democratic Party (PDI) which groups together secular nationalists. And within these parties there are still further state controls which pose considerable difficulties for a critical opposition. All members must pass government vetting before becoming eligible candidates: though Megawati was a sitting MP, neither she nor her faction members passed the test in 1997. The 1997 campaign also included a tightening of election rules, making it the most stringent of the New Order regime:

> During the 25-day campaign, the large outdoor rallies and motorcades that made a festival of past elections [were] banned. Lists of campaign speakers [were] submitted for Government approval and texts of radio and television speeches [were] reviewed in advance.[47]

Although party politics is banned from rural areas between elections, Golkar was able to campaign for years in advance through its local organizations. This included military harassment of opposition candidates in 1997. Campaigning was actually limited to nine days; in an effort to limit political conflict between partisans of the three parties, candidates could only campaign on every third day. The review of campaign literature was necessary because candidates were not allowed to criticize either the government or its policies. Golkar candidates could more easily obtain permits to hold campaign events, and studies showed that they received more and positive coverage in the media.

In addition to such 'tacit support' Indonesian elections experience outright violations of election law in both voting and counting. Civil servants, who are by definition members of Golkar, are often issued with two voting cards: one for their home address, and the other for the office. Vote counting is also not transparent: though representatives of all parties are allowed to be present at the counting, poll watchers from opposition parties are often not allowed to see the count. Electoral fraud is thus systemic rather than haphazard; its purpose is to ensure Golkar's victory.[48]

If candidates are lucky enough to overcome all these hurdles, when they take their seats in parliament the MPs are subject to recall if they speak critically of the regime.[49] Thus any opposition is caged in parliament, leading many in Indonesia to see the role of MPs as confined to *datang, duduk, dengar, diam, duit* (turn up, sit down, listen, keep quiet, get paid).[50]

There have been various responses over the years to such blatant manipulation of the electoral process. It should be noted that there is nothing inherently undemocratic about Indonesia. Indeed its multiparty election in 1955 has been described as the 'most open and participatory elections held anywhere in Southeast Asia since World War II: full adult suffrage, a competitive press, very little violence or gerrymandering, remarkably little emphasis on money, and so on.'[51] But since political parties and voting procedures have been very much under state control under Soeharto's New Order, the main political tactic has not been to vote for an opposition party, but to boycott the sham elections entirely. For example, prominent student activists organized a 'boycott the vote' campaign after the abuses in the 1971 election. With such continued interference in the 1997 election, voters again opted for the 'golput – white group'. Since the three official parties are known by their colors, support for Golput means a boycott of the official parties. Heryanto argues that far from being an example of de-politicization, the boycott campaigns can be quite participatory and vigorous. As the newspaper *Media Indonesia* writes: 'Golput is like a fourth contesting party' (Mydans, 6). The Golput campaign was also supported by Megawati who announced that she would not vote (Eklöf, 1188).

Curiously, parallel to the rise of Megawati and the oppositionalist politics of the PDI in 1996, other groups responded to the government's manipulation of the election in a new way. The Independent Election Monitoring Committee (KIPP) was set up on 15 March 1996 by a group of human rights workers, unionists, environmentalists and religious leaders, and enjoyed broadbased support.[52] Both established (opposition) parties also welcomed KIPP. One of the major organizers of KIPP was the Legal Aid Institute (LBH) which was initially formed by former supporters of the New Order regime who had been alienated by the 'bulldozer tactics' of 1971 and 1977 elections. The LBH has always seen itself in a much broader context than legal issues, increasingly seeing itself as an 'engine of democratization' (Aspinall, 228). The KIPP organizers were in contact with Namfrel and PollWatch, and organized a series of seminars to benefit from the Philippine and Thai experience.[53]

Unfortunately, the high-profile campaign against Megawati was preceded by a campaign waged against the establishment of KIPP. Various official groups, including the youth wing of the ruling Golkar Party which is known for its strong-arm tactics, sought to ban KIPP and harassed its members in various ways. Critics of KIPP argued that an independent election monitoring body was unnecessary since there was already a government-sponsored watchdog in place for the 1997 elections.[54] Other groups were more forceful in their arguments: Golkar youth members burned down the LBH office where KIPP activists had been holding meetings in Medan, Sumatra. Soon after, the secretary general of KIPP was denounced as a communist, which as we saw above, is a very serious thing in Indonesia.[55] Thai and Filipino representatives from NAMFREL and PollWatch were also harassed when they were invited to come to Indonesia to share their experiences with KIPP.[56] In the end, KIPP was another casualty of the 1996 Jakarta riots; though it was not dissolved, its activities were severely limited to monitoring a few hundred polling stations. Thus people opted again for boycott tactics.

Such a pattern of crushing independent groups (even when they pose comparatively little threat) and co-opting civil society in an arm of the ruling party is characteristic of the New Order of Indonesian politics: independent political parties were crushed in the 1960s, student organizations in the 1970s, NGOs in the 1980s, and the media in the 1990s. As soon as independent groups start to challenge the regime, they are targeted for control.[57] Thus the ruling party does not need to buy votes to maintain its power, it merely needs to utilize the political machine that is already in place. The distinction between state and society has been effaced to the benefit of the ruling party.

This is what makes the prospect of political reforms promised by Soeharto's replacement B.J. Habibie so exciting. He guided the country towards general elections in mid-1999, and has scheduled a special meeting of the MPR on 22 December 1999 to select a new president. More than simply scheduling new elections, there is strong pressure for reforming the entire election system. The 'Commission II' has been charged with formulating three basic laws covering political parties, elections, and membership of the House and MPR. Political parties were already starting to form as of August 1998. These changes are not as drastic as might appear. A plan for such election reforms already existed; it was commissioned by Soeharto in 1994, but he decided then to hold back on the changes.[58] It is likely that the limit on the number of political parties will be lifted, and all expect that Golkar will not survive these changes. It is too closely associated with the Soeharto regime, and more importantly, 'bereft of Soeharto's patronage and government largesse, only a third of Golkar's 325 legislators would win votes in a fair election.'[59] Though Megawati was not an active participant in the May revolution, she and the PDI are well-placed to benefit from electoral reforms.

### Singapore and Malaysia

The governments of Singapore and Malaysia also have had comparable patterns of co-opting the independent and critical organizations of civil society into the sphere of ruling party control – a very different relationship from PollWatch's critically co-operative relationship with the Thai government. In Malaysia the ruling United Malays National Organization (UMNO) – which is the leading party in the Barisan Nasional (United Front) coalition – has also presided over an 'uneven and probably unsystematic erosion of democratic institutions' which brought the media, the bureaucracy and the judiciary under government control in the 1980s, and compromised the independence of the constitutional monarchy in the 1990s.[60]

In Singapore the policy has been to domesticate all sites of opposition, as well as co-opting the bureaucracy and the judiciary. Organized labour was the first casualty in the 1960s, and then student activism led to the Societies Act (1967), which restricted legally registered independent organizations from commenting on politics outside their narrow expertise under threat of de-registration. This was quite successful in limiting the institutional influence of civil society because it prevented groups from forming alliances amongst themselves or with opposition political parties.[61] In the mid-1980s NGO and religious activism were severely restricted (Rodan 1996:114, 100–1). Unlike Thailand and the Philippines which have segments of the media which are independent and critical, the domestic media in Singapore – television, radio and newspapers – is either owned or controlled by people sympathetic to the ruling People's Action Party (PAP).[62] This, like a similar media configuration in Malaysia, is an important part of collapsing the distinction between state and society. The official and sympathetic media have been instrumental in aiding the ruling parties in turning their own ideology into official ideology which excludes opposition: Shared Values in Singapore, Vision 2020 in Malaysia, and Pancasila in Indonesia.

Certainly, even with such strong government intervention, democracy has been more stable and elections are much freer and fairer in Malaysia and Singapore than in Indonesia. Although vote-buying and money politics was an issue in the 1995 Malaysian general election[63] and the 1996 UMNO election,[64] Singapore and Malaysia both generally pride themselves on being free from corruption[65] – especially in comparison with their Southeast Asian neighbours of Indonesia, the Philippines, and Thailand.[66] But such surface judgements of corruption-free democratic politics are misleading, for political space is defined quite narrowly in Singapore and Malaysia.[67] Politics is largely restricted to professional politicians in government-approved political parties in Singapore.[68] The rule of law in Malaysia and Singapore does not protect civil society. Rather the law serves as a tool that the state uses to restrict activity in civil society. So a legal concept of corruption does not do much to help us understand the workings of politics in these countries. But if we conceptualize corruption and political life in a broader moral sense, then corruption can be seen as more than the legal transgressions of individuals giving or taking bribes; it can be seen as indicative of the 'moral health' of a society.

> Corruption occur[s] . . . not because exchanges took place between politicians and a citizen, and not because of what was exchanged or the motives we might attribute to the participants. Rather, the transactions were corrupt because they avoided the democratic process, which is not to be regarded simply as the institutional

formalities of politics but as embodying major values – representation, accountability, open debate, equality – in its own right.[69]

With this broader understanding of corruption then the 'unhealthy' practices of politics in Singapore and Malaysia become clearer.

The electoral corruption in these two countries is not so obvious as the vote buying and the faulty counting in Thailand and the Philippines. The balloting is not rigged; the ruling parties' strategies and techniques of electoral fraud are more subtle and sophisticated. They work more through the manipulation of the electoral process where biased government officials use tried-and-true methods such as political co-optation, gerrymandering, and selective coercion (Jesudason, 129; Jomo 1996; Rodan 1996a:102; Rodan 1996b; Crouch 1993, 153–4; Rodan 1997). Thus there is a difference of kind rather than of degree between the electoral practices in Singapore and Malaysia on the one hand, and the Indonesian state's use of 'occasional political violence, witch hunts, and propaganda' on the other (Heryanto, 242). In Singapore and Malaysia it is hard for meaningful elections to be held in an 'electoral system where the rules are stacked against' non-ruling parties (Jesudason, 142). For example, since elections in Singapore and Malaysia involve very short official campaigns of nine days, most of the canvassing happens between elections. Since the media is very close to the government, it is difficult to get opposition views across in the press. It is also difficult to spread the campaign message through more traditional methods; state officials tend to use regulations selectively to harass opposition parties. Candidates need to apply for permits to talk to constituents; while the ruling party MPs get them easily, applications made by opposition candidates are often denied. Likewise, permits for public fora organized by opposition parties typically come only a day or two before the event. Thus these fora cannot be properly publicized in advance, because the permit can require a change of venue.[70] It is therefore difficult to run a campaign from outside the ruling party.

Still, the electoral fraud is not obvious, and certainly does not fit the narrow legalistic definitions of corruption in Singapore and Malaysia.[71] If opposition members complain publicly about such harassment, they risk the arbitrary wrath of the Internal Security Act (ISA) of both Singapore and Malaysia, where the state can hold people indefinitely without charge. Though the ISA originated as a move against communist insurgency and race riots, the ISA has also been effectively used to limit the scope of debate among opposition politicians and members of civil society.[72] More recently, the method of choice in Singapore has been to sue opposition politicians for defamation in civil court, thus leading to the bankrupting of numerous leading opposition politicians.[73] Because – as in many other countries – bankrupt citizens lose their right to run for parliament, this is an effective way of controlling critical voices. Understandably, among Singaporeans there is a 'strong fear of persecution for involvement with opposition parties. The long list of candidates and activists taken to court by government members serves as a strong negative example to would-be participants in the political process' (Rodan 1996a:114).

And if voters did consider electing opposition candidates, both UMNO and the PAP have shown that there would be a 'political recession'; the provision of public services and development funds has suffered considerably in opposition territory.[74] Thus the practice in Singapore and Malaysia often is to threaten voters rather than woo them.[75] With this in mind, it is not surprising that between 1968 and 1981 the PAP held a parliamentary monopoly. Likewise, the UMNO-led BN coalition has not only won all nine elections in Malaysian history, it consistently gains the two-thirds majority necessary to change the Malaysian constitution. But as Rodan concludes for Singapore, in a way that is also meaningful for Malaysia, 'parliamentary elections constitute a stunted political expression, not the end product of broad contests over social and political power.'[76]

## Avenues for anti-corruption reform in Southeast Asia

As we have seen, corruption works differently in different political economies and different political cultures, and thus reforms to combat corruption need to address the specificities of each case. In other words, the reforms that might effectively control corruption in the United States might just as easily encourage corruption in China; reforms that might work to reduce corruption in Thailand might exacerbate it in Malaysia. Michael Johnston has put forward a schema for understanding the complexities of corruption in a way that recognizes the particularities (and morals) of each society while still making meaningful generalizations in terms of four 'ideal types' of corruption. Certainly, as we will see, some of the Southeast Asian countries fit into the categories more snugly than others, and Johnston's approach to the politics and economics of corruption is quite useful in encouraging a more complex discussion.

Johnston argues that corruption is not an absolute judgement, but rather comes from an imbalance in the relationship between state and society on the one hand, and in the relationship between wealth and power on the other. Thus such a framing of political and economic relationships reinforces the idea that state and society are not contradictory, wealth and power are not ideally separated: rather than being sets of polar opposites they are balanced on a continuum.[77] Serious imbalances on either continuum foster corruption, and Johnston argues that 'political and economic reforms can aid both democratization and anti-corruption efforts'.[78] In this way he ties together political and economic issues with the stated goal of sustainable democracy in mind; a goal that is shared by the election monitoring groups in Thailand, the Philippines and Indonesia, as well as many elements of civil society in the other Southeast Asian countries.

To categorize a country and thus suggest suitable reforms, Johnston suggests that we examine the balances and imbalances along two general continua. Firstly, the balance between the accessibility and autonomy of political elites: is the system closed where the elite are not subject to public scrutiny, thus too autonomous, or is it not professional and thus open to manipulation by specific interest groups? Secondly, Johnston suggests we examine the balance between wealth and power. Where are the opportunities: do people use wealth to buy power or power to acquire wealth? Reforms seek to restore the specific balances: where the elites' autonomy decisively outweighs their accessibility, reforms need to open up channels of mass participation, accountability and bureaucratic access. But where accessibility to elites weakens their professionalism, reforms need to be made to protect elites from excessive private influence. Where economic opportunities greatly exceed political opportunities, the depth and equality of political competition needs to be enhanced. And where political opportunities greatly exceed economic opportunities, broad-based economic growth needs to be encouraged (Johnston, 1997:68).

By assessing the imbalances in these two categories, Johnston charts four syndromes of corruption and suggests four distinct reform strategies. I will briefly outline these four syndromes and relate them to the five Southeast Asian countries considered in this chapter. Firstly, Johnston discusses 'Interest group bidding' where the accessibility of elites exceeds autonomy, and economic opportunities are more plentiful than political ones. Thus interest groups are strong and use economic pressure – campaign contributions, gifts, bribes – to seek influence from political elites who are vulnerable because they lack sufficient autonomy. Johnston states that this form of corruption is typical of liberal democracies, and gives the United States, Germany and the United Kingdom as examples. The PAP in Singapore justifies its firm control over civil society and opposition because it is trying to avoid such strong interest group politics; but as we have seen, it goes to the other extreme and thus creates an imbalance of elite hegemony. There are hints of 'Interest group bidding' in Malaysia's recent 'money politics' scandals; still one commentator notes that they are not necessarily for the benefit of interest groups, so much as 'blatant abuses of power for self-aggrandizement' (Jomo, 1996, 97).

The reforms suggested by Johnston to re-establish a balance include strengthening official autonomy and protecting the boundaries between state and society, while enhancing internal bureaucratic accountability (Johnston 1997:75). Reforms should also include such things as campaign finance laws and lobbying regulations which are intended to protect political competition, and thus even-out the imbalance between economic and political opportunities – such political reforms are suggested by Jomo for Malaysia (1996, 110–11).

Johnston's second category of political corruption, 'Elite hegemony', is characterized as more ominous. In this situation, political opportunities outweigh economic ones, while the elite is more autonomous than accessible. Thus an entrenched political elite faces little political competition and few demands for accountability. Johnston points to the examples of China and Japan where the boundaries between state and society are weak. Thus there is a danger of an organized and systemic 'hypercorruption'. Reform efforts in Elite hegemony are sporadic, and are usually manipulated to the elite's political advantage.

This is helpful in describing the situation in Singapore and where the political and economic elites are intertwined. A close collaboration between government and business elites is seen as one of the defining features of the 'East Asian economic miracle'.[79] But as the previous section demonstrated, the imbalance between state and society in Singapore and Malaysia is quite serious, and was one of the causes of the severity of the 1997 economic crisis. In such a situation, Johnston writes that genuine reform efforts should encourage broader political competition and the opening of more routine lines of accountability and access to elites, re-making them into 'public servants' (Johnston 1997:77). This would entail enhancing mass participation, opening up and routinizing bureaucratic channels, emphasizing legality, and expanding political competition. Johnston recommends that this can be done by enhancing the independence of the bureaucracy, the judiciary and the press from the entrenched elites, as well as promoting more competitive elections and nurturing a stronger civil society. Unfortunately, Johnston writes that in 'Elite hegemony' anti-corruption campaigns are usually directed at specific opposition politicians: this is certainly true of Singapore where key opposition leaders have been charged with corruption. Though Jomo suggests such broad-based political reforms for Malaysia, he does not consider the full complexity of the situation; economic reforms are not part of his anti-corruption strategy (Jomo, 1996, 110–11).

Though the imbalance between wealth and power is not as serious as it is in China, it is still an important issue that needs to be addressed in tandem with political reforms in Singapore and Malaysia. As Johnston recommends, property rights and economic enterprises also need to be protected. For example, the fragility of Singapore's economic success was shown in the crisis of 1997, as well as the negative growth of the 1985–6 recession. The economic downturns are so sudden and extreme because Singapore's economy relies on a combination of state enterprises and multinational capital which are seriously out of balance with domestic capital.[80] The Singaporean bourgeoisie has been squeezed by the government's development policies, and thus is not a strong force. One reason for Singapore and Malaysia's courting of multinational capital is that these foreign concerns are not in a position legitimately to demand political power, as would a domestic bourgeoisie. Economic reforms that encourage local enterprise, and thus restore the balance, are needed to ensure economic and political stability. Social justice has become an important theme in Malaysian politics, and to a lesser extent in Singapore. Rapid economic growth has led to an increasing gap between the rich and the poor, and when the economy soured, it led to social unrest.

Johnston's third category is 'Fragmented patronage/extended factionalism' which also has the distinct danger of becoming 'hand-over-fist' corruption. In such systems, political opportunities exceed economic ones, and the bureaucrats are more accessible than autonomous. Thus the elites seek power in a setting of intense political competition with few economic opportunities. The path to power involves cultivating personal politics rather than institutionalizing political parties. Because access to wealth and power is based on personal ties, Fragmented patronage is difficult to control: followers always have political alternatives. Johnston argues that this quadrant is the most politically unstable of the four categories, and the danger of extreme corruption is most pronounced (Johnston 1997:73, 78).

Though corruption in Thailand used to take the form of Elite hegemony,[81] the rapid economic growth and the weakening of the bureaucracy in relation to economic forces and parliamentary power has Fragmented patronage and led to powerful factions. The transition is not complete, thus the ill-fit at times with Johnston's categories and prescriptions. Even with these caveats, Johnston's description of Fragmented patronage/extended factionalism reads like a catalogue of Thai and Philippine political practices. Political parties are transient and/or weak. For example, one of the most damning criticisms of Cory Aquino is that she did not institutionalize the 'People Power' movement into a political party to carry on the democratic reforms past her administration. The results of the 1992 presidential campaign attest to the fragmented nature of Philippine electoral politics: Fidel Ramos won the election with just over 20 per cent of the vote. Thailand's parliamentary system invariably produces a weak coalition government which is characterized by infighting among political parties as well as factions within the major parties. In both countries, bureaucrats and police are not independent, often being in close personal relationships with elected politicians and provincial capitalists. Political opportunities outweigh economic ones in the Philippines where there was an elected office for every 1400 voters in the mid-1980s (Anderson, 1996, 24); the number of offices certainly increased with the 1991 Local Government Code. Opportunities are similarly skewed towards politics in the Thai countryside, while they are more balanced in Bangkok where economic growth in the private sector has been quite strong from the the early 1980s to 1997.

Johnston notes that it is difficult to reform such systems since balanced and orderly political competition will be difficult to establish as long as it is clear that playing the role of opposition is of little value for its own sake: the real political opportunities lie in the scramble for the spoils. Indeed, election expenses (including vote-buying and bribing officials) are commonly seen as investments that will pay off from the use of ministerial offices. Banharn Silapa-acha, the Prime Minister chosen in the 1995 Thai election, is well-known for saying that he could not 'afford' to be in opposition for too long. Johnston notes that in such a situation, anti-corruption reforms are often raised as a club to use against political enemies, and are unlikely to be much more than a slogan. This was a common criticism of Chuan Leekpai's 1995 election campaign which focused more on negative campaigning than outlining what his Democrat Party could do for Thailand. Furthermore, Johnston notes that law-enforcement officials will be as politically vulnerable as politicians and bureaucrats, for neither side can count on much support from the other – PollWatch and the Philippine election monitoring groups' frustrations with police and bureaucrats bear this argument out.

To address the corruption in Fragmented patronage, Johnston suggests that reforms increase elite autonomy and broad-based economic growth (Johnston 1997:78). Reforms need to establish a clearer distinction between public and private. This would involve enhancing the professional standards and protections for jurists, bureaucrats and law enforcement personnel. To balance the fragmentation of this scenario, Johnston recommends reforms which would facilitate the consolidation of a limited number of strong broad-based political parties and the proliferation of interest groups in civil society beyond the personal domination of political figures. The Philippines is certainly strong in its wide array of groups in civil society; Thailand's popular sector is also growing, but needs more institutional support and space.[82] Once there is meaningful law enforcement and the protection of civil liberties, Johnston reasons, then people can deal with the state through official channels rather than personal connections. Indeed, he notes that such a package of reforms needs to entail 'a real commitment, on the part of both citizens and elites, to the value and necessity of the state – not as a coercive force, and certainly not as a resource to be plundered, but rather as a guarantor of important processes and rights whose rules must be taken seriously' (Johnston, 1997:78).

Lastly, Johnston argues that broad-based and sustained economic growth must be coupled with these political reforms. This of course is a major problem in all of East Asia, where the economies are contracting rather than growing – and there is a risk that the IMF prescription for Thailand and Indonesia is wrong, leading to austere economic conditions. But even in the heyday of the economic miracle the growth was uneven. Even when the Philippines' economic growth was increasing in the early 1990s, it still needed to be spread out from the ruling elites to farmers and workers throughout the archipelago if corruption was to be curbed. Even while Thailand's economic growth was strong, it was uneven, benefiting Bangkok and a few provincial cities while leaving the countryside behind. As many of the Thai commentators note, a more prosperous village community would not be as easily manipulated by political elites.

Johnston's fourth scenario is 'Patronage machines', where political opportunities exceed economic ones and elite autonomy exceeds the accessibility of elites (Johnston 1997:73–4, 78–9). In this situation, a well-entrenched elite manipulates scarce economic rewards to control political competition even where there are significant political opportunities. Political parties are well-disciplined, hierarchical and extend elite power into society. Such systematic corruption can be accompanied by intimidation and violence. Johnston argues that this is characteristic of machine politics often found in early twentieth-century America (Tammany Hall in New York),[83] as well as rapidly urbanizing nations in the late twentieth-century. He cites Indonesia as an example of a well-oiled Patronage machine, and our analysis serves to confirm this. Though the IMF prescription aims to uproot systemic corruption in the political economy, politics remains the path to wealth; the reform movement in Indonesia has yet to touch the fabulous fortunes of Soeharto's children and other favourites. Still, Johnston notes that the elite's monopoly over patronage means that the operatives in this system do not need to be bribed again and again. Though there are contradictions in Patronage machines, Johnston argues that they are not likely to produce rampant corruption since the elites profit – both economically and politically – from the status quo. As opposed to the Fragmented patronage style of corruption, the Patronage machines are long-term ventures; the main damage to the political system comes from stagnation and postponed change rather than a sudden crisis or collapse. Though Soeharto is now gone, his regime remains in place. B.J. Habibie's cabinet contains many familiar faces.

Reforms to a Patronage machine involve enhancing access to elites and expanding economic opportunities. Enhancing access to elites reduces the need to work through political patrons, Johnston argues, while expanding economic opportunities reduces dependency on the machine's favours. Economic growth must be accompanied by political changes, otherwise it could be transformed into the Elite hegemony with its more extreme forms of corruption. Once again, Johnston's prescriptions sound as if they are directed squarely at the Indonesian situation: opening up electoral politics, increasing the independence of parliamentarians and civil servants, non-politicized access to civil servants from private interests, and a general strengthening of independent groups in civil society. It remains to be seen whether the 'reform' team of B.J. Habibie will be able to deliver these changes.

## Conclusion

This chapter has considered the politics of corruption and reform in Southeast Asia through a short description of corruption and society in Thailand, the Philippines, Indonesia, Malaysia and Singapore. In a sense, Thailand and the Philippines have more 'developed' forms of corruption because electoral fraud comes not just from state manipulations – as in the other three states – but from more recognizably political-economic forces. Though the state's looser grip on society has led to fragmented forms of patronage and corruption in Thailand and the Philippines, it also opens up avenues for change. The media and civil society in general have more leeway – this is certainly why independent election monitoring bodies have been active in Thailand and the Philippines – and thus afford more popular (as opposed to elite) solutions to the challenges of corruption and development.

Johnston's analysis also shows that the reforms necessary for these five states differ considerably according to their specific imbalances.

For example, while Singapore, Malaysia and Indonesia need to address the problems of elite autonomy by opening up bureaucratic channels, Thailand and the Philippines need to strengthen state–society boundaries in order to protect administrative autonomy from political manipulation. While Thailand and the Philippines need to reform their political systems to encourage fewer and stronger political parties, reforms for the other countries entail an enhancing of mass participation. While Thailand, the Philippines and Indonesia need to professionalize their civil service and listen more to technocrats, Singapore's civil service and government are too technocratic, not responding well to popular pressures.

The analysis also suggests that the lesson for all five countries is that political and economic problems are linked, thus reforms need to address both of these areas. For example, it is common to hear that a comparison of reform strategies in China and Russia has shown that there is a trade-off between economics and politics: economic reforms need to come before political reforms. But Johnston's arguments suggest that each path to development leads to its own set of serious problems of corruption: China has Elite hegemony, while Russia has Fragmented patronage. In Southeast Asia this suggests that Thailand's and the Philippines' focus on democratic reform and Indonesia, Singapore and Malaysia's dominant interest in economic development also lead to their own sets of problems. The economic crisis of 1997 has only served to reinforce these prescriptions. Rather than economic development and political openness being at odds, each country needs to find a balance along both the continua of economic and political affairs.

## Notes

1  Adam Schwarz interview with Amien Rais, 'A Sense of Disgust', *Far Eastern Economic Review,* 14 May 1998, pp. 26–7.
2  Richard Robison, 'Currency Meltdown: the End of Asian Capitalism?' *NIAS nytt: Nordic Newsletter of Asian Studies,* No. 2, June 1998, pp. 5–9. An expanded version of this article appeared *World Development,* August 1998.
3  A comical case in point is the writings of Francis Fukuyama. In February 1998 he finished an article called 'Asian Values and the Asian Crisis' by declaring, 'The remaining years of the 20th century thus promise to be difficult and eventful ones for people on both sides of the Pacific. It would be nice if, for the duration, we could be spared further lectures either about the special advantages or about the special deficiencies of Asian values' (*Commentary,* February 1998). This is certainly good advice. Unfortunately,

Fukuyama has been playing both sides without explaining his change of heart. In 1989 he triumphantly declared the final victory of Liberalism and Western values in his famous essay, 'The End of History?' (*National Interest*, Summer 1989). In 1995 he switched triumphant mode to extol the uniqueness and success of Asian values ('Confucianism and Democracy', *Journal of Democracy*, 6:1, January 1995).

4  For a view of the crisis of Asian values in the Korean press, see Kim Young-hie, 'Debate on Asian Values', *Korea Focus*, 6:2, May–June 1998, pp. 121–3; and Junn Sung-chull, 'Economic Crisis and Asian Values', *Korea Focus*, 6:2, May–June 1998, pp. 126–8.

5  There is an ancient Thai word for corruption, *charatbungluang*, which means 'cheat the people, deceive the government'. But for various reasons it is not always used, and the new loan-word was forged.

6  Lucian W. Pye, 'Money Politics and Transitions to Democracy in East Asia', *Asian Survey*, 37:3, March 1997, pp. 213–28.

7  Chalmers Johnson, 'Tanaka Kakuei, Structural Corruption, and the Advent of Machine Politics in Japan', *Journal of Japan Studies*, 12:1, 1986, pp. 1–28.

8  Chalmers Johnson, *Japan: Who Governs? The Rise of the Developmental State*, New York: WW Norton & Company, 1995, pp. 210–11.

9  Pasuk Phongphaichit and Sungsidh Piriyarangsan, *Corruption and Democracy in Thailand*, Bangkok: The Political Economy Centre, Faculty of Economics, Chualongkorn University, 1994.

10  Singapore has had an uninterrupted constitutional regime since independence, while Malaysia has had a parliamentary regime except for a two-year period of emergency powers after the 1969 racial riots.

11  Edmund Terence Gomez, 'Electoral Funding of General, State and Party Elections in Malaysia', *Journal of Contemporary Asia*, 26:1, 1996, pp. 90–1.

12  Inspect the Front (column), 'A concise handbook of electorocrats in 1995', *The Manager Daily*, 20–21 May 1995, p. 18.

13  Also see Gordon Fairclough, 'Rural Reality', *Far Eastern Economic Review*, 29 June 1995, pp. 15–16.

14  Vitit Muntarbhorn and Charles Taylor, *Roads to Democracy: Human Rights and Democratic Development in Thailand*, Montreal: The International Centre for Human Rights and Democratic Development, 1994.

15  Editorial, *Thai Rat*, 28 October 1990, as cited in Daniel Arghiros, *Rural Transformation and Local Politics in a Central Thai District*, PhD dissertation, University of Hull, 1993, p. 152.

16  Sombat Chantornvong, *Leuktangwikrit: panha lae thang ok* (Thai elections in crisis: problems and solutions), Bangkok: Kopfai Publishing, 1993, pp. 13–16.

17  On Thai parties and the workings of factions see James Ockey, 'Political parties, factions and corruption in Thailand', *Modern Asian Studies*, 1994, 28:2, pp. 251–77.

18  Also see Pasuk and Sungsidh, *Corruption and Democracy*, pp. 51–97, and James Ockey, 'Thai Society and Patterns of Political Leadership', *Asian Survey*, 36:4, April 1996, pp. 345–60.

19  Surin Maisrikrod and Duncan McCargo, 'Electoral Politics: commercialization and exclusion', in Kevin Hewison (ed.), *Politics in Thailand: Democracy and Participation*, London: Routledge, 1998.

20  For more on the religious aspect of vote-buying in Central Thailand, see Arghiros 1993.

21  Duncan McCargo, Interview with Yuttapol Srimungkun, 1 July 1995; Somrudee Nicro, 'Thailand's NIC democracy: studying from general elections', *Pacific Affairs*, 66:2, Summer 1993, pp. 167–82; and Surin and McCargo 1998.

22  'B17 billion likely to be circulated over 45 days', *Bangkok Post*, 24 May 1995. This was a considerable rise from 12 billion baht circulated in 1992. In 1995 a US dollar was worth approximately 25 baht.

23  For a detailed description and analysis of local campaigns, see William A. Callahan and Duncan McCargo, 'Vote-buying in the Thai Northeast: the July 1995 General Election', *Asian Survey*, 36:4, April 1996, pp. 376–92; and William A. Callahan, *Pollwatching, Elections and Civil Society in Southeast Asia*, Aldershot: Ashgate, 1999.

24  *The Nation*, 23 March 1992, p. A3.

25  'Poll-related police raids net 12 000', *Bangkok Post*, 10 July 1995, p. 1. Also see Paul Handley, 'Gave Gun, Will Kill', *Far Eastern Economic Review*, 27 February 1992, p. 20.

26  'Canvassers easy targets on fierce political battlefield', *The Nation*, 7 June 1995, p. A6.

27  Interview in Pichit PollWatch Office, 24 June 1995; 'Local administrators at grave risk', *The Nation*, 7 June 1995, p. A6. 14 canvassers were killed in the September 1992 general election campaign (*Bangkok Post*, 18 June 1995, p. 3).

28  A.B. Villaneuva, 'Parties and Elections in Philippine Politics', *Contemporary Southeast Asia*, 18:2, September 1996, p. 181.

29  National Citizens Movement for Free Elections, *The NAMFREL Report on the February 7, 1986 Philippine Presidential Elections*, Manila: Namfel, 1986, p. 2.

30  David Wurfel, *Filipino Politics: Development and Decay*, Quezon City: Ateneo De Manila Press, 1988, p. 76.

31  *Report of the Commission on Elections to the President and Congress of the Republic of the Philippines On the Conduct of the Synchronized National and Local Elections of May 11, 1992*, Vol. I, Manila: Comelec, 31 January 1993, pp. 1–2.

32  *Election Laws in the Philippines: The Omnibus Election Code*, Quezon City: LEGIS, 1995, pp. 15–20.

33  Kaa Byington, *Bantay ng Bayan: Stories from the Namfrel Crusade 1984–86*, Manila: Bookmark, 1988, p. 81.

34  Miranda argues from survey data that public opinion credited the 'smooth running of the 1992 elections' as one of Aquino's main achievements, especially since they did not see any substantial improvement in 'public welfare' under the Aquino regime (Felipe B. Miranda, 'Democratization in the Philippines: Recent Developments, Trends and Prospects', *Asian Journal of Political Science*, Singapore, 1:1, 1993, pp. 85–112).

35  Editorial, 'Indecisive Comelec', *Philippine Daily Inquirer*, 13 May 1995, Virigilio Galvez, 'Sin, Aquino launch second crusade', *The Nation*, 14 June 1996. Also see editorials in the *Philippine Daily Inquirer*, especially for 10, 13, 14, 17, 24 May 1995. Many thanks to the Friedrich Naumann Stiftung's Manila office and especially Miel Moraleda for providing press clippings.

36  Editorial, 'And foolishness', *Philippine Daily Inquirer*, 10 May 1995.

37  Regalado E. Maambong, 'Memo-Report: Analysis of Corrections Made Based on Retabulations of the Statement of Votes (SOV) Attached to the Provincial/City Certificates of Canvass (COC)', 9 June 1995; Regalado E. Maambong, Interview, 9 August 1995.

38  Aquinaldo Pimentel, Interview, 8 August 1995; Editorial, 'Admission of failure', *Philippine Daily Inquirer*, 24 May 1995.

39  See The Internet Center for Corruption Research's annual Corruption Perception Index where Indonesia scores in the top ten corrupt countries (http://www.gwdg.de/~uwvw/ ).

40  Ariel Heryanto, 'Indonesian Middle-Class Opposition in the 1990s', in Garry Rodan (ed.), *Political Oppositions in Industrializing Asia*, London: Routledge, 1996, p. 258.

41  For an account of the riot and crackdown, see Alliance of Independent Journalists, FORUM-ASIA, and ISAI, *Jakarta Crackdown*, Bangkok: FORUM-ASIA, 1997.

42  Heryanto argues that the New Order regime's legitimating myth of the '30 September 1965 Movement' has 'generated a master narrative of "Communist threats" that has been the crucially determining principle in the restructuring of social relationships and the redefining of social identities and notions of "reality".' (p. 260)

43  Stefan Eklöf, 'The 1997 General Election in Indonesia', *Asian Survey*, 37:12, December 1997, p. 1183; Philip Eldridge, 'Human Rights and Democracy in Indonesia and Malaysia: Emerging Contexts and Discourse', *Contemporary Southeast Asia*, 18:3, December 1996, p. 303.

44  Heryanto, pp. 257–8. Still, Heryanto notes the oblique significance of Megawati's election to the leadership of the PDI: 'What Megawati and her party realistically could do after the election was questionable, but the dramatic defeat of an old authoritarian regime by the common people in a public contest created the perception that a new phase was approaching' (p. 258). And they were right.

45  Golkar is not a revolutionary party, but was formed in response to the founding of the New Order after the blood-bath of 1965–6. Likewise, Golkar is not the ruling party, but the party of the rulers; it does not determine the membership in the government, but on the contrary, its membership is determined by the government, since civil servants are required to join (Richard Robison, 'Indonesia: Tensions in State and Regime', in Kevin Hewison, Richard Robison, and Garry Rodan (eds), *Southeast Asia in the 1990s: Authoritarianism, Democracy & Capitalism*, Sydney: Allen & Unwin, 1993, pp. 45, 67). Others note that Golkar is not a party at all, but an umbrella group of anti-communist organizations formed by the military in 1964G. (Eklöf, p. 1183).

46  Before the parliamentary elections in May 1997, the governing party had already announced its winning total – 70.02 per cent of the vote – which was a 2 per cent rise from the previous election. This prediction enraged the other parties since it seemed to guarantee manipulation. Golkar actually received 74.5 per cent of the vote, mainly because it had undermined the PDI (see Eklöf, pp. 1190–9).

47  Seth Mydans, 'Rulers Spoil Suspense for Voters in Indonesia', *New York Times*, 20 April 1997, p. 6.

48  Eklöf, p. 1192.

49  Heryanto, p. 243.

50  Edward Aspinall, 'The Broadening Base of Political Opposition in Indonesia', in Garry Rodan (ed.), *Political Oppositions in Industrializing Asia*, London: Routledge, 1996, pp. 234–5.

51  Anderson also notes that 'There is not much evidence that the [1955] electoral regime created, in itself, intense social conflict, but the evidence abounds that an electionless Guided Democracy did so' (Benedict R. Anderson, 'Elections and Participation in Three Southeast Asian Countries,' in R.H. Taylor (ed.), *The Politics of Elections in Southeast Asia*, Cambridge: Cambridge University Press, 1996, pp. 29, 31).

52  Eldridge, p. 304; Andreas Harsono, 'Golkar youth seek to ban election monitor', *The Nation*, 26 April 1996, p. A6.

53  I went on the first of these trips in January 1996 to meet with people interested in the workings of a neutral election monitoring group. Trips were planned for Filipino and Thai activists later in 1996.

54  The official election monitoring committee, which was headed ex officio by the attorney general, was not very effective: as of 1995, none of the 462 violations reported in the 1992 election had led to legal action (Eklöf, p. 1193).

55  'Watchdog chief will be denied vote in election', *The Nation*, 25 April 1996, p. A9.

56  The NAMFREL representative's passport was stolen the day before he was scheduled to leave Manila, and thus did not make it to Indonesia. This theft became doubly suspicious when it was reported on the front pages of Jakarta newspapers the next day. The Thai representatives were able to talk to various KIPP groups in Indonesia, but were harassed by the police and local officials throughout their trip. The last meeting on their itinerary was held at an LBH office, and the meeting was broken up by armed police. This office was burnt down later in July 1996 (Laddawan Tantiwittayaphitak, Interview, 14 September 1996).

57  Though it sounds systematic, Crouch observes that 'Authoritarian controls are not usually introduced according to grand design but incrementally as political leaders deal with particular challenges to authority.' (Harold Crouch, 'Malaysia: Neither Authoritarian nor Democratic', in Kevin Hewison, Richard Robison, and Garry Rodan (eds), *Southeast Asia in the 1990s: Authoritarianism, Democracy & Capitalism*, Sydney: Allen & Unwin, 1993, pp. 153–4).

58  John McBeth, Michael Vatikiotis, and Margot Cohen, 'Into the void', *Far Eastern Economic Review*, 4 June 1998, p. 18.

59  McBeth, Vatikiotis, and Cohen, p. 18.
60  Jomo K.S., 'Elections' Janus Face: Limitations and Potential in Malaysia', in R.H. Taylor (ed.), *The Politics of Elections in Southeast Asia*, Cambridge: Cambridge University Press, 1996, p. 90; also see James V. Jesudason, 'The Syncretic State and the Structuring of Oppositional Politics in Malaysia,' in Garry Rodan (ed.), *Political Oppositions in Industrializing Asia*, London: Routledge, 1996, p. 152.
61  Garry Rodan, 'Elections Without Representation: The Singapore Experience under the PAP', in R.H. Taylor (ed.), *The Politics of Elections in Southeast Asia*, Cambridge: Cambridge University Press, 1996b, pp. 61–89; Garry Rodan, 'Singapore in 1996: Extended Election Fever', *Asian Survey*, 37:2, February 1997, pp. 175–80.
62  State control of the media has even extended beyond the shores of Singapore. In the mid-1980s, the captive media forced many Singaporeans to turn to foreign media outlets to get critical commentary of their own government. In response to this trend, the Singapore authorities passed another law which gave the government power to restrict distribution of foreign newspapers and magazines which 'interfered' with domestic politics. It has been quite successful in controlling foreign media coverage of Singaporean politics (Rodan 1996b, ibid.).
63  An opposition leader declared that the 1995 elections were the most 'unfair, unfree and unclean in Malaysian history' (cited in James Chin, 'The 1995 Malaysian General Election: Mahathir's Last Triumph?' *Asian Survey*, 36:4, April 1996, p. 398). For more discussion of 'money politics' see Jomo, pp. 95–7; Jesudason, p. 137; Gomez, 1996.
64  James Chin, 'Malaysia in 1996: Mahathir-Anwar bouts, UMNO Election, and Sarawak surprise', *Asian Survey*, 37:2, February 1997, pp. 181–7.
65  Singapore scores high (9.26 out of 10) on the Surveys of Public Service Corruption of business executives (cited in Arnold J. Heidenheimer, 'The Topography of Corruption: Explorations in a Comparative Perspective', *International Social Science Journal*, 149, September 1996, p. 338). Also see The Internet Center for Corruption Research's annual Corruption Perception Index where Singapore scores in the top ten corruption-free countries (*http://www.gwdg.de/~uwvw/*).
66  Though Malaysian and Singaporean leaders are well-known for their critical view of Western civilization, their cultural criticism is also often directed at their Southeast Asian neighbors – including each other.
67  An experience I had when I discussed election irregularities at a seminar of 'liberal and democratic' political party leaders from Pacific Asia was instructive. After my presentation about the problems of vote-buying, the response of a Malaysian MP from a ruling coalition party was quite instructive. He was fascinated with the process of vote-buying, and asked me how a candidate could guarantee that the money was well spent. When I refused to answer how Thais enforce vote-buying, the Philippine host of the seminar took up the slack and listed the tried and tested methods of effective vote-buying. Now it is still not clear to me who was more naive: an urban politician from Malaysia who was not familiar with vote-

buying, or an academic for thinking that Malaysia is generally free of the practice.

68  As Rodan notes, 'the PAP's brand of authoritarian rule has been effective in direct repression of political opposition and in carefully defining the limits to political space outside the state' (Rodan, 1996a, p. 101).

69  Michael Johnston, 'The Search for Definitions: the Vitality of Politics and the Issue of Corruption', *International Social Science Journal*, 149, September 1996, pp. 332.

70  Interview with an opposition party leader, 23 January 1996.

71  Corruption is also quite narrowly defined in the United Kingdom; the undisclosed campaign contributions that are very illegal in North America and continental Europe are still quite legal in Britain. Though such corruption was unpopular – and became a major issue in the 1997 British general election – it was not illegal.

72  Jesudason notes that 'emergency powers [have been] used against opposition state governments while the Internal Security Act has been used to detain individual opponents of the government' (Jesudason, p. 132).

A recent example of UMNO's interference in state politics occurred in 1994 when the Governor-General of Sabah refused to swear in the Chief Minister whose opposition party had won the state election. While the Chief Minister-elect was waiting, defections of over three-quarters of the state MPs from his party to the Barisan Nasional's party forced him to resign. Even though a party hostile to the federal government had won the election, a new administration more favourable to Kuala Lumphur was engineered (Chin, pp. 404–5).

For a discussion of how the ISA works in Singapore from the point of view of a former prisoner, see Francis T. Seow, *To Catch a Tartar: A Dissident in Lee Kuan Yew's Prison*, New Haven, Connecticut: Yale Southeast Asian Studies, 1994.

73  Between 1971 and 1993, the Singapore judiciary bankrupted 11 opposition politicians. For example, the leader of one of the opposition parties had to pay then-Prime Minister Lee Kuan Yew S$740 000 when he was found guilty of defamation for comments he made at an election rally in 1988 (Rodan 1996a, pp. 123–4. Also see Donald K. Emmerson, 'Singapore and the "Asian Values" Debate', *Journal of Democracy*, 6:4, October 1995, p. 98.

74  In Malaysia, this primarily affects rural projects. In Singapore, this affects the upkeep and up-grading of flats in the public housing programme. For the politics of Singapore's public housing programme, see Beng-Huat Chua, *Communitarianism and Democracy in Singapore*, London: Routledge, 1995, pp. 124–46.

75  In response to a minuscule gain of a few opposition seats in the 1984 election, Singapore's second deputy prime minister warned that 'if it is an attempt by voters to blackmail the government (to compromise on important issues or principles), then we must show that we cannot be blackmailed' (cited in Rodan 1996b, p. 71).

76  Garry Rodan, 'Preserving the One-party State in Contemporary Singapore', in Kevin Hewison, Richard Robison, and Garry Rodan (eds), *Southeast*

*Asia in the 1990s: Authoritarianism, Democracy & Capitalism*, Sydney: Allen & Unwin, 1993, p. 77.

77   In this way Johnston is more in line with descriptions of Asian politics which reject notions that state and society are competitors in a struggle.

78   Michael Johnston, 'Public Officials, Private Interests, and Sustainable Democracy: Connections between Politics and Corruption', in Kimberly Ann Elliot (ed.), *Corruption and the Global Economy*, Washington, DC: Institute for International Economics, 1997, p. 68.

79   Considering the British policies in Hong Kong, one could say that such elite hegemony is an outgrowth of the British colonial regime rather than a modern form of Asian values.

80   Walden Bello and Stephanie Rosenfeld, *Dragons in Distress: Asia's Miracle Economies in Crisis*, London: Penguin, 1990, pp. 287–336.

81   See James C. Scott, *Comparative Political Corruption*, Englewood Cliffs, NJ: Prentice Hall, 1972, pp. 56–75.

82   See William A. Callahan, *Imagining Democracy: Reading the Events of May in Thailand*, Singapore: ISEAS, 1998.

83   There are still defenders of patronage machines among the political elite in the United States. Though the Supreme Court ruled that such practices were illegal in 1996, two judges wrote a dissenting opinion praising patronage politics as 'a venerable and accepted tradition' in American politics (see John C.H. Oh and Bruce Wiegand, 'Democracy, Development and Corruption: The Case of Korea', *Korean Observer*, 26:4, Winter 1996, pp. 499–500).

# 8
## Conclusion: Problems and Prospects

*Robert Williams*

One study of campaign and party finance in North America and Western Europe suggests that 'the main problem in political finance is not corruption but rather the *appearance* of corruption.'[1] At the same time it is asserted that political parties are inevitable and indispensable 'instruments of democratic government'.[2] But political competition requires resources and the issue of how political parties acquire and use money is central to understanding the relationship of the party system to the wider political system. The main challenge appears to be how to find a model of party finance that successfully reconciles the needs of party building, competition and campaigning with the need to inhibit and minimize the corruption of the electoral and policy processes. Meeting one set of needs at the expense of the other only exacerbates particular problems. Starving political parties of funds in order to bear down on corruption would impede or deny the ability of political parties to perform their functions. Disregarding corruption in order to protect the financial strength of political parties would tend to denigrate democratic values in favour of preserving and enhancing the political advantages of the economically privileged.

If the need to balance competing aims is recognized, the point of balance is a matter for political judgement, cultural traditions and local circumstances. In some countries, an acute shortage of finance seems to encourage and facilitate corruption. But scandals occur in countries where state funding is substantial and even lavish. In considering models of party finance, there is clearly no 'gold standard' against which actual examples can be measured. No system is both free from corruption and yet able to produce adequate funding for a range of political parties. The problem is exacerbated by escalating costs and benefits. As 'retail', face-to-face campaigning has declined, the costs of technology, of electronic media and advertising have increased. Buying television time is the prime electoral cost in regimes as different as Russia and the United States and attempts to regulate it have met with commercial and constitutional objections. Yet parties who lack the funds to buy television and radio time are severely handicapped and their opportunities to attract wider support are correspondingly reduced. The ability of new parties to compete effectively crucially depends on conveying their message to a mass audience and, where access to mass media is rationed by price or by government restrictions, the party system will tend to ossify.

When the same parties regularly win elections, it is almost inescapable that they will command the overwhelming share of private and state funding. It is no accident that the only credible challenge to the dominance of the Democratic and Republican parties in recent American presidential elections came from one of the richest individuals in the United States. Ross Perot was able to escape from the normal funding constraints experienced by minor parties by drawing directly on a huge personal fortune. Media owners themselves, such as Berlusconi in Italy, enjoy special advantages. The examples of Perot in the United States, Berlusconi in Italy or Goldsmith in Britain are few and far between because, for obvious reasons, such personal wealth is, in most societies, restricted to a handful of individuals. Money clearly does not guarantee political success for minor parties but, if not a sufficient condition, it certainly appears a necessary one.

If party systems are not to ossify because of the financial problems facing new challengers, state funding is frequently advocated as an effective way of creating a more even playing field. But one danger here is that 'state funding may be a Trojan horse for state intervention and control.'[3] A further concern is that state subsidy will diminish the need for parties to create, consult and sustain large memberships. The consequence may be that parties become detached from and unresponsive to their grass-roots followings. Much depends, of course, on the principles which inform the distribution of public subsidies and the extent to which already dominant parties are able to establish cartels. Public subsidies may encourage competition but they can also help preserve the status quo.

A crucial element in the relation between party finance and corruption is the extent, clarity and implementation of regulation. These regulatory frameworks evolved over long periods in established democracies and, as the Italian and British cases demonstrate, they are still subject to radical overhaul. What was once regarded as effective is now no longer sufficient. Whereas scandals were once depicted as isolated lapses and their central figures characterized as 'rotten apples' in otherwise wholesome barrels, the modern tendency is to seek structural, procedural or regulatory reform. Many countries and especially developing and transitional democracies have great problems in enforcing party finance regulations. But this is not surprising because their capacity to enforce other sorts of laws and regulations is also weak. Where governance capabilities are limited, the enforcement of party finance regulations is rarely a high priority.

When electoral competition is still a novelty and where the regulations governing party activity and fund-raising are both new and poorly understood in a context of overstretched and under-resourced governments, the regulatory framework takes on a cosmetic character. When asked by prospective aid donors or international political and financial institutions whether they have appropriate regulatory provisions for party finance, the answer will invariably be affirmative. But regulations on paper are one thing, effective enforcement is quite another. In the absence of enforcement, the opportunities for corruption multiply and, where the risks of detection are minuscule, temptations are harder to resist. Western business enterprises which are deterred by the risks of exposure, prosecution, blacklisting and humiliation from engaging in corrupt practices at home are more likely to do so in political settings where the risks are much lower. This combination of inadequate enforcement and increased opportunity is difficult to resist and difficult to reform.

In Western democracies political parties emerged and developed in very different circumstances. When the Democratic and Republican parties crystallized in the mid-nineteenth century, the reach of government was much shorter and lighter and party-funding arrangements were seen primarily as private matters rather than legitimate issues of public concern. There was a distinct shortage of international role models to serve as comparative yardsticks. In mature democracies rules and restrictions on party finance gradually evolved after the party system had been established. Only recently has it been necessary to

bring vibrant party systems under control. But developing and transitional countries face multiple and competing challenges: how to
develop, for the first time, a party system and how, simultaneously,
to find ways of regulating the funding arrangements of the fledgling
parties which meet the expectations and standards of mature democracies. As Burnell observes, 'the presence of internationally sanctioned norms and expectations can be particularly intrusive for the
emerging democracies in fiscal crisis, desperate for foreign debt relief
and beholden to the IMF, World Bank and bilateral donors.'[4] In
short, the newer democracies have to build and regulate party systems
in accordance with standards derived from different contexts which
were not applicable to the early phases of party development in mature
democracies.

But applying Western judgements about finance and corruption to
non-Western situations is fraught with difficulty. The political contexts
are fundamentally different and party-finance models based on
wider assumptions about the role of government and the strength
of civil society do not always fit local circumstances. Singapore and
Malaysia conduct elections which are relatively free from corruption
but this is partly because the governing parties have devised political
arrangements which impede the ability of opposition parties to compete effectively. Where political space is narrowly defined and the
ideology of the dominant party is represented as the official ideology
of the nation, opposition parties are marginalized. If the law serves as
an instrument of the state rather than as a protection for individuals
and groups, legally inspired understandings of corruption are of limited analytical relevance. Such states are free from the blatant vote-
buying seen in other Asian contexts but, as Callahan documents,
they employ a variety of devices to silence critical voices and minimize the threat of electoral challenge. Securing adequate sources of
party finance is never a problem for a party with a virtual guarantee
of exercising political power, as the Singapore and Malaysian cases
confirm. The corruption in such cases is of a broader moral kind in
which the moral health of the body politic is at issue.

It might be argued that elections are seldom absolutely free and
fair in the sense that all competitors enjoy equal access to resources
but, as Sakwa notes, what is crucial is that the judicial and regulatory
terrain remain impartial for all competitors, and here the Russian
case is deeply flawed. Where the advantages of incumbency are dispro-

portionate, those in power will be tempted to manipulate the political and electoral process to preserve their position. The periodic campaigns against corruption launched by President Yeltsin are therefore not to be accepted at face value. Sakwa suggests that they were substitutes for substantive change and their purpose was symbolic and political. When anti-corruption campaigns start to catch those close to the centre of power, the head of the anti-corruption unit is in grave jeopardy. The first head of the Russian General Control Inspectorate was forced to resign precisely because he was not concentrating exclusively on Yeltsin's enemies. In April 1999, President Yeltsin suspended Prosecutor-General Shuratov, apparently because he was investigating alleged financial misconduct by Yeltsin, his family and close associates.[5] The dual character of the Russian system so clearly delineated by Sakwa means that it is possible to see a tightening up on party finance through the creation of a Central Electoral Commission, which requires declarations from parties about the source and amount of campaign donations, while the regulatory framework governing the financing of election campaigns remains unclear and implementation remains problematic.

The consequence of political upheaval for Russia is a system of party finance which is suffused with informal, quasi-legal aspects. The rise of organized crime in a political system which lacks public confidence and legitimacy makes the corruption of the political finance system almost unavoidable. Without established rules and when secrecy rather than transparency prevails, the prospects for meaningful reform of party finance are remote. For reform to have any impact, it will have to be wider and deeper, embracing the entire political and economic system. The failure of attempts to regulate party finance is less surprising than the fact that any attempts have been made.

While the problems of developing and transitional countries are particularly acute in terms of party finance and corruption, as in so many other areas, there are few grounds for complacency when considering the position in Western Europe and North America. The two major European states to experience the rigours of fascism, Italy and Germany, present contrasting examples. Superficially, both presented stable party systems with competitive elections which were usually won by Christian Democrats and their electoral allies. But the democratic renewal after 1945 proved to be less authentic in the Italian setting than in the German. What is equally remarkable is that, despite the democratic deficit in both states, little or no attention was given to the problems of funding the nascent political formations which emerged in the 1940s and 1950s.

As Newell reminds us, party funding in Italy has only been formally regulated since 1974. The previous system was unregulated but before and after 1974 the systems were essentially corrupt. This corruption was generated by the depth and extent of party penetration of the Italian state and society. The complex tentacles of the 'partyocracy' made subsequent attempts to clean up Italian politics much more difficult. The legitimacy of the state was intimately related to the legitimacy of the political parties which formally controlled it. The overlap between the personnel of parties, interest groups and bureaucracies made it more difficult to make the distinction between private and public regarding conduct which is central to the public-office understanding of corruption.

The corruption of party finance in Italy displayed an inner logic which meant that, once established, corruption grew and spread. The informal networks within the political parties acted as conduits for illicit funding and the formal party organizations became a veneer or facade behind which corruption flourished. Party loyalty rested more and more on corrupt motives as party membership became less associated with ideology and policy and more with material ambition. Ultimately, corruption undermined the party organizations and, when the *Tangentopoli* scandals broke, the parties collapsed. The efforts of the 1990s to introduce new systems of party financing have emphasized a greater judicial role in scrutinizing accounting practices. There has been a tightening up in procedures but loopholes and ambiguities remain. Parties remain weak and do not command public confidence. The rise of Berlusconi's *Forza Italia* suggests the current weakness of the Catholic and Marxist traditions in Italian political movements. When party membership is low and demoralized, it provides opportunities for parties to become personal vehicles for the rich and powerful.

While Italian parties were exposed as fragile and weak, German political parties are sometimes depicted as too strong and too powerful. Alternatively, German parties are presented as heavily dependent on public funding and thus dependent on the state. Prior to the 1980s, West Germany was relatively untouched by scandals involving political finance. But the Barschel, Flick and Amigo scandals helped change the political climate and the Flick affair in particular raised concerns about the funding of political parties. Saalfeld argues that the Federal Constitutional Court has played a crucial role as an external institutional check on the parties and prevents, or at least limits, the capacity of the main parties to pass self-serving legislation. Nevertheless, German parties resemble 'cartel parties'[6] and serve less as links between civil society and the state and more as agents of the state. But, as Saalfeld points out, the rise of the Green Party created a challenge to the consensus on party finance that had developed between the established parties.

State funding may reduce the dependence of parties on powerful economic interests in society but it also raises questions of accountability. The parties in parliament award themselves public funds and this raises questions of propriety and legitimacy. Party competition on party finance issues has often been suspended but this truce has not allowed the established parties to exclude new parties. Public funding provisions, as interpreted by the Federal Constitutional Court, have played a part in facilitating the break-up of the parliamentary cartel. The scandals of the 1980s have ensured that party finance will continue to receive media attention and the German public are now more sensitized to corruption issues than was the case in the heyday of the cartel.

The contributions to this book have helped highlight not only the differences between developed and less developed countries but also the differences between North America and Western Europe. The approach to party finance issues pursued in the United States is manifestly different to the German approach. Where one focuses on organizations, the other focuses on individuals. Where one focuses on legislative subsidies, the other rejects such subsidies. While Germany has its 'party state', the United States treats political parties almost as if they were just like other interest groups. While one grants no free television and radio time but allows individual candidates to buy it, the other prevents candidates from buying time but gives free time to parties. By German standards, American parties are hollow and weak. By American standards, German parties are too strong and creatures of the state.

The debate in the United States centres around campaign finance reform rather than party finance reform for the simple reason that parties spend and receive only a relatively small proportion of campaign money. As McSweeney notes, a distrust of political parties has been a recurrent theme in American political history since the eighteenth century. Successive reforms served to weaken party organization and limit the parties' electoral role. In consequence, American electoral politics was atomized and individual candidates were left with the responsibility of funding their campaigns. As American parties have never had members in the European sense, it followed that candidates would be dependent on income from external sources, or what McSweeney calls 'interested money' seeking returns on investments.

The history of campaign finance in the United States is a history of a series of legislative measures preventing companies, banks and trade unions from funding election campaigns, coupled with a variety of ingenious methods of evading these regulations. The laws were formal restrictions both in the sense that they were widely evaded and in the sense that attempts to enforce them were infrequent and unsuccessful. The most spectacular scandal in American history, the Watergate scandal, had its roots in illicit campaign contributions and part of the Watergate fallout was to separate still further candidates from party funding. The reality is that while regulation in Europe tends toward protecting political parties from the pernicious influence of special economic interests, campaign finance law in the United States treats parties as special interests.

The current system of campaign finance in the United States has few defenders inside or outside the political system. Suspicion of corruption understood as improper or undue influence is widespread. Analyses of contributions from Political Action Committees suggest they reward existing allies with donations rather than attempt to subvert opponents but the impression that money 'talks' remains. In recent years, much concern has been expressed about the influence of foreign money and the implications for American foreign policy. At the congressional level, the high-profile Keating Five scandal suggested that, although not illegal, the conduct in question had raised concerns about the expectations of reciprocal favours implicit in some kinds of fund-raising.

Despite persistent demands for change, there has been no effective reform because there is no consensus on how to remedy the current system. Divisions between parties, legislative chambers, and ideologies, and between incumbents and challengers, have meant that competing and irreconcilable perceptions of electoral self-interest preclude agreement. By definition, all current members of Congress are beneficiaries of the present rules and a radical revision of them seems to fall into the 'turkeys voting for Christmas' category of reform proposal. But because dissatisfaction with the system is so strong, political leaders in both parties almost ritually propose their different and incompatible schemes for reform. Members of Congress have proved incapable of reforming the system of campaign finance but are loathe to allow any other agency to do it for them. The consequences of reform are difficult to anticipate and those who succeed under the present rules need substantial and as yet undiscovered incentives to change their ways.

Compared to the United States and continental Europe, party finance in Britain has been relatively unregulated. Its pragmatic evolution has, according to Fisher, been untroubled by major scandal or serious concerns about corruption. Yet, paradoxically, a major inquiry has recently recommended wholesale reform of party finance in Britain. The significance of these reform proposals appears far-reaching but it is not clear whether they represent a timely and appropriate response to an increasingly important problem, an over-reaction to a temporary political difficulty, or a cosmetic and ineffective reaction to structural and deep-seated problems in British party finance. Britain is entering its post-modern era of party finance in which the old practices are being swept away but the shape of the system to come is unclear.

The pattern of British party finance up to the 1980s has been well described in Pinto-Duschinsky's study[7] but, since its publication, there have been a number of innovations in party fund-raising which partly triggered the inquiry by the Committee on Standards in Public Life. British parties found their traditional sources of income declining and, in the 1990s, they became more entrepreneurial and diversified in their fund-raising techniques. The previous structure of regulation was aimed at the local level but modern elections are essentially national and orchestrated by national parties. At the national level, fund-raising and spending by parties were essentially unregulated.

British parties have a tradition of not disclosing their contributions and, especially in the case of the Conservative Party, this highlights the issue of whether political parties are public or private organizations. Under British law, the Conservative Party is an unincorporated association with no legal status and therefore its accounts are not open to external scrutiny. The Labour Party – which had made much political capital about the Conservative Party and its wealthy, and sometimes foreign, financial backers – was itself embarrassed by the disclosure of a substantial donation from motor racing boss Bernie Ecclestone. The size of the contribution, one million pounds, was difficult to explain, given Ecclestone's previous lack of public identification with the Labour Party but, even more embarrassing, was the link that was made to the exemption the new government had given Formula One racing from its projected ban on tobacco advertising in sport. The potential for scandal was quickly recognized and Prime Minister Blair sought to defuse the issue by asking the Committee on Standards in Public Life to review the issue of party finance. Blair was presumably further encouraged to take this step by the refusal of his Conservative predecessor, John Major, to make a similar referral. The circumstances of the 1997 election were such that the new administration was determined to be seen to act decisively to deflect sleaze allegations.

Increased sensitivity to issues of party finance and the possibility of corruption is, if not general, much more common than it used to be. In Britain and Italy major reforms have been, or are being, enacted. Scandals related to finance and corruption have become common in established democracies and the collapse of authoritarian regimes in East Europe and East Asia has permitted a freer expression of public concern and outrage about the corruption of political leaders. This volume demonstrates that there is no single template, no ideal type of party finance which can be imitated or emulated by diverse countries. Local circumstances, particular traditions and cultures, as well as economic realities, will play their part in shaping the party finance system.

There will always be those opposed to reform, those who wish to cover up misconduct and who do not value transparency and accountability. In some states, the prospects for reform are poor and, as in Russia, the political leadership is increasingly desperate. But, in parts of East Asia, there is hope and even excitement at the prospect of building democracy with genuine and independent political parties. In Europe, complacency has given way to concern. Public and political sensitivity to and awareness of party finance issues has increased and reform is on many agendas. The United States has reform on its agenda but has not yet demonstrated a capacity to reconcile the interests of the competing forces in the debate.

Political parties will always need to solicit funds from social and economic interests in society. Even in Germany, state funding has proved inadequate and, in developing and transitional countries, the economic and political realities exclude it as a possibility. Where reform is possible, it is not a once-and-for-all solution. Whatever regulatory framework is put in place, some interests will seek loopholes and ingeniously exploit ambiguities and gaps in the regulations. Where party finance and corruption are concerned, periodic review is necessary if the aims and objectives of regulation are not to be undermined by the ambitions of politicians and those who seek to influence them.

## Notes

1  Arthur B. Gunlicks (ed.), *Campaign and Party Finance in North America and Western Europe*, Boulder: Westview Press, 1993, p. 11

2  Karl-Heinz Nassmacher, 'Comparing Party and Campaign Finance in Western Democracies', in Gunlicks (ed.), p. 233

3  Peter Burnell, 'Introduction: money and politics in emerging democracies', in Peter Burnell and Alan Ware (eds), *Funding Democratization*, Manchester: Manchester University Press, 1998.

4  Burnell, p. 17.

5  *Guardian*, 3 April 1999, p. 15.

6  See R. Katz and P. Mair, 'Changing models of party organization and party democracy: The emergence of the cartel party', *Party Politics*, 1, 1995, pp. 5–28.

7  Michael Pinto-Duschinsky, *British Political Finance 1830–1980*, Washington: American Enterprise Institute, 1981.

# Index

211